199

Fun and Effective

Fundraising Events

for Nonprofit Organizations

By

Eileen Figure Sandlin
and Richa

199 Fun and Effective Fundraising Events for Nonprofit Organizations

Copyright © 2010 by Atlantic Publishing Group, Inc.
1405 SW 6th • Ocala, Florida 34471 • 800-814-1132 • Fax 352-622-1875
Web site: www.atlantic-pub.com • E-mail sales@atlantic-pub.com
SAN Number: 268-1250

Library of Congress Cataloging-in-Publication Data

Sandlin, Eileen Figure.
  199 fun and effective fundraising events for nonprofit organizations / Eileen Figure Sandlin and Richard Helweg.
     p. cm.
  Includes bibliographical references and index.
  ISBN-13: 978-1-60138-148-4 (alk. paper)
  ISBN-10: 1-60138-148-4 (alk. paper)
  1. Fund raising. I. Helweg, Richard, 1956- II. Title. III. Title: One hundred ninety nine fun and effective fundraising events for nonprofit organizations.
  HG177.S26 2010
  658.15'224--dc22

                         2010033487

Printed on Recycled Paper

Printed in the United States

We recently lost our beloved pet "Bear," who was not only our best and dearest friend but also the "Vice President of Sunshine" here at Atlantic Publishing. He did not receive a salary but worked tirelessly 24 hours a day to please his parents. Bear was a rescue dog that turned around and showered myself, my wife, Sherri, his grandparents Jean, Bob, and Nancy and every person and animal he met (maybe not rabbits) with friendship and love. He made a lot of people smile every day.

We wanted you to know that a portion of the profits of this book will be donated to The Humane Society of the United States. *–Douglas & Sherri Brown*

The human-animal bond is as old as human history. We cherish our animal companions for their unconditional affection and acceptance. We feel a thrill when we glimpse wild creatures in their natural habitat or in our own backyard.

Unfortunately, the human-animal bond has at times been weakened. Humans have exploited some animal species to the point of extinction.

The Humane Society of the United States makes a difference in the lives of animals here at home and worldwide. The HSUS is dedicated to creating a world where our relationship with animals is guided by compassion. We seek a truly humane society in which animals are respected for their intrinsic value, and where the human-animal bond is strong.

Want to help animals? We have plenty of suggestions. Adopt a pet from a local shelter, join The Humane Society and be a part of our work to help companion animals and wildlife. You will be funding our educational, legislative, investigative and outreach projects in the U.S. and across the globe.

Or perhaps you'd like to make a memorial donation in honor of a pet, friend or relative? You can through our Kindred Spirits program. And if you'd like to contribute in a more structured way, our Planned Giving Office has suggestions about estate planning, annuities, and even gifts of stock that avoid capital gains taxes.

Maybe you have land that you would like to preserve as a lasting habitat for wildlife. Our Wildlife Land Trust can help you. Perhaps the land you want to share is a backyard— that's enough. Our Urban Wildlife Sanctuary Program will show you how to create a habitat for your wild neighbors.

So you see, it's easy to help animals. And The HSUS is here to help.

2100 L Street NW • Washington, DC 20037
202-452-1100 • www.hsus.org

For Dan the Man
Long may you wave

From Eileen Sandlin

For Karla and Teach a Kid to Fish
From Rick Helweg

Table of Contents

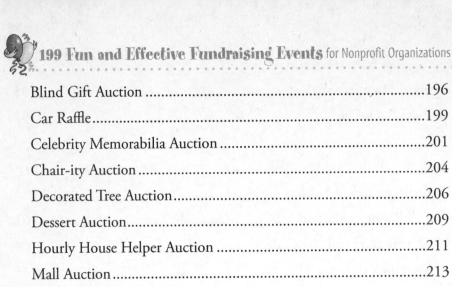
Chapter 12: Dances 223

Chapter 13: Food and Drinks 241

Chapter 18: Themed Events 387

Chapter 19: Miscellaneous 431

Introduction

If you belong to one of the more than 1.5 million nonprofit organizations in the U.S. today, whether it is a charity, a school, a religious group, or another not-for-profit organization, fundraising is a key element of success. Yet, no matter the size and scope of your organization, it can sometimes be difficult to come up with fresh, fun, and profitable ideas to obtain support. Perhaps your group is struggling in this tough economy and is in need of some inspiration to stay afloat. Perhaps the thought of another bake sale or car wash makes you want to scream. Or, perhaps you just need guidance on where to begin. Regardless of your group's needs, this book is here to help.

In today's troubled economy — only 18 percent of nonprofits expect to exceed breaking even at the end of 2010 — profitable, creative fundraisers are needed more than ever. In spite of the economic depression, people are still willing to donate their time and money to a worthwhile cause —especially if they can have a little fun doing so. *199 Fun and Effective Fundraising Events for Nonprofit Organizations* will help you secure some of these contributions, which reportedly still exceeded 1.4 trillion in 2009, and find volunteers, a category that approximately 26.8 percent of Americans fell under in 2008 to 2009.

In this book, you will find 199 fresh event ideas that have proven successful for various organizations. The events have been divided into two categories: simple and complex. You will find 100 fundraising ideas for each type. The simple events require less effort and are less expensive to put together. However, they may not produce the same return as the complex events, which call for more effort and larger investments (not to mention several months of planning and plenty of advertising) to be successful.

For each event listing, you will find the name of the fundraiser and a description of what it entails. Thus, you will be able to determine which events meet your financial capabilities and suit your social objectives. The estimated cost for putting the event together is represented by up to five dollar signs to give you a general idea of expense — with one dollar sign representing the lowest cost involved and five representing the highest cost.

Each event also requires a certain amount of effort to organize. This is why, with each listing, you will find five gauges representing the level of difficulty to host the fundraiser. The gauges measure five parameters: obtaining sponsorship, finding a venue, recruiting volunteers, preparation, and execution of the event. Each parameter is rated on a scale of one to five, with one indicating the least amount of difficulty and five representing the most.

If any special equipment or materials are needed, they are also described in the event listing. Ideas to obtain sponsors and donations are included, along with possible venues for your event. Depending on the nature of your fundraiser, a rough estimate of volunteers is provided for each event. Furthermore, you will find directions on how to prepare and execute each fundraiser, and, where applicable, variations of events and special tips.

You will also encounter case studies throughout the book. Experts will introduce you to various nonprofits and how they operate, and they will share experiences from working in the field and offer advice about running a successful event in a tough economy. Furthermore, they describe the fundraising techniques that have worked best for their groups — and those that have not.

Keep in mind that the goal of this book is not to instruct you on how to run your organization. Rather, it provides you with innovative and effective ways to raise money for your cause. So, as you start planning your next fundraiser, be sure to keep this valuable resource within arm's reach.

Good luck with all of your fundraising endeavors!

The Number Scale Event Chart

Each event in this book has a chart to show its amount of difficulty in six major areas: Estimated Cost, Obtaining Sponsors/Donations, Finding a Venue, Recruiting Volunteers, Preparation, and Execution.

On the left side of the chart, there is a number scale from 1 to 5 with one being the easiest and 5 the most difficult. For example:

1 – The fundraiser is very easy or costs little to nothing.

2 – Although still easy to do, events with this ranking need slightly more work, planning or money to pull off.

3 – A moderate amount of work or money is necessary. You might have to find volunteers who are willing and able to sell somewhat expensive products or tickets. You might have to book a venue, which is at least moderately challenging.

4 – More than the average amount of time, effort, or funds is required.

5 – The event is somewhat difficult or expensive. It might require plenty of preparation or hands-on work. It may require many materials or resources.

The chart looks like this:

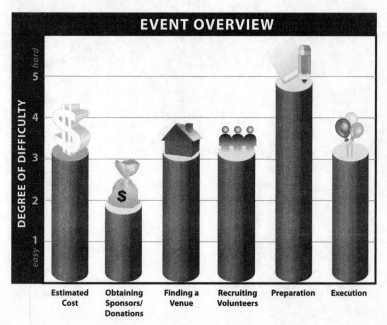

This would be a medium difficulty event, with the most challenging or time consuming portion being the preparation. Each chart is designed to let you know at a glance whether the event described is a good fit for the resources of your organization.

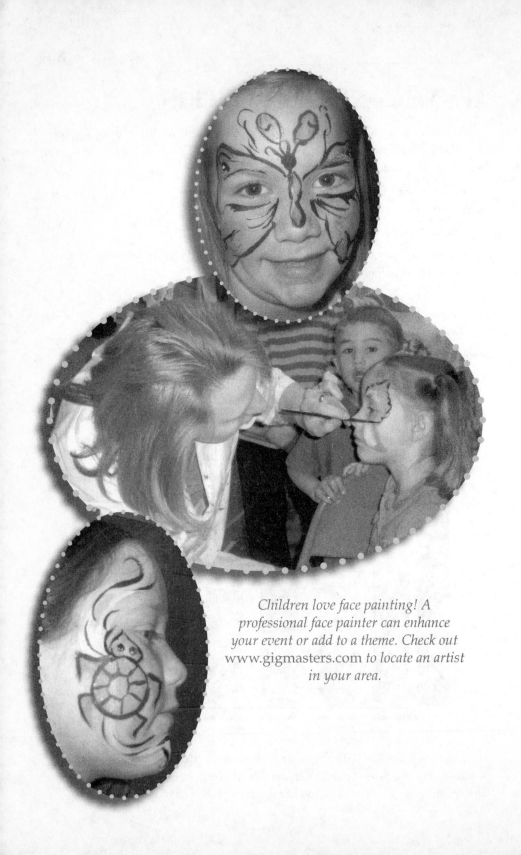

Children love face painting! A professional face painter can enhance your event or add to a theme. Check out www.gigmasters.com to locate an artist in your area.

SECTION 1

Simple Events

A student Art Show is a popular fundraiser at St. Charles School in Genoa, WI. Here the winner of the Best Painting displays her award-winning work.

Chapter 1

Arts and Crafts

The events in this chapter can be put together with minimal fuss but will take maximum advantage of your members' creativity. The projects you will find in this chapter include:

- ◎ Community Mural Project
- ◎ Custom Art Yearbooks
- ◎ Family Portraits
- ◎ Student Art Gallery
- ◎ Tie-Dye Station
- ◎ Van Painting

Community Mural Project

Invite the community to create a colorful mural using various media. Charge an entry fee, and either display the finished artwork or auction it off to raise additional funds.

OVERVIEW: Community Mural Project

(Degree of Difficulty, easy to hard, for: Estimated Cost, Obtaining Sponsors/Donations, Finding a Venue, Recruiting Volunteers, Preparation, Execution)

Special Materials/Equipment
- Art materials (such as paint, pencils, fabric, tile, clay, and brushes)

Sponsors/Donations
- Contact an art supply store for donations of art materials.
- Ask a tile store for donations of colorful tiles.
- Approach a fabric store for scraps and remnants.

Possible Venue(s)
Community or church meeting facilities, public parks (for an art-in-the-park event), sports arenas, or playing fields work well.

Recommended Volunteer
10+ to create and install the mural

Preparation
Talk to local business owners to find out whether they would be interested in having a community mural installed on a wall inside or outside of their buildings. Have a local artist draw a sketch, then cut it into 6-inch squares that participants can work on.

Promote the event heavily in local media, and stress that no previous art experience is necessary. Recommend that participants bring their own art materials, if possible.

Execution

Charge an entry fee to participate in the project. Allow participants to choose the section they wish to work on using their choice of art materials. Assemble the completed sections into the finished art project, which can be displayed or auctioned off.

Tip(s)

- Ask a local artist to donate his or her services to oversee construction of the project.
- Choose a theme for the mural to give it cohesiveness.
- If the finished artwork will be displayed outside, choose waterproof and wind-resistant media.

Variation(s)

- Create a tile mosaic community project using donated materials.

Custom Art Yearbooks

Take orders from parents at the start of the school year to create yearbooks of the art their children made at school throughout the year. You can either create custom scrapbooks using the actual art, or you can photograph the best pieces and use them to make an attractive photo album.

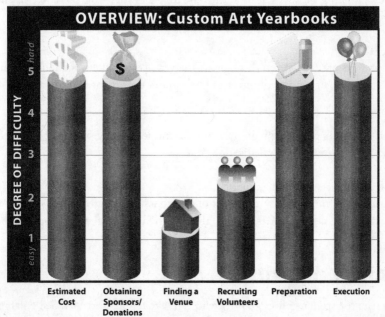

OVERVIEW: Custom Art Yearbooks

DEGREE OF DIFFICULTY — hard / easy

Estimated Cost | Obtaining Sponsors/ Donations | Finding a Venue | Recruiting Volunteers | Preparation | Execution

Special Materials/Equipment
- One scrapbook or photo album per order (preferably in school colors)
- Other scrapbooking paraphernalia (including page embellishments, decorative stamps, stencils, and adhesives)

Sponsors/Donations
- Art, craft, and scrapbooking stores might be willing to donate clearance and past-season merchandise.
- Ask retail stores for cash donations to cover the cost of the scrapbooks or photo albums.

Possible Venue(s)
Preschools and elementary schools are best, but it might also be possible to interest a high school art department in a high-end product.

Recommended Volunteer
12+ depending on the number of orders you secure. If you have experienced "scrappers" among your members, be sure to recruit them to help. A volunteer who is good with a digital camera might also be needed.

Preparation
Create a sales flier to mail or send home with children at the beginning of the school year to advertise the product. Enclose an order form with the flier. Add a shopping cart to your website so parents can place orders online. Create original page layouts. If you are photographing the art, schedule with the teachers when you can come in and take photos before projects are graded and sent home.

Execution
As art projects are completed throughout the year, collect them for inclusion in each child's yearbook, or send a volunteer to photograph the art for a photo album.

Tip(s)
- Put the child's photograph on the cover. Parents love seeing photos of their children.
- Let the children make a dedication page.

Variation(s)
- Take orders from parents at the start of the school year to create books of the writing (essays, poetry, short stories, reports) their children did at school throughout the year.

Family Portraits

Find a talented student photographer who can take family portraits. Sell enlarged and matted portraits or photo packages.

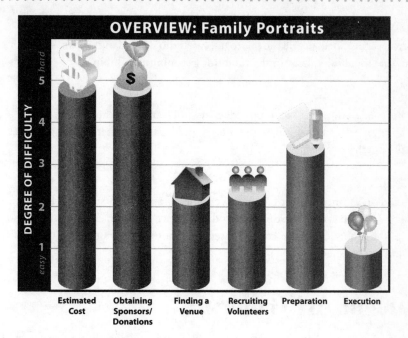

Special Materials/Equipment
- Attractive backdrop
- Digital photography equipment
- Chairs or benches (to pose family members on)

Sponsors/Donations
- Contact a creative arts school or studio to find a student photographer who might donate his or her services.
- Ask a photo studio for permission to borrow a photo backdrop, or for permission to use studio space during off hours. Raise funds to have the digital pictures printed and matted, or make arrangements to have the student's school do the honors.

Possible Venue(s)
A photo, dance, or music studio with neutral-colored walls, or an uncluttered community or church meeting facility works well.

Recommended Volunteer
4 to 5 to set up backdrops, take photos, and keep track of orders.

Preparation
Promote the portrait sale through the local media, notices in church and school newsletters, fliers on vehicles, and notices on public bulletin boards. Add a notice about the event to the home page of your website. Set up an appointment schedule.

Execution

Set up a staging area outside the photography studio where families can wait their turn. Make sure there is a mirror in the room for last-minute primping.

Tip(s)

- Locate an online source to provide mats and frames for the photos.
- Take orders when you show the proofs, and have the materials shipped directly to the purchaser.

Variation(s)

- Find an online portrait company to handle your photo sessions. Typically, your organization can sell certificates good for a free portrait in exchange for a donation ($10 or more), and the company sends a photographer out to snap the pictures and sell packages.

Student Art Gallery

Partner with a school art department to hold a student art exhibition and auction off artwork in various media. Turn the event into a gala by serving hors d'oeuvres with champagne for the adults and sparkling grape juice for the youngsters. Charge an entry fee to raise money for your organization, and auction the student art to benefit the school's art department.

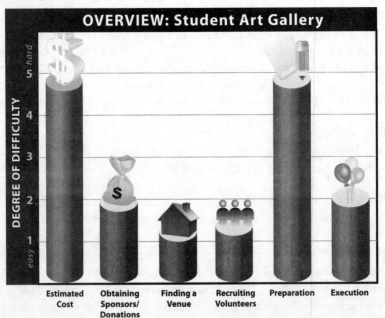

Sponsors/Donations

- Ask several local restaurants to donate a few trays of hors d'oeuvres each.
- Contact a wine shop and several grocery stores for bottles of champagne and sparkling juice, or ask local businesses for cash donations to purchase beverages.
- Speak with an art or craft store about having pictures matted.

Possible Venue(s)

A student art show is best held at the school itself, but a library, museum, or civic center would also be appropriate.

Recommended Volunteer

5 to 10 well-dressed volunteers, including several people to pour beverages and walk around with trays of hors d'oeuvres. A professional auctioneer would be ideal, but a volunteer with a gift of gab would also work.

Preparation

Work with the art teacher(s) to plan the exhibit. Promote the event in local media. Add a notice to the school's and your origination's website inviting people to attend. Print a program giving the names of each contributor. Set an opening bid for each art piece.

Execution

Start the event with appetizers and beverages. Have the student artists available to meet the public.

Tip(s)

- Have donation canisters on hand for those who wish to contribute directly instead of bidding.

Variation(s)

- Hold an exhibition and sale of student-made craft items.

Tie-Dye Station

Kids and adults alike will agree that this fundraiser is to "dye" for. Set up a tie-dying station, and let participants enjoy swirling dyes onto a rubber banded T-shirt, towel, canvas bag, or other cloth item. Charge a fee per item.

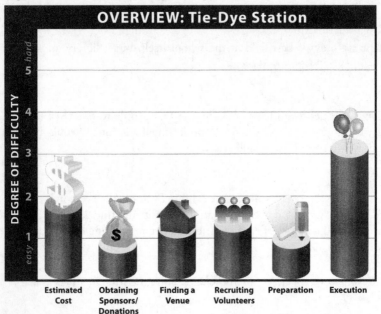

Special Materials/Equipment

- Rubber gloves
- Squirt bottles
- Buckets of water
- White T-shirts, and towels, or other cloth items to dye
- Dye
- Rubber bands
- Zip-close bags

Sponsors/Donations

- Ask a craft store to donate tie-dye kits and items to tie-dye.

Possible Venue(s)

Any outdoor location, like a park pavilion or a table in the grass, is a good place to not have to worry about making a mess with this fundraiser.

Recommended Volunteer

2+ to set up the station and help tie-dye.

Preparation
Have volunteers wear tie-dye shirts to advertise the event. Dye the shirts about a week in advance so you have time to wash and dry them beforehand. Tie-dye other items to hang up on a clothesline around your station with prices.

Execution
Supply volunteers with gloves and have them wear clothes that they would be OK getting dye on. Assist customers in tie-dying the items of their choice. Place customers finished products in zip-close bags for them to take home, and give them washing instructions.

Tip(s)
- Have customers pay before they start tie-dying, and designate one volunteer to handle the money.

Variation(s)
- Set up a T-shirt decorating station with puffy paint, permanent markers, or iron-on decorations.

Van Painting

Invite kids to let their creativity loose by using washable paint to decorate the sides of a white van. Charge a small fee for the privilege of turning the van into a moving piece of art. Circulate a donation canister among those who stop by to watch the kids work.

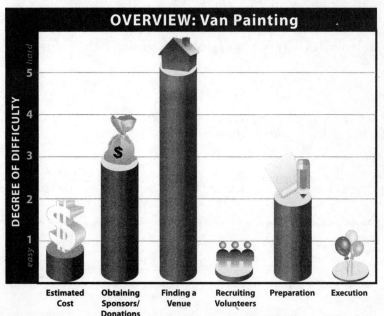

Special Materials/Equipment

- White van
- Brushes
- Washable paints

Sponsors/Donations

- If you cannot borrow a member's white van, ask a used car dealer or your municipality's vehicle pool manager to loan a van for a set period of time. Offer to display the donor's name in the side windows or another safe place during that time.
- Ask a print or sign shop to donate a sign that can be used during the event. Obtain washable paint from a school supply or office supply store, as well as paper towels for clean up.

Possible Venue(s)

A mall, shopping center, civic center, or school parking lot. A lot on a busy street is preferable, because more people will see the art event in action and might stop to watch (and donate to your cause).

Recommended Volunteer

3 to 4 to get supplies, oversee the event, and collect money

Preparation

Contact a school to line up budding artists, or place an ad in free community papers to seek participants. Send news releases to the media to promote the event.

Execution

Little effort required — just arm the kids with paint and brushes and let them go wild.

Tip(s)

- Make sure there is a water source close to where the kids will be painting to clean up paint spills and wash hands.

Variation(s)

- Try this with any vehicle (car, truck, bus), or have a wall painting fundraiser.

Auctions and Raffles

Everyone enjoys winning prizes, and these events let you raise money while still giving away fun prizes. The projects you will find in this chapter include:

- ⊚ Be the Boss for a Day
- ⊚ Bingo Night
- ⊚ 50/50 Raffle
- ⊚ Lunch with the CEO
- ⊚ Parking Space Auction
- ⊚ Quilt Auction
- ⊚ Reverse Raffle
- ⊚ Stick Lottery

Be the Boss for a Day

Give local companies' employees the opportunity to sit in their boss's chair for a day or an afternoon by raffling off a top executive's job. Add to the hilarity of the event and up your organization's take by also requiring the boss to do the winner's job that day, including wearing a uniform, if appropriate. Choose a large company so the chances of raising a significant amount of money are greater.

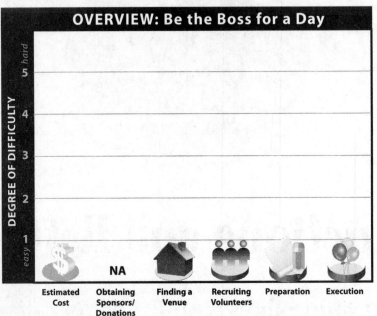

Special Materials/Equipment
• Roll of two-part raffle tickets

Sponsors/Donations
• If you wish to offer a few more prizes, approach local retail stores, restaurants, and service providers (such as tanning salons or fitness gyms) for gift cards or other rewards.

Possible Venue(s)
Large corporations and mid-sized companies, government agencies, schools and universities, and hospitals and medical centers work well.

Recommended Volunteer
2 to 3 to sell tickets and conduct the raffle

Preparation

Identify target companies and make arrangements with the human resources department to schedule the event. Submit a brief article for the employee newsletter promoting the event and giving details about the cost, and where and when to purchase tickets. Prepare a short reminder e-mail that can be sent to employees the day before the raffle.

Execution

Sell tickets in a high traffic area, such as the lobby or employee lunch room. Personally escort the executive to his or her "new" job amid much fanfare.

Tip(s)

- Make sure the selected executive is onboard and has a schedule that will allow him or her to honor the commitment.

Variation(s)

- Pay to play Trading Spaces with a coworker. Trade office spaces for a few hours, and bring or buy decorations to re-do the look of their desk or cubicle.

Bingo Night

Host a community bingo party complete with prizes and refreshments. Add a 50/50 raffle to generate more profit.

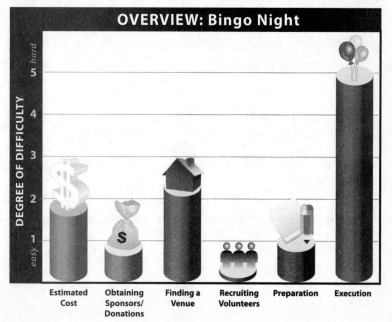

Special Materials/Equipment
- Plastic bingo chips
- Numbered bingo balls
- Bingo cards (available at party supply stores or for print from online sites)
- Bingo cage or other container from which to draw the balls

Sponsors/Donations
- A bingo hall might be willing to supply bingo cards and other paraphernalia for your fundraiser, as long as it is not held on the same night as its own event(s).
- Ask several members of your organization to go to different sites online and print free bingo cards.
- Approach local businesses for gift cards and other small prizes that can be awarded to winners.

Possible Venue(s)
Any room with long tables and chairs, including church halls, community centers, and school cafeterias, is good. It is a plus if there is a raised platform on one end where the caller can hold court.

Recommended Volunteer
3 to 4 to run the game and concessions

Preparation
Advertise the event in free community newspapers and through news releases sent to local media. Circulate fliers in parking lots and post them on free bulletin boards.

Execution
Charge a set amount per game (say, $1) or give a discount for multiple card purchases.

Tip(s)
- Check discount department stores or toy stores for inexpensive bingo sets, or make your own bingo balls by writing letters and numbers on ping-pong balls with a permanent marker.
- Check with the state to see if you will need a gaming license to operate legally.

Variation(s)
- Host a bingo party for the employees of a local company.

50/50 Raffle

This simple fundraiser entails selling tickets, drawing a winning ticket, and splitting the jackpot with the winner.

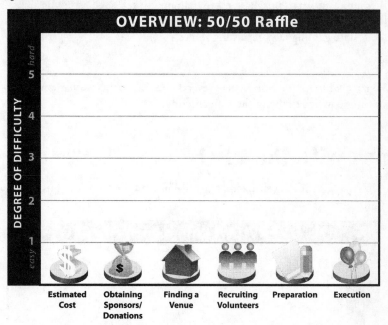

Special Materials/Equipment
- Roll of two-part tickets (available at office supply stores or online)

Possible Venue(s)

City fairs, church festivals, school events like sporting events. You might also be able to persuade mall, grocery store, bank, or office building management company representatives to allow your volunteers to sell tickets in their building or lobby.

Recommended Volunteer

1 to 2 to handle tickets

Preparation

Buy the two-part tickets and set up a table from which to sell them.

Execution

When holding a 50/50 raffle as part of another event, like a city festival, turn it into a special event of its own. Have a display board showing how much money has been raised each hour. Make regular announcements encouraging more sales. Count down the time to the drawing, and issue a last call for tickets. To ramp up the excitement, require that the winning ticket holder be present to claim the jackpot. Then, make a special production of handing over the cash to the lucky winner.

Tip(s)

- Offer an incentive to purchase more than one ticket, such as selling tickets for $1 each, or three tickets for $2, or five tickets for $4. This will increase profits fast.
- Check state gaming laws regarding raffles.

Variation(s)

- Make it a Chinese Auction, where several items are being raffled, and participants can choose which drawing they are entering.

Lunch with the CEO

Auction off a meal with a well-liked and well-known CEO or other business leader in your community.

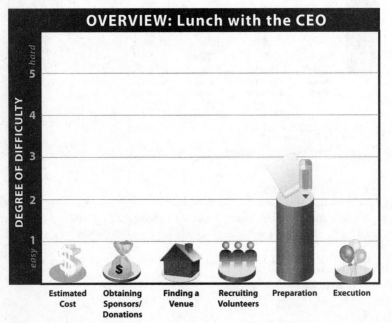

OVERVIEW: Lunch with the CEO

Sponsors/Donations

- To maximize the amount of money your organization will receive, approach a local restaurateur to donate the cost of the meal or provide a gift certificate.
- Ask a professional auctioneer to donate his or her services to make the auction experience more exciting.

Possible Venue(s)

Because audience interaction and participation are necessary to conduct a successful auction, it is best to hold it as part of another event that will attract many people. A city or church festival, concert, art show, or sporting event is ideal. If the CEO is employed at a large company with many employees, a company event like a picnic or holiday party will also work well.

Recommended Volunteer

2 to 3 to set up the lunch and run the auction

Preparation

Create signs to draw attention to the auction site. Promote the event in local media. Send out personal invitations to potential big bidders.

Execution

Make an announcement to draw participants to the auction site.

Tip(s)

- Promote the lunch as an opportunity to network, build a relationship, or otherwise hobnob with a community business leader. But, make it clear that it is *not* an opportunity to ask for a job or promotion.

Variation(s)

- Auction off an opportunity to play golf with a popular or well-known CEO.
- Line up several CEOs or other business leaders and local personalities and hold a silent auction to win a lunch or dinner with each of them.
- Auction off a job-switch opportunity, in which the CEO switches jobs for a few hours with the winning bidder in his or her company.

Parking Space Auction

Auction off a prime parking spot in a company parking lot or parking structure to benefit your charity. Conduct either a live auction in conjunction with another company event, or hold a silent auction on site.

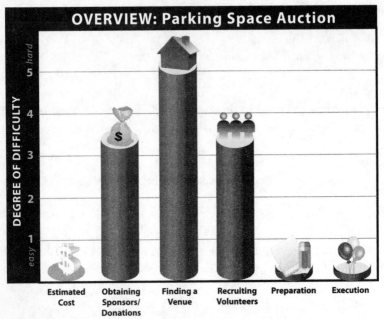

OVERVIEW: Parking Space Auction

DEGREE OF DIFFICULTY — hard (5) / easy (1)

Estimated Cost · Obtaining Sponsors/Donations · Finding a Venue · Recruiting Volunteers · Preparation · Execution

Sponsors/Donations

- Approach the CEO or other executive in companies that have their own parking lot or structure, especially those with assigned parking. Ask him or her to donate a spot for a set period of time (perhaps a month).
- If holding a live auction, ask a professional auctioneer to donate a small block of time for the event.

Possible Venue(s)

Companies with their own parking facilities and a large number of employees are preferable so there will be plenty of bidders. Also, companies in downtown areas that offer only executive parking work well, because regular staff members are likely to be eager to have a chance to get preferred parking for a specific period of time.

Recommended Volunteer

2 to 3 to oversee the auction

Preparation

Advertise the auction in the company newsletter and by e-mail. If holding a silent auction, scout out a central location in the building, and prepare bid sheets. Determine a minimum incremental bid (perhaps $1 or $5).

Execution

Decorate the auction venue (meeting room, cafeteria) with balloons or other decorations to create a festive atmosphere. Present the winning bidder with a token representing his or her prize, such as an oversized ticket for 30 days of parking.

Tip(s)

- Make sure the parking spot is in a premium location. If the budget allows, have a "Reserved for (Name)" sign made. You can find companies that offer affordable signs on the Internet.

Variation(s)

- Let the winner paint his or her parking spot to personalize it.

Quilt Auction

Sell a hand-stitched quilt in an online auction or offer it as a raffle prize to raise funds. The quilt could be made by members of your own organization or by a person or group who donates it to your organization.

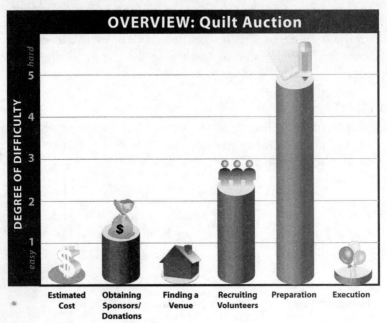

Special Materials/Equipment

- Fabric
- Other quilting materials (needle and thread or sewing machine, etc.)

Sponsors/Donations

- Ask craft store owners to donate fabric scraps for the quilt.
- Ask quilting clubs to create and donate a handmade quilt to your organization.

Possible Venue(s)

Raffle tickets for quilts can be sold at another event (like a church or art fair) or through your organization's website. You can also sell the quilt through an online auction like on eBay or through Etsy.com, a website that sells specialized, handmade goods.

Recommended Volunteer

3 to 4 or more, including experienced quilters to create quilted squares and assemble the quilt; 1 person to list the quilt on eBay or Etsy.com, then mail it to the winning bidder or seller; and, if the quilt is raffled, 1 to 2 volunteers to conduct the raffle

Preparation

Sign up for an online auction account, write an item description, and photograph the quilt. List the quilt with a reserve (minimum) price, or designate a "Buy It Now" price. If the quilt will be raffled, reserve a table for the event.

Execution

Mail the quilt once the auction closes. If raffled, display it at the event to encourage ticket sales.

Tip(s)

- Make a winter-themed quilt to remind people of the warmth it will provide in the cold weather and the festive decoration it will add to your home for the holidays.

Variation(s)

- Raffle or auction other handmade quilted goods, like placemats, table runners, or handbags.

Reverse Raffle

Imagine holding a raffle in which no one wants the prizes. That is the premise of the reverse raffle, where everyone automatically receives a chance to win a highly undesirable prize, such as a donkey, a buzz haircut, or a tacky house decoration. If they do not want the prize — which is likely if the prize is outlandish enough — they can "sell" their ticket back for a set price. This works best as part of an organization's meeting or other major event.

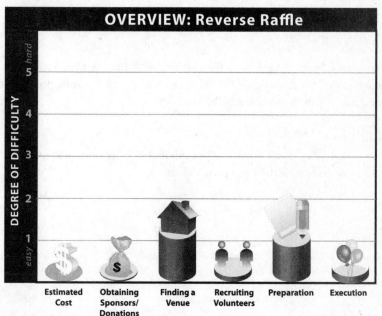

OVERVIEW: Reverse Raffle

Special Materials/Equipment
- Roll of two-part raffle tickets

Sponsors/Donations
- Find a host venue or organization where you can run the raffle as part of an event.

Possible Venue(s)
Membership meetings, stockholders meetings, church and community events, and fundraising events for related causes work well.

Recommended Volunteer
2 to 3 to come up with an undesirable item and sell tickets

Preparation
Send a news release to local media. Create a professional-looking sign to display at the event. Determine the ticket buy-back price (typically $1 to $10 or more, depending on the event).

Execution
Give attendees half of a two-part ticket and explain the raffle. Direct them to a nearby table where they can sell back their ticket. Just before the end of the event, give attendees one last chance to sell back their ticket to get a last surge of donations.

Tip(s)
- If you must award the gag prize because all tickets have not been sold back, allow the winner of the drawing a final chance to sell it back — or be prepared to load that donkey into the winner's SUV.

Variation(s)
- Offer a real prize in addition to the undesirable prize and enter into a drawing those who "sell" back their gag prize tickets.

Stick Lottery

Raise funds by having people select a stick from among a bunch standing upright in a box filled with sand. Those who select the specially-marked lucky sticks win prizes. Drawing a stick can cost $1 to $10 or more; just make sure the higher the fee, the higher the prize values are.

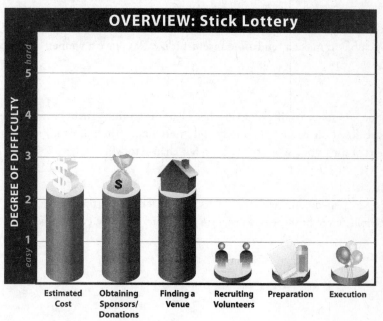

Special Materials/Equipment:

- Box filled several inches high with sand
- Large number of identical sticks (such as wooden craft sticks, meat skewers, or toothpicks)

Sponsors/Donations

- Ask a nursery to donate a few bags of sand.
- Approach a craft store for craft sticks, or a kitchenware store for meat skewers.
- Request gift card donations from stores and restaurants.

Possible Venue(s)

Community and school fairs, and church and city festivals are great options.

Recommended Volunteer

2 to 3 to setup up the sticks and box and to run the lottery

Preparation

Set the cost to draw a stick and the prize amounts. For example, 200 sticks at $5 will raise $1,000, so you might offer five $20 prizes, or donated gift cards in varying amounts. Using a marker, mark the ends of the predetermined number of winning sticks, and then mix them with the unmarked sticks. Insert them upright into the box of sand, making sure the colored ends are completely submerged.

Execution

Collect cash and make a loud announcement like "We have a winner!" when a lucky stick is selected.

Tip(s)

- If the fundraiser is still going on when all of the winning sticks have been selected, close down the game temporarily and insert a new batch of winning sticks out of sight of the public so everyone has a fair chance to win.

Variation(s)

- Use sharpened pencils at school fairs, or golf tees at sporting events.
- Use lollipops to further entice people to participate. That way, everyone wins something.

Chapter 3

Food and Drinks

Everyone eats, and you can put together delicious deals to raise money for your organization. The projects you will find in this chapter include:

- ⦾ Cakewalk
- ⦾ Create a Cookbook
- ⦾ Donations for Fortune Cookies
- ⦾ Lollipop Sale
- ⦾ Popcorn Concession Stand
- ⦾ Potluck Dinner
- ⦾ Restaurant.com Gift Card Sale

Cakewalk

Similar to musical chairs, competitors walk around a set of marked squares and freeze when the music stops. The participants who are standing on specially marked squares when the music stops win cakes to take home. Cakewalkers pay a fee to play.

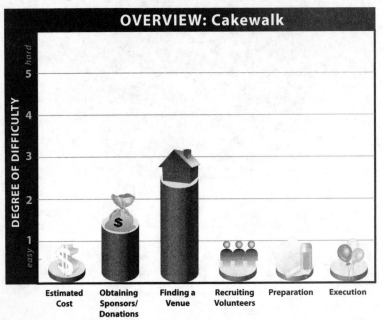

Special Materials/Equipment

- Cakes
- Bakery boxes (for winners to carry cakes home in)

Sponsors/Donations

- Call on the members of your organization to make cakes.
- Contact bakeries or grocery stores that have in-house bakery departments for donations of baked goods and cake boxes.

Possible Venue(s)

Any room large enough to hold the expected number of participants, such as your organization's home, a community center, or a banquet room, works well.

Recommended Volunteer

2 to 3 to bake and to run the game

Preparation

Promote the event in as many free media as possible. Prepare the cakes and make specially marked winners squares.

Execution

Tape or securely fasten the squares in a circle on the floor, creating the path participants will follow in their walk. Display the cakes, and collect participants' entry fees. Play music, stop it, and award cakes. There can be one or more winners per round.

Tip(s)

- Print a booklet containing the recipes for the cakes, and sell it for a nominal price.

Variation(s)

- Ask the best bakers among your donors to create more elaborate cakes, such as holiday-themed cakes or even gingerbread houses.

Create a Cookbook

Gather tasty recipes and compile them in a professional-looking cookbook that you can sell.

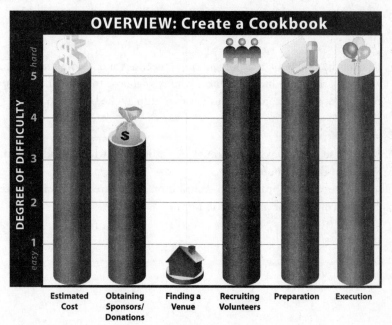

OVERVIEW: Create a Cookbook

DEGREE OF DIFFICULTY — hard / easy

Estimated Cost | Obtaining Sponsors/ Donations | Finding a Venue | Recruiting Volunteers | Preparation | Execution

Sponsors/Donations

- See if you can find a company that can professionally design and bind a cookbook for a discount. Several companies listed online specialize in making fundraising cookbooks at an affordable price.
- Although you can solicit donations to offset the cost of compiling and printing the book, it is usually best to sell advertising pages in the book to fund the project. Local companies that recognize the value inherent in a cookbook's long shelf life will be happy to be included.
- Additionally, you might charge each person who submits a recipe a nominal entry fee (perhaps $1 or $5) as a way to raise additional cash.

Possible Venue(s)

Stores, office buildings, craft shows, or online sales through your website are good venues.

Recommended Volunteer

10+ to collect recipes and sell cookbooks

Preparation

Collect recipes from contributors and type them into a word document. E-mail the document to the company that will lay out and print the cookbook. Proof the final version before printing. Also, set a retail price, and draw up a distribution plan.

Execution

Bring copies of the cookbook to all organization meetings and fundraisers. Send copies to all local media that have lifestyle editors who may choose to write or talk about the cookbook. Ask local bookstores and businesses to display the book.

Tip(s)

- Arrange to sell the cookbook through Amazon.com, which handles both hard copy and on-demand books.
- Obtain advance book orders from contributors, who surely will want to see their names and culinary contributions in print.

Donations for Fortune Cookies

Used in concert with another fundraiser or on its own, selling fortune cookies is a fun way to generate interest in your cause. Look for a manufacturer that can produce customized messages for the cookies so you can place inspirational messages inside, along with your organization's phone number and website and a request for a donation. Give a cookie in exchange for a donation. The cookies themselves cost as little as 10 cents each.

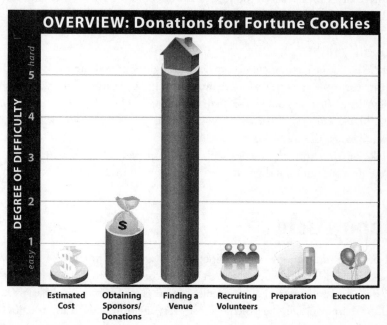

Sponsors/Donations

• Partner with another organization to give away cookies during its fundraising event.

Possible Venue(s)

Try holding this event at community and school events and fairs.

Recommended Volunteer

1 to 2 to order the cookies and hand them out for donations

Preparation

Write the custom message, place the online order, and reserve a booth or table at the community event where funds will be solicited.

Execution

Ask passersby to donate to your cause and present them with a cookie in exchange for a donation.

Tip(s)

- Time cookie giveaways or sales to coincide with the Chinese New Year (which can begin any time between late-January and early-February, depending on the year).
- Note that commercially-produced fortune cookies have a shelf life of 2 to 3 months.

Variation(s)

- Make gourmet fortune cookies to sell through your website or online. Offer to create customized fortunes for organizations that pay extra for the service. Package them in a fortune cookie box tied with a red ribbon (red is considered lucky in Chinese culture). Check with your state to see whether you will need a food license to sell the cookies commercially.
- Make origami fortune cookies with colored paper, fill them with candy, add a paper fortune, and sell them at organization functions.

Lollipop Sale

Small, portable, and inexpensive, lollipops make a great fundraising item. Typically, lollipops sell for $1 each, which is pocket change for most people, plus they come in a variety of shapes and colors. You can generate a 50 percent profit on these sweet treats, and selling them could not be easier, because everyone from kids to adults enjoys them. Add gourmet options like cherry cheesecake flavor or chocolate roses on sticks to your selection and watch the "big kids" line up.

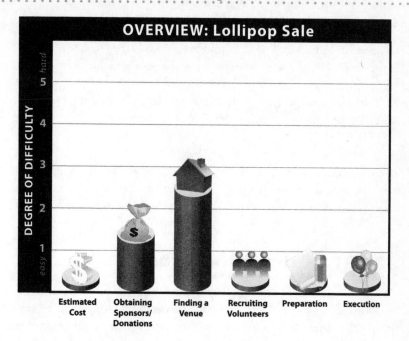

Special Materials/Equipment
- T-shirts emblazoned with your organization's logo and/or hats (to identify your volunteers)

Sponsors/Donations
- Ask local businesses that cater to kids for donations. This might include pizza parlors, day care businesses, and kid-friendly hair salons. Offer to include the name of their business on your promotional materials, or affix a sticker with both the organization's and the business's name on the product.

Possible Venue(s)
Schools, school cafeterias, school sporting events, dance recitals, shopping centers, malls, and community get-togethers are great.

Recommended Volunteer
3 to 5+ to order the lollipops and handle sales

Preparation
Obtain permission to use a venue. Purchase the product at least two weeks in advance.

Execution
Have volunteers mingle with event participants, or set up a table near the entry to the event to attract as many potential buyers as possible

Tip(s)

- Sell hearts and/or lips lollipops around Valentine's Day.
- Sell other holiday-themed lollipops to mark occasions like Christmas, Easter, Halloween, and Thanksgiving.
- Sell sports-themed lollipops at sporting events (especially during football season).
- Add curled ribbons to the sticks to add to the presentation.

Variation(s)

- Let customers add personalized cards (provided by you) to the lollipops and offer to deliver them to the recipients in their offices or classrooms for an extra fee.
- Make your own using lollipop mix or melted chocolate, plastic molds, and sticks.

Popcorn Concession Stand

This popular snack comes in different flavors, offers healthy options, and can be served in sports-themed bags. It is a versatile, inexpensive fundraising food that everyone loves. It runs the gamut from convenient microwave packages to pre-popped gourmet selections, to reduced-fat or trans fat-free and cholesterol-free options.

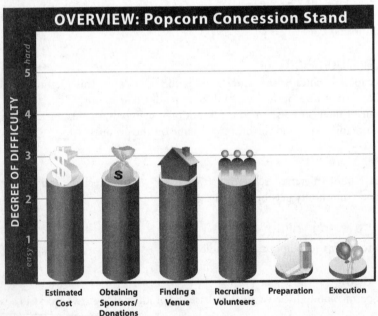

OVERVIEW: Popcorn Concession Stand

Special Materials/Equipment

- T-shirts emblazoned with your organization's logo and/or hats (to identify your volunteers)
- Money pouches and/or aprons (for holding cash)

Sponsors/Donations
- Approach local businesses for financial assistance with product purchases. Offer to display signs at the venue to identify them as sponsors, and include their names in all other publicity efforts (news releases, ads in community newspapers).
- Request free space at venues and other places where people gather to socialize.

Possible Venue(s)
Sporting facilities and playing fields, movie theaters, amusement parks, carnivals, shopping centers, and malls work well.

Recommended Volunteer
3-5 to order the popcorn and run the stand

Preparation
Using the amount of money you would like to raise as a guide, order sufficient product at least two weeks before the fundraiser. Expect to pay about 50 percent of the product's retail price in your calculations.

Execution
Station volunteers at the entrance to the venue to advertise. Set up a table a few feet from the door where buyers also can stop conveniently.

Tip(s)
- Popcorn can be salty, so be sure to sell drinks and sweets to bring in more profit and complement the snack. Offer combos for discounts.

Variation(s)
- Time sales for right before the Super Bowl, World Series, Final Four, or other popular sporting events.
- Set up a retail display in a video rental store to sell packaged products.
- Rent concession equipment and pop this delicious treat right on site for hungry customers.
- Charge more for specialty bags that you dipped in chocolate or caramel or tossed in powdered cheese.

Potluck Dinner

Invite your organization's members to share their favorite recipes while raising funds during a potluck dinner.

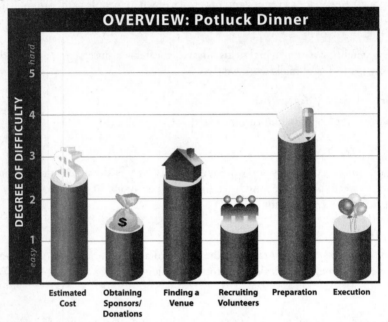

OVERVIEW: Potluck Dinner

Special Materials/Equipment

- Slow cookers
- Ice-filled coolers
- Chafing dishes

Sponsors/Donations

- Approach grocery stores, membership warehouses, and party stores for food donations.
- Ask florists to donate table arrangements, and party supply stores to donate paper plates and cups, plastic cutlery, and disposable tablecloths.

Possible Venue(s)

Look for a location where many people gather. Church and city festivals are ideal, as are sports booster events, block parties, and municipal parks. Check with the local municipality and the state to see if a food vendor license is necessary.

Recommended Volunteer

10+ to sell tickets and collect money, oversee the food tables, refill serving containers, and clean up; dozens to make food and desserts

Preparation

Develop a budget and line up food donations. Create a sign-up sheet divided into courses (appetizers, meat, vegetarian dishes, salads, desserts, and so on), and circulate it among the volunteers. Make sure you have enough entries in each category. Establish a meal price, and promote the event in local media and in free community newspapers.

Execution

Set up food tables, and invite the public to enjoy the party.

Tip(s)

- Sell a potluck recipe booklet and offer simple party games to raise additional funds.
- Hand out information about your organization to interested parties.

Variation(s)

- Hold a fundraising potluck lunch at your volunteers' workplaces.
- Host a potluck that features ethnic foods and music.

Restaurant.com Gift Card Sale

Your organization can order Restaurant.com gift cards for less than the value price and then sell them at the value price to make a nice profit. You can purchase $25-value cards for $15, $50-value cards for $25, and $100-value cards for $40. Customers can redeem cards online for use at 15,000 restaurants nationwide, and the cards have no expiration. You can also customize them with your organization's logo and marketing message.

Special Materials/Equipment

- Signs (to advertise)
- Table (to sell the cards)

Sponsors/Donations

- You might ask the largest participating restaurant in your town for permission to sell cards or post a sign about the availability of the cards in its establishment.

Possible Venue(s)

Retail stores, shopping centers, malls, school athletic events, community fairs, and bank and grocery store lobbies are possibilities.

Recommended Volunteer

3 to 5 to order and sell the gift cards

Preparation

Check the list of participating restaurants on Restaurant.com to make sure the gift cards can be redeemed in your area. Order the cards and promote them on your website and in your organization's newsletter. If you are selling the cards at a community event, inform the local media by sending out press releases.

Execution

Set up a table from which to sell the cards. Be sure to tell passersby that their donation will buy them a delicious meal (or many) at any of 15,000 restaurants.

Tip(s)

- This fundraiser may not work as well in smaller towns, where there may not be as many participating restaurants.
- Around the holidays, pitch the gift cards as a perfect, low-cost stocking stuffer.

Variation(s)

- Get restaurants to donate special coupons, and sell special coupon packets.

Chapter 4

Games and Contests

This chapter brings out the friendly competition, as your supporters compete for prizes or pride, all while you raise funds. The projects you will find in this chapter include:

- Baby Photo Competition
- Cutest Baby Competition
- Draw-the-Boss Competition
- Dunk Tank
- Executive Chair Chase
- Fish for a Prize
- Game Night
- Penny Pile-Up
- Quiz Competition
- Rubber Ducky Race
- Spelling Bee
- Ugliest Tie Contest
- Video Game Challenge

Baby Photo Competition

Collect baby photos from 15 to 20 well-known members of a social community (such as a church, school, club, or athletic association), and then take pictures of the same individuals today. Shuffle the photos and create a contest sheet showing both the old and current photos, then ask participants to match each baby picture to the current picture. Charge a fee to participate and award a cash prize. This fundraiser works best as part of another community event, such as a church fair, club activity, city fair, or anywhere else the participants are well-known.

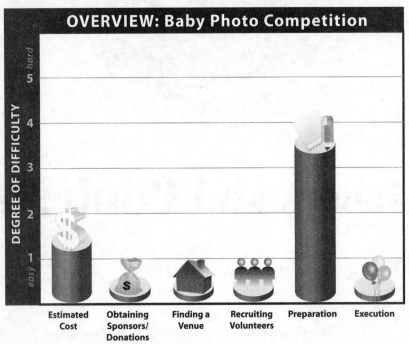

Special Materials/Equipment
- Digital camera (to take present-day photo)
- Scanner
- Collection canisters

Sponsors/Donations
- Ask a quick print shop or office superstore to donate the printed contest sheets.

Possible Venue(s)
Churches, clubs, municipal meeting rooms, schools, or membership organizations are good options.

Recommended Volunteer

3 to 4 to collect photos, create the contest sheet, and sort through contestants' entries

Preparation

Contact prominent members of the target organization for baby photos, and scan the photos so they can be returned safely to donors.

Execution

During the designated community event, display the photos, charge a small fee to participate in the contest, and collect completed entry forms. Draw entries at random until you find one with a perfect score. If no one matches every picture correctly, award the prize to the entry with the most correct matches.

Tip(s)

- If possible, post the photos (or scanned copies) in a centrally located place in the organization's facility (mount them on poster board or place them under glass in a display case).
- Print the contest sheets using a high quality printer or photocopier so the picture quality is as good as possible.

Variation(s)

- Have a celebrity look-alike photo contest. Charge a fee for entrance, choose a panel of judges, and award the winner with a red-carpet experience or a trip to Hollywood.

Cutest Baby Competition

Hold a contest to choose the cutest baby from among submitted photos. Charge a small entry fee for each contestant, and have people vote for their favorites by placing dollars into collection canisters. The person whose picture collects the most vote money is crowned "Cutest Baby" and wins a trophy or a selection of baby-themed products.

Special Materials/Equipment

- Collection canisters
- Signs (to promote the contest)
- T-shirts with the name of your organization (for volunteers)

Sponsors/Donations

- Contact baby stores for donations of gender-neutral clothes, toys, and other items for the grand prize.
- Approach a sign company about donating signs.

Possible Venue(s)

Baby clothing and toy stores, department stores, grocery stores, preschools, or community centers work well.

Recommended Volunteer

10+ to scan and print photos, post them, monitor donation canisters, collect and count money

Preparation

Advertise for pictures in local media and on community bulletin boards. Set up a post office box to collect pictures and entry fees, or have a secure drop-off box at a central location (like a participating baby clothing store). Distribute signs to baby clothing and toy stores and day cares. If displaying the photos in numerous locations, scan each photo and print the appropriate number of copies. Be sure to have one collection canister per photo. Print signs with the date of the contest and details about how to vote. Post photos at least a week before the competition in order to generate excitement.

Execution

Pair up numbered canisters with a photo. Have volunteers available at each venue to explain the contest and safeguard the canisters. Award the title of "Cutest Baby" to the person whose canister has the most money.

Tip(s)

• Have a "Baby Shower" party for the winner.

Variation(s)

• Have a Cutest Pet Contest.

Draw-the-Boss Competition

A charming fundraiser that will make everyone smile. Take or obtain current pictures of two top executives at a business workplace, then hold a contest in which the children of the organization's employees draw pictures of the executives. Charge an entry fee for each drawing submitted. Post the drawings in the company cafeteria or a meeting room, and charge employees $1 or more to cast a vote for their favorites. Award a prize to the child whose drawing receives the most votes.

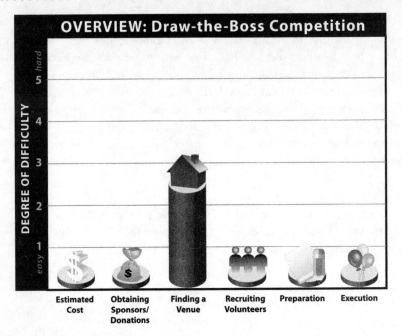

Special Materials/Equipment
- Digital camera (to photograph the executives)
- Canisters (to collect vote money in)

Sponsors/Donations
- Ask a local business to donate money or other prizes for the winning artists.

Possible Venue(s)
Any organization that has a fairly large number of employees, including corporations, government agencies, large retail stores, hospitals and medical centers, schools and universities, is a good option.

Recommended Volunteer
3 to 5 to prepare promotional materials, collect and post pictures, and collect entry fees and voting fees

Preparation
Contact the human resources department of the target company to get permission to hold the fundraiser. Prepare a short article for the company's newsletter to announce the contest and its details. Get approval from the human resources department to send e-mails to employees that remind them about the contest. Also, prepare and hang posters announcing the event.

Columbus Metropolitan Library

Date: 6/8/2019

Time: 11:11:30 AM

Name: BRAATEN, BRENDAN L

Fines/Fees Owed: $0.00

Total Checked Out: 4

Checked Out

Title: Star Wars : Darth Vader : dark lord of the
Sith. Vol. 1, Imperial machine
Barcode: 1337609121
Media Type: Juvenile Book
Due Date: 06/29/2019 23:59:59

Title: Star wars. Darth Vader, dark lord of the Si
Vol. 3, The burning seas
Barcode: 31869004500642
Media Type: Book
Due Date: 06/29/2019 23:59:59

Title: Star wars. Darth Vader, dark lord of the Si
Vol. 2, Legacy's end
Barcode: 1337880879
Media Type: Juvenile Book
Due Date: 06/29/2019 23:59:59

Title: 199 fun and effective fundraising events f
nonprofit organizations
Barcode: 30231006482066
Media Type: Book
Due Date: 06/29/2019 23:59:59

Execution

Collect the entries and entry fees, and hang the pictures in the designated location. Place canisters under each submission so employees can deposit cash into the canisters to vote for their favorites.

Tip(s)

- Request that all drawings be made on the same size paper, such as 8 ½-by-11-inch.

Dunk Tank

Simple to run and plenty of fun to observe, a dunk tank fundraiser is a crowd pleaser that gives people a chance to lob balls at a target upon which a direct hit triggers a mechanism that drops a volunteer seated above a large vat of water right into the tank. Rather than operating as a standalone event, this activity works best as part of another outdoor event, such as a carnival or church fair.

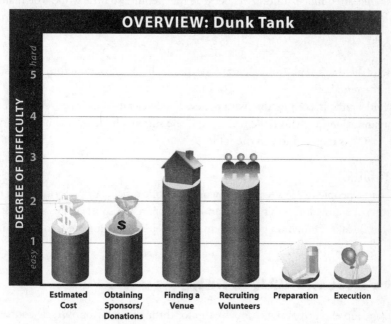

Special Materials/Equipment

- Dunk tank
- Water source (Tanks can be rented by the day starting at around $120, or by the hour usually for a minimum of 3 to 4 hours.)

Sponsors/Donations

- Solicit companies with a water tie-in (car washes, auto detailers, marinas) for donations or sponsorships.

Possible Venue(s)

Carnivals, church fairs, school fairs, or city festivals are ideal.

Recommended Volunteer

4 to 5 to collect money, take tickets, dole out balls to participants, and sit in the tank

Preparation

Rent the dunk tank and balls, promote the event, and line up volunteers willing to take a dip for a good cause. All "dunk-ees" are welcome, but also invite local celebrities, public officials, and school officials and teachers (for school fundraisers) to participate.

Execution

Dunk tanks are popular fundraisers because they require so little work. The main tasks include selling tickets, collecting money, and handing out and retrieving balls.

Tip(s)

- Rent the dunk tank from a company that includes delivery, setup, and insurance in the rental fee.
- Hold a raffle in conjunction with the event to generate even more revenue for your organization (a 50/50 raffle works well). Be sure to check with your state to see if a license is required to run the raffle.

Variation(s)

- Charge people to pie a teacher, coworker, public official, or celebrity in the face in front of a crowd. Do this during an intermission at a sports game, show, or other event. Make a donation goal that must be met in order for them to be pied.

Executive Chair Chase

Challenge top executives at a company to race through a relay or obstacle course while seated in their office chairs. This is best held in an outdoor location like a parking lot, but it can be hilarious when held right in the office through a maze of cubicles and office equipment. Charge employees $1 or more to bet on their favorite executive, and give a prize to the competitor with the best time.

Special Materials/Equipment
- Canisters (to collect vote money in)
- Stopwatch (to record official finishing times)

Sponsors/Donations
- Ask a local restaurant or other business to donate a gift certificate or other non-monetary prize that can be awarded to the chair champ.

Possible Venue(s)
To raise the most money, select an organization with a large number of employees, like a corporation, government agency, large retail store, hospital and medical center, school, or university.

Recommended Volunteer
3 to 5 to prepare promotional materials and collect voting fees from employees

Preparation
Contact the human resources department of the target organization to propose holding a fundraiser. Create posters advertising the event and submit a story to the company's newsletter to build excitement. Set a vote price (such as $1). Alert the local media, who undoubtedly will be delighted to see top executives in suits and ties engaging in such a lighthearted activity for a good cause.

Execution

Place canisters at the starting line for employees to cast their money into. Have each canister labeled with a competitors name.

Tip(s)

• Write a post-event story for the company newsletter, giving the total amount raised and thanking employees for their generosity.

Variation(s)

• Make it an Office Olympics, and come up with other creative office games. Have a small award ceremony.

Fish for a Prize

Let participants cast a toy pole into a kiddie pool full of numbered plastic fish. Award them with prizes such as gift cards, stuffed animals, or bags of candy that correspond with the numbers on their fish. Charge per time they cast.

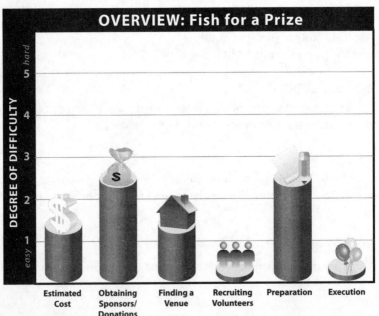

Special Materials/Equipment

• Toy fishing set with poles and fish
• Kiddie pools or other pond-like displays

Sponsors/Donations

- Ask restaurants and local stores to donate gift cards that you can give out as prizes.
- Ask toy stores to donate other fun prizes.

Possible Venue(s)

Try holding this event at a carnival or in conjunction with a picnic. It could also be set up in a school cafeteria during lunchtime.

Recommended Volunteer

2 to 3 to collect prizes, set up, and run the game

Preparation

Try to get prizes donated that vary in value. Consider setting up a few "fishing ponds" and charge more for participants to cast a pole into ponds with more expensive prizes. Create signs advertising the possible wins for each pond.

Execution

Recruit participants, collect entry fees, and give out prizes that correspond with their catches.

Game Night

A friendly competition that pits teams of game players against each other. Organizations can raise cash by charging individuals or teams a low admission fee (to encourage them to return on subsequent game nights), or by asking the host business to donate a percentage of its profits for the evening. To encourage participation, offer a cash prize to the winning team.

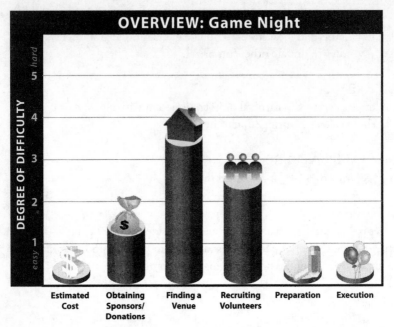

Special Materials/Equipment

- Game of your choice (i.e. Trivial Pursuit, bingo, poker, Texas Hold 'em, Monopoly or Scrabble)

Sponsors/Donations

- If the cash prize is low enough (perhaps $75), it can come out of the night's proceeds. Otherwise, ask the sponsoring venue to donate the prize money.

Possible Venue(s)

Try hosting this event at bars, taverns, pubs (best for Trivial Pursuit, poker, and Texas Hold 'em), bingo halls, or community centers (for all types of games).

Recommended Volunteer

4 to 5 including 1 to run the game (like calling out the Trivial Pursuit questions) and 3 or 4 to collect cash, judge the validity of answers, etc.

Preparation

Obtain the appropriate game and promote the event.

Execution

Designate a volunteer to take the microphone and read questions, call numbers, or otherwise lead the game players. Circulate among players to referee and judge answers.

Tip(s)

- Check to see if you need a gaming license from the state to legally hold such events.
- Ask the sponsoring organization to consider a recurring game night to build a loyal following and bring in a couple of bucks on a regular basis.
- Ask the venue to offer reduced fair and drink prices to attract more players (and thus increase your organization's take of the profits).

Penny Pile-Up

Set out collection canisters at point-of-sale locations like store check-out counters, or public places like libraries and community pools, and ask people to toss in every penny in their pocket or purse.

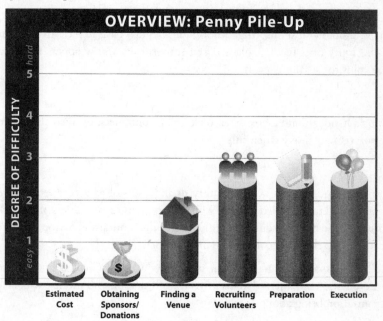

OVERVIEW: Penny Pile-Up

Special Materials/Equipment

- Collection canisters
- Penny wrappers
- Penny sorters

Sponsors/Donations

- Contact a bank that offers a coin counting service to its customers and ask if it will count your pennies at no charge.

Possible Venue(s)

Retail stores, libraries, government buildings, banks, and anywhere else you might find people with money in their pockets works well.

Recommended Volunteer

5 to 6 to distribute collection canisters, pick up filled containers, count and wrap pennies, and take the rolls to the bank

Preparation

Distribute the containers. Put a label on each container explaining the reason for the fundraiser, the name of your organization, and the day the penny drive concludes. Ask the sponsoring location to call your organization when the container fills up.

Execution

Volunteers should visit sponsoring locations on a regular basis to pick up full containers and leave empty ones in their place. Use penny sorters and wrappers to prepare the donated coins for a bank deposit.

Tip(s)

- Bring a handcart and a box when picking up containers. Even small canisters will be surprisingly heavy when full.

Variation(s)

- Run the fundraiser in an elementary or high school as a competition between classes, sometimes called Penny Wars. Supply larger containers like buckets or empty plastic milk cartons, and at the end of the fundraising period, throw a pizza party for the class that collects the most copper.

- Collect all spare change, and call it Money Wars or Change for Change, and write on the container what positive transformation the money will help your organization bring about.

Quiz Competition

Offer players the opportunity to show off their knowledge of popular culture, current events, or general know-how in a fast-paced quiz competition. Charge an entry fee to compete, and award cash prizes to the winners. Sell snacks and beverages to keep players energized and happy.

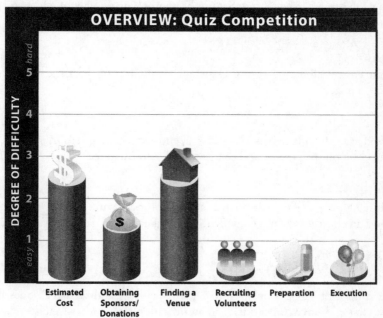

Special Materials/Equipment

- One game (like Trivial Pursuit), or list of about 50 quiz questions and answers as well as several tie-breaker or grand prize challenge questions, per table

Sponsors/Donations

- Approach a vending company for donations of packaged snacks, soft drinks, and water. Ask volunteers to donate baked goods for a bake sale.
- Seek a sponsor among local business owners to cover the cost of cash prizes, and tables, chairs, and microphone rentals.
- Ask a local celebrity or government official to serve as master of ceremonies/quiz master.

Possible Venue(s)

Community centers, church meeting halls, school auditoriums, or gymnasiums are good options.

Recommended Volunteer

5 to 6 to come up with questions, recruit participants, run the quiz show, and check answers

Preparation

Rent a microphone. Determine how individuals will compete (in teams or as individuals) and how long each game will run. Set up the appropriate number of tables and chairs. Create an answer sheet for each participant or team to use during play.

Execution

Have the emcee call out questions. Designate a volunteer to check the answers before awarding a prize.

Tip(s)

- Hold a 50/50 raffle to increase profits. Set up a spectator area so friends and family can cheer on the players, and charge a small admission fee.

Variation(s)

- Host a topic-specific event, such as an "Earth Bowl" with geography questions.
- Host an electronic gaming competition using handheld games or PlayStations.

Rubber Ducky Race

Release a flock of rubber duckies into a local waterway and see which ones float to victory. Charge $5 to $10 per duck and award cash prizes to top winners.

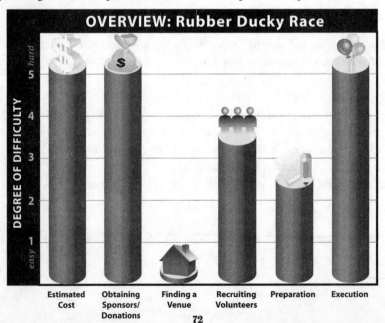

OVERVIEW: Rubber Ducky Race

Special Materials/Equipment
- Identical toy rubber ducks (at least several hundred)
- Waterproof markers
- Canoes and/or kayaks for duck chasing
- Walkie-talkies for volunteers
- Bullhorn to announce the winning numbers
- Fishnets to retrieve runner-up ducks

Sponsors/Donations
- Contact local businesses for donations to buy the ducks or offset the cost of renting canoes and walkie-talkies. Seek corporate sponsorships for flocks of ducks.

Possible Venue(s)
Any small body of water with a current, such as a stream or creek, works well. A waterway with bridges and stable banks along which people can stand to cheer on the ducks is ideal.

Recommended Volunteer
5+ to set up, monitor the race, follow the ducks, and declare the winners

Preparation
Promote the event in local media. Number each duck on its sides using a waterproof marker. Sell ducks until just before the race begins. Keep a log of the purchasers' names and contact information so winners can be notified. Prepare posters showing who owns which duck(s).

Execution
Release the ducks at the starting line. Have volunteers take canoes and kayaks out to untangle the ducks that get stuck in the brush, and use a bullhorn to relay play-by-play commentary. Station duck catchers at the finish line to log the winning numbers and collect the ducks.

Tip(s)
- Use ducks with a weighted base so they remain buoyant and stay upright. These tend to be a bit more expensive (about $2 each), but if you collect all the ducks at the end of the race, they can be used again.

Spelling Bee

Challenge an office or group to an old-fashioned spelling bee. Raise funds by organizing participants into teams and charging an entry fee. Offer a prize to the team still standing at the end of the bee. Engage others in the event and raise more cash for your organization by having them pay a small fee (like $1) to vote for the team they think will be victorious.

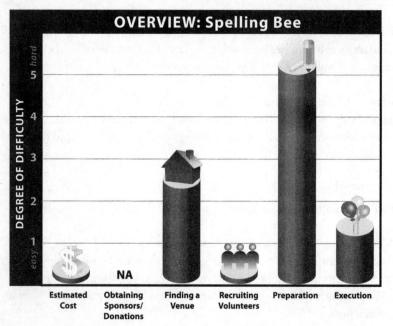

Special Materials/Equipment
- Podium and a microphone (for the moderator)
- Two tables surrounding the moderator with a microphone on each (for the teams competing)

Sponsors/Donations
- Contact local companies for prizes like gift cards. Try to obtain enough prizes to award first-, second-, and third-place teams.

Possible Venue(s)
Large businesses, such as corporations, government agencies, schools and universities, and medical facilities, or businesses that thrive on word play, like newspapers and advertising agencies, are great to ensure a large pool of players.

Recommended Volunteer

5+ including a moderator and a team to come up with a list of words

Preparation

Search a dictionary for spelling words, noting the root of each word and an example of how it is used in a sentence. Choose words that are commonly misspelled or unusual rather than obscure terms. Sign up teams a few weeks before the event.

Execution

Set up a playing area, preferably on a stage or other raised area in an auditorium or meeting room. Invite observers to come cheer on the players.

Tip(s)

- Invite a local celebrity to serve as emcee for the event.

Variation(s)

- Have a Geography Bee.

Ugliest Tie Contest

Hold an "Ugly Tie Day" fundraiser. Charge each participant an entry fee (perhaps $5 to $10), and $1 or more to cast a vote for the worst-looking tie. Award prizes to the people who are the proud owners of the top three ugliest ties.

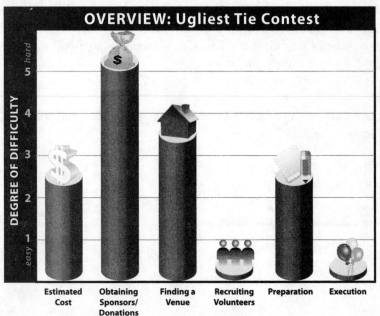

OVERVIEW: Ugliest Tie Contest

DEGREE OF DIFFICULTY (easy 1 – hard 5)

| Estimated Cost | Obtaining Sponsors/ Donations | Finding a Venue | Recruiting Volunteers | Preparation | Execution |

Special Materials/Equipment
- Collection canisters (in which to collect vote money)

Sponsors/Donations
- Have gift cards and other prizes donated by local businesses and vendors. To justify a large entry fee for tie wearers ($10 or more), make sure the prizes are valuable, such as dinner for two at a local restaurant or a luxury spa treatment.
- You also can collect cash from businesses and purchase gifts on your own.

Possible Venue(s)
This is best held at a corporate or company workplace, where the potential for good-natured ribbing and competition is highest. Hold the event during lunchtime so business day disruptions are minimal.

Recommended Volunteer
4 to 5 including people to monitor donation canisters and announce the winners

Preparation
Contact the human resources department of larger companies, and pitch the idea. Obtain collection canisters, and label them with numbers.

Execution
Have the participants meet in the lunchroom or conference room at a specified time. Assign a number to each participant that corresponds to a collection container. Ask other employees to vote for their favorite tacky tie by dropping money into the appropriate numbered container. Have a mini ceremony to award the winner and runners-up prizes after the voting is over.

Tip(s)
- Take a digital photo of each tie in contention, print them, and affix them to the appropriate collection canister.

Variation(s)
- Host an Ugliest Earrings Contest.
- Put on a Craziest Hat Contest.
- Have a Look-Alike or Costume Contest.

Video Game Challenge

Host a day-long video game tournament, focusing either on a single type of game or having several different game tournaments going on at one time. Charge an entry fee to play, and a small entrance fee to watch. Award prizes to the winners. Sell food and beverages.

Special Materials/Equipment

- Video game consoles
- TV sets or video monitors
- Scoreboard (a chalkboard, whiteboard, or computer and LCD projector work)
- Sound equipment (microphone and speakers for game time announcements)

Sponsors/Donations

- Contact video game retailers and department stores, or any type of business that caters to kids and young adults, including cell phone stores or bike shops.
- Approach businesses for gift cards that can be awarded as prizes.
- Ask grocery stores, restaurants, and party stores to provide snacks and other food.

Possible Venue(s)

A community or municipal center, school gym or auditorium, or bar or tavern (if players are of legal drinking age) is a good option.

Recommended Volunteer

5 to 6 to handle registrations and collect cash, update the tournament scoreboard, sell refreshments

Preparation

Promote the event in free community papers and through news releases to local media and local, youth-oriented organizations. Distribute fliers and post them on free bulletin boards. E-mail everyone in your own organization to drum up players.

Execution

If more than one game will be played, group players by game. Update the scoreboard often. Periodically announce leaders' names. Circulate among the players to sell food and beverages.

Tip(s)

- If the challenge is for one game, have elimination rounds and a final championship round.
- If several games are underway, allow players to try to top the highest scores right up to the event's end time.

Chapter 5

Holidays and Special Occasions

The events in this chapter tap into the holiday theme and combine a good cause with a seasonal event. The projects you will find in this chapter include:

- Corsage Sale
- Holiday Cookie Dough Sale
- Holiday Gift-Wrapping
- Holiday Money Tree
- Pumpkin Carving
- Seasonal Items Sale

Corsage Sale

Sell fake flower corsages as a lasting, wearable gift and a special expression of love and appreciation. Set up stands outside of popular date and occasion spots. As potential customers arrive, ask men if they would like to buy a corsage for their date. These can also be marketed as beautiful gifts for moms or graduates.

Special Materials/Equipment

- Fake flowers
- Ribbons
- Pipe cleaners

Sponsors/Donations

- Florists or hobby/craft stores are perfect sponsors to donate supplies.

Possible Venue(s)

If there is space, it might be easiest to assemble the corsages at your organization's home. For prime sales locations, you might want to set up a stand at the entrance to dances, graduations, churches, or popular date and occasion spots, like movie theaters and nice restaurants.

Recommended Volunteer

3+ to make and sell the corsages

Preparation

Plan for a one to two week production period (depending on how many corsages you sell) to assemble the corsages.

Execution

Bring a starter box of cash to make change. Set up your stand(s) and approach potential customers for sales. Appeal to the idea that the honoree can wear her corsage immediately.

Tip(s)

- Sales can be planned to correspond with Valentine's Day, Mother's Day, Easter, graduation, homecoming, or prom.
- Sell small cards that buyers can customize to accompany the corsages.

Variation(s)

- Sell small flower bouquets (fake or real), tied with ribbons or presented in decorated vases.
- Sell chocolate roses. To make them, put two Hershey's Kisses together base-to-base, and wrap them in colored plastic wrap. Attach the rosette to a pipe cleaner or fake vine stem with a green rubber band or twist tie and add ribbon.

Holiday Cookie Dough Sale

Having prepared cookie dough on hand during the holidays makes it easy to serve fresh, delicious cookies to your family and guests. Stress the time-saving, mess-free convenience of this crowd pleaser, and it will practically sell itself to prospective customers. There is no inventory to store and no up-front cost to your organization. Rather, you take orders for the cookie dough, which is shipped directly to the customer, and you keep a share of the profit.

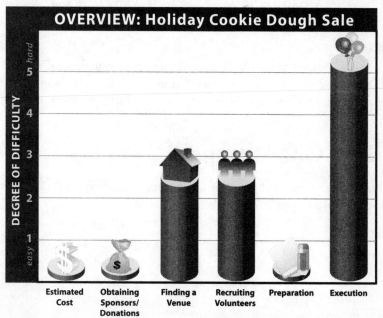

Special Materials/Equipment
- T-shirts emblazoned with your organization's logo and/or hats (to identify your volunteers)

Possible Venue(s)
Grocery store and bank lobbies, shopping centers and malls, or holiday craft shows are good options.

Recommended Volunteer
4 to 5 to find potential buyers and assist them with the paperwork

Preparation
Go online to locate a company that specializes in cookie dough fundraisers, and request fundraising brochures and order forms. Advertise the event in free community newspapers and church newsletters. Send a news release to the lifestyle editor at newspapers. Create signs with your organization's name prominently displayed.

Execution
Set up a table in your preferred venue. Arm volunteers with brochures that they can show to prospective customers.

Tip(s)
- Stress to prospective buyers how easy it is to bake fresh cookies during the holidays when starting with prepared cookie dough.

Variation(s)
- Choose a company that sells dry cookie mix if you prefer to direct sell rather than take orders. However, be aware that there is likely to be a minimum order requirement; order conservatively so you are not stuck with excess product.

Holiday Gift-Wrapping

Help Santa and all the tired shoppers out during the gift-giving season by offering gift-wrapping for a charge.

Special Materials/Equipment

- Wrapping paper
- Tape
- Gift tags
- Scissors
- Ribbons

Sponsors/Donations

- Ask stationery stores, florist shops, card stores, and discount retail stores for donations of wrapping materials.
- Ask neighbors, friends, and organization members to donate their extra wrapping paper and other materials.

Possible Venue(s)

Malls, shopping centers, and department stores of all kinds are great places for this event. Book stores are especially good venues because the gifts are small and easy to wrap, and your wrapping supplies will go much further.

Recommended Volunteer

4 to 5 who can do a neat job of wrapping. It is a good idea to have volunteers audition, because a certain amount of patience and precision is necessary to wrap gifts well.

Preparation

Promote the event through news releases sent to the media, ads in free community newspapers, and bulletin boards. Write an announcement that can be read over the mall's or department store's broadcast system to direct shoppers to your wrapping station.

Execution

Set up the wrapping station in a highly visible place. Display the rolls of paper so shoppers can make their choice. Talk to the people who walk by, especially those who are laden with packages, to encourage them to stop.

Tip(s)

- If you have a secure area where packages can be stored, offer to hold the wrapped packages while people shop. Charge a small fee for keeping them safe.
- Find out if there is a store, like certain Barnes & Noble stores, that will supply you with everything you need, including wrapping paper, ribbon, cards, scissors, tape, table, and a donation box. All you need to supply is the volunteers, which is a huge money-saver.

Variation(s)

- Offer a gift bag option or gift basket option.
- Provide an assortment of fancy bows and ornaments to be used as decorations for an extra fee.

Holiday Money Tree

Challenge people to help cover an evergreen tree with paper ornaments that they purchase to benefit your cause. Though the December holidays are the best time to hold this fundraiser, it is also a cute activity year-round, including for Valentine's Day, St. Patrick's Day, Easter, Mother's Day, Father's Day, Independence Day, Halloween, and Thanksgiving.

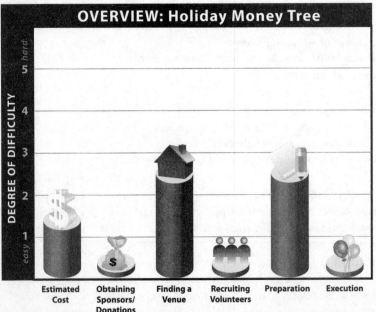

OVERVIEW: Holiday Money Tree

Special Materials/Equipment
- Seasonal ornaments
- Cut evergreen tree in a stand, or a potted evergreen
- Paperclips or ornament hangers

Sponsors/Donations
- Approach a mall or shopping center to sponsor the tree.
- Other potential sponsors might include companies that sell live plants, such as a nurseries, florists, or grocery stores.

Possible Venue(s)
A mall, shopping center, busy community center, office building, or any other place where many people congregate has potential for this event.

Recommended Volunteer
3 to 4 to talk to potential donors, collect money, and hang "money" on the tree

Preparation
Promote the event in local media. Use a home computer to print ornaments in different colors and shapes (such as wreaths, shamrocks, or hearts), and indicate prices. Set up a table with a few chairs at the designated venue.

Execution
Ask people who pass by your table to buy a paper ornament to hang on the tree. Have the donor write his or her name on the front of the ornament.

Tip(s)
- Do not hang real money on the tree to prevent theft.
- Group ornaments by donation amount on the tree, like putting all $1 donations at the bottom, $5 donations in the middle, and so on.

Variation(s)
- The tree can also be dedicated to and decorated with local or national sports team memorabilia for use as a "Spirit Tree."

Pumpkin Carving

Participants are challenged to carve an imaginative, crazy, or outrageous pumpkin right on site and can win a prize for their best effort. This fun contest is best held around Halloween or as part of a fall harvest festival. Each participant pays an entry fee of $5 or more, and supporters can vote for their favorites by paying a small fee, like $1 per vote.

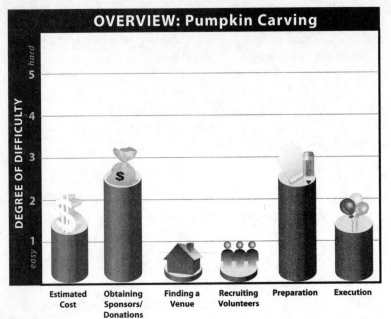

Special Materials/Equipment

- Pumpkins
- Tables (to display carved entries)
- One canister per pumpkin (to collect voting money in)
- Signs (to promote the event on site)

Sponsors/Donations

- If held at a fall festival, request complimentary space for the carving contest.
- Tap pumpkin patches and local companies for donations of pumpkins and non-monetary prizes.
- Contact a cider mill to donate cider, doughnuts, and candied or caramel apples that can be sold by your volunteers during the competition.

Possible Venue(s)

Community or church festivals, state fairs, cider mills, or public parks are great options.

Recommended Volunteer

4 to 5 to prepare promotional materials, collect entry and voting fees, handle the refreshment concession

Preparation

Advertise the competition in free community papers and on bulletin boards. Send a news release to the media. Post signs, if permitted, at the venue in advance of the event.

Execution

Set up a table where fees can be collected. Establish a refreshment concession with cider and doughnuts. Circulate among viewers to urge them to vote for the best entries.

Tip(s)

- Create categories for entries, such as best traditional pumpkin, most creative carving, most intricate entry, and so on.

Variation(s)

- Have local celebrities judge the entries and award the grand prize. Select all other winners based on how many $1 votes their fans cast.

Seasonal Items Sale

Make the seasons a little more festive by selling fun, seasonal plants and items to benefit your organization. A Valentine's Day rose sale, a spring flower sale, an Easter lily sale, a Halloween pumpkin sale (complete with cider and doughnuts), and a Christmas tree or December poinsettia sale are naturals.

OVERVIEW: Seasonal Item Sale

Special Materials/Equipment

- Tables (to display merchandise)
- T-shirts emblazoned with your organization's logo and/or hats (to identify your volunteers)
- Cash box with startup funds

Sponsors/Donations

- Appeal to farmers, growers, nurseries, and even florists for fresh products and wrapping materials.
- Offer a sponsorship in exchange for a cash donation.
- Ask grocery stores for donations of snack foods and beverages to sell.

Possible Venue(s)

Try parking lots or grocery store and bank lobbies for small portable items. A sale held at a school event, festival, or sporting activity could be very profitable as well.

Recommended Volunteer

10+ to help pick up and move merchandise, transport it to the sale site, handle cash transactions, and promote the sale

Preparation

Make up signs directing customers to the venue. Promote the event in free community newspapers and on bulletin boards. Inform the media about the sale and the cause it will support.

Execution

Have a full crew of volunteers on site to quickly serve customers. Play holiday-related music. Have volunteers dress to the theme; for example, they can wear Halloween costumes for pumpkin sales. Sell themed snacks and beverages.

Tip(s)

- Donate leftover perishable products like flowers to hospitals and nursing homes.

Variation(s)

- Hold a holiday bake sale with goodies donated by members of your organization.

Chapter 6

Shows

These events are larger productions but you can put them together without much hassle. The projects you will find in this chapter include:

- ◈ Family Movie Night
- ◈ Lip-Sync Show
- ◈ Dog Show

Family Movie Night

Show a family-friendly film, and sell movie snacks like popcorn, soft drinks, boxed candy, and hot dogs. Hold a 50/50 raffle to raise more money.

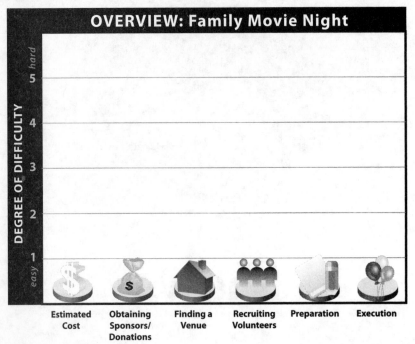

OVERVIEW: Family Movie Night

DEGREE OF DIFFICULTY (easy 1 – hard 5)

| Estimated Cost | Obtaining Sponsors/ Donations | Finding a Venue | Recruiting Volunteers | Preparation | Execution |

Special Materials/Equipment

- Age-appropriate film

Sponsors/Donations

- Contact a local movie theater or drive-in to arrange the showing. Ask for a percentage of the ticket sales for your organization in exchange for bringing in patrons. Any other facility that has a multi-purpose room with seating and a large screen, including municipal centers and schools, can be considered.
- Approach restaurants, membership warehouses, party stores, grocery stores, and other businesses for donations of snack food.
- Ask a video rental store to donate a film and a sign company to donate a sign announcing the event.

Possible Venue(s)

Consider a movie theater, drive-in theater, church gathering room, community center, civic center, or school gymnasium.

Recommended Volunteer

5 to 10 to take tickets, act as ushers, work the concession stand, and clean up after the event

Preparation

Promote the event in local media. Distribute promotional fliers throughout the community, and post them on bulletin boards. Place a sign outside the host facility at least a week in advance to drum up interest. Test the equipment and DVD in advance to make sure there are no glitches.

Execution

Arrange the seats in rows, pop some popcorn, open the doors, and collect the ticket money.

Tip(s)

- Check your state's copyright laws to see whether a special license is needed to show a film for profit, or show the film for free and charge for food, soft drinks, and games for children.
- Put volunteers on skates to sell concession food.

Variation(s)

- Have a family theater night.

Lip-Sync Show

Everyone wants to be an American Idol — but unfortunately, not everyone has a knack for singing. Give every frustrated singer a chance at the spotlight by holding a lip-sync show. Let participants take center stage while simply mouthing the words to their favorite songs. Charge participants a fee for the chance to wow the audience with their enthusiastic facial expressions and dance moves, and pass the hat among the spectators to gather more donations.

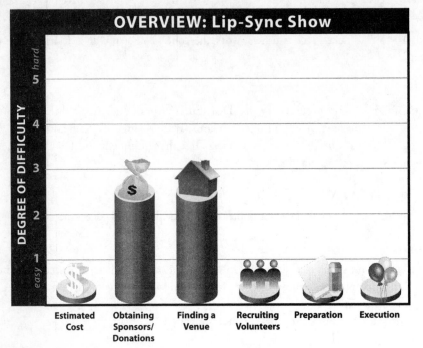

OVERVIEW: Lip-Sync Show

DEGREE OF DIFFICULTY — *hard* 5 4 3 2 1 *easy*

| Estimated Cost | Obtaining Sponsors/ Donations | Finding a Venue | Recruiting Volunteers | Preparation | Execution |

Special Materials/Equipment
- Sound equipment
- Selection of popular songs on a CD or an MP3 player

Sponsors/Donations
- Contact a music store for used demo CDs it can loan or donate.
- Offer an exclusive sponsorship to the store in exchange for a cash donation.

Possible Venue(s)
This is best held as part of another event, such as at a school talent show or community or church festival.

Recommended Volunteer

3 to 4 to play tunes, collect cash from singers, circulate in audience with donation canisters, and act as an MC to introduce performers

Preparation
Put up "save the date" signs at the venue. Promote the event in local media, including radio stations, and on free bulletin boards. Collect donated CDs or download music from iTunes. Compile a list of available songs for participants to choose from.

Execution

Collect the entrance fee, review the song list with each singer, and treat each singer like a rock star.

Tip(s)

- Borrow popular music on CD from the local library.
- Be sure to check the warning stickers on CDs to make sure the music is appropriate for children in the audience.

Variation(s)

- Encourage contestants to come dressed as a rock star or as their favorite singer, and have a costume contest in addition to the lip-sync.

Dog Show

Invite dog lovers to show off their canine pals during this fun community event. Hold either a "serious" event with qualified, professional judges or a casual event for house pets and mixed breeds. Charge a fee for each show category, offer refreshments for sale, and sell dog-related merchandise.

Special Materials/Equipment
- Agility equipment (ramps, hurdles, barriers, etc.)
- Rosettes (to award to pooches who place first, second, and third in each show category)
- Dog bowls
- Plastic bags, gloves, and covered receptacles (for disposing of pet waste)

Sponsors/Donations
- Contact pet food and toy manufacturers for donations.
- Ask dog show judges or local breeders to donate time to judge professional events.
- For fun events, ask veterinarians or local celebrities to do the honors.
- Speak to a trophy company to acquire rosettes.

Possible Venue(s)
There should be good parking and an available clean water source (to fill dog bowls) near outdoor tracks, municipal parks, or other grassy open areas.

Recommended Volunteer
10+ to set up equipment, register entrants, judge, and run other sales

Preparation
Determine the different competition classes, which may include age, breed, or function (such as working dogs). Write news releases to promote the event in local media and encourage pet owners who sign up to enter the dogs in several categories to increase profits.

Execution
Designate the main show ring. Set up agility barriers and ramps if agility events are planned. Set up and monitor dog water stations.

Tip(s)
- Beside pedigree categories, have a variety of fun categories, like prettiest dog, funniest bark, or most soulful eyes.

Variation(s)
- Make it a charity cat show or open it up to all animals, and see what interesting critters you get.

Chapter 7

Sports

Combine your cause with sporting events and activities with the events found in this chapter. The projects you will find in this chapter include:

- ◉ Day-Long Sports Competition
- ◉ Earth-Friendly Fun Walk or Ride
- ◉ Go-Kart Challenge
- ◉ Halftime Contest
- ◉ Polar Plunge
- ◉ Putt-Putt Golf
- ◉ Stair Step Challenge
- ◉ Tailgate Party
- ◉ Water Balloon Fight
- ◉ Workplace Mini-Golf

Bowl-A-Thon

Invite bowling teams, kids, families, and others for an afternoon of bowling and refreshments. This low-cost fundraiser is easy to run and requires no special equipment other than the bowling balls and rental shoes already provided at the alleys.

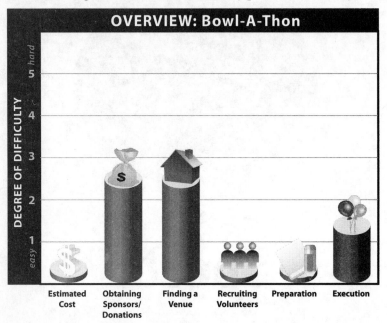

Sponsors/Donations

- Persuade your favorite bowling alley to give your organization a percentage of the money generated by supporters who attend the fundraiser.
- Contact local businesses for sponsorships in exchange for publicity at the event and in any promotional materials that are sent out.
- Ask retail businesses to donate raffle prizes and a pizzeria to donate food that can be sold to raise additional cash.

Possible Venue(s)

A large bowling alley in a metropolitan area is ideal.

Recommended Volunteer

5 to 10 to promote the event, collect money, run the concession, and award prizes

Preparation

Promote the event in local media through ads in free community papers, signs on bulletin boards, and news releases sent to radio and TV stations.

Execution

Crank up the music, throw open the doors, and watch the money roll in. Have volunteers circulate among bowlers and offer to deliver snacks and drinks alley-side.

Tip(s)

- Find a bowling alley that offers Cosmic Bowling to create a party atmosphere. Consider charging a higher-than-usual flat fee to increase profits, but be sure to let participants know up front how much they must pay.

Variation(s)

- In addition to charging an admission fee, have participants collect pledges tied to their bowling prowess. Pledges can be based on the number of pins knocked down, the number of gutter balls, or some other criteria.

Day-Long Sports Competition

Challenge other groups and organizations to compete in friendly games against the members of your organization for 24 hours straight. The games can be traditional and organized, like softball, or whimsical, such as juggling unusual objects or running races dressed as gladiators. Advertise to attract opponents who are well-known or beloved in the community, such as a group of firefighters or a team of the coaches from all the local sports teams. Charge each group an entry fee, and sell refreshments to spectators.

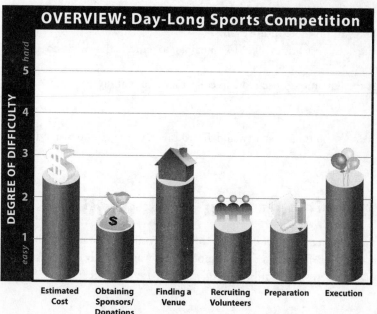

OVERVIEW: Day-Long Sports Competition

Special Materials/Equipment
• Appropriate sports equipment

Sponsors/Donations
• Sporting goods stores, sports drink companies, and athletic apparel companies might be interested in sponsorships.

Possible Venue(s)
Sports arenas or stadiums, college campuses, or shopping centers are great options.

Recommended Volunteer
20+ because the games will run around the clock

Preparation
Include a link to an official entry form on the organization's website. Invite potential competitors personally. Advertise the event in local media and by posting notices on free bulletin boards.

Execution
Start the action at the appointed time and keep the coffee brewing and the music playing during the wee hours. It does not matter if the players are any good — just have fun!

Tip(s)
• Ask the community access cable station to cover the event so you will have footage to show to promote future events.
• Invite local celebrities like TV anchors to emcee the event to generate more interest.
• Pass the hat among spectators to collect more donations.

Variation(s)
• Have a 24-hour dance party, and award prizes to the last ones standing at the end of the full day.

Earth-Friendly Fun Walk or Ride

Be kind to Mother Earth while raising funds for your organization with a "green" fun walk or ride. Walkers and those on any mode of environmentally friendly transportation, including bicycles, skateboards, and rollerblades, are welcome.

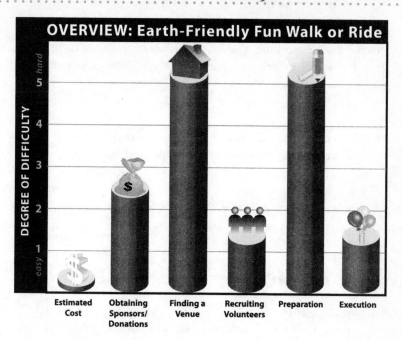

OVERVIEW: Earth-Friendly Fun Walk or Ride

DEGREE OF DIFFICULTY (hard 5 — easy)

Estimated Cost | Obtaining Sponsors/ Donations | Finding a Venue | Recruiting Volunteers | Preparation | Execution

Sponsors/Donations

Solicit sponsors among local business owners to cover promotion, snacks, the cost of T-shirts emblazoned with the name of the event, and licenses. Have participants collect pledges based on the number of miles or laps they will cover. Provide them with a simple computer-generated form on which pledges can be recorded (see sample form and rules in Appendices).

Possible Venue(s)

City streets, high school track, racetrack, or fairgrounds have potential.

Recommended Volunteer

6 to 10 including 1 to lead the event and 5 to 10 to pass out T-shirts, cheer participants on, and run concession stands

Preparation

Contact a sign company to obtain a donated event sign. Establish the starting time and publicize your event in all advertising materials. Map out a safe route with the assistance of local law enforcement. Check with the appropriate local municipality to determine whether a parade license or other permit is necessary. Obtain a food permit to sell food prepared on site (such as hot dogs). Set up a (donated) tent or canopy from which to sell snacks and bottled water.

Execution

Have a ceremonial kick-off during which someone says a few words about caring for the Earth and the importance of environmentally friendly transportation. Have a cheering section to greet those who cross the finish line.

Tip(s)

- Time the event to coincide with Earth Day, which falls on April 22, or even Valentine's Day as a way to show Mother Earth some love.

Variation(s)

- Hold a midnight fun run or ride that you end with a midnight breakfast and information session about your organization.

Go-Kart Challenge

An old-fashioned go-kart rally is sure to encourage creativity while raising funds. Require all entrants to build homemade go-karts that will either be paraded down a street or track or raced in a traditional go-kart derby. Collect an entry fee from each participant. Offer a cash prize to the fastest derby participant, or give prizes to go-karts that are judged to be the best decorated, most creative, cleverest, or most eccentric. This can be a standalone event or one that is part of a city fair or church fundraiser.

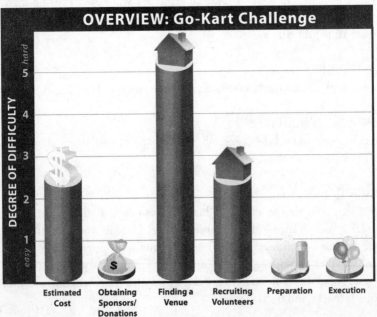

Special Materials/Equipment

None (unless you wish to build a go-kart as an organizational project)

Sponsors/Donations

• Contact local businesses to serve as event or team sponsors.

Possible Venue(s)

Try holding this at a high school track, sports field, city street (with municipal and police permission), or municipal park.

Recommended Volunteer

5 to 6 to set up, register participants, judge, and award prizes

Preparation

Create different competition categories (such as kids, teens, parents). Obtain permission from the municipality and police department to hold the event on a city street, if applicable. Promote the event in local media, including community newspapers.

Execution

Little work needed, other than to collect entry fees, help line up entrants, and – if it is a race – drop the checkered flag. A brief ceremony should be held to award prizes and allow pictures to be taken.

Tip(s)

• Collect additional money by lining up the go-karts before the derby, placing a donation bucket in front of each one, and asking the public to vote for their favorite by tossing in their spare change. Give a prize to the person whose go-kart earns the most money.
• Sell refreshments and baked goods along the sidelines.

Variation(s)

• Have a scooter, skateboard, or rollerblading race. Pick a theme of attire for participants, like the '80s, for even more fun.

Halftime Contest

Sell tickets for a chance to play a sports-themed game of skill during intermission at professional, university/college, or amateur sporting events. Games can include kicking a field goal, sinking a basket, or shooting a puck. For something different, consider a potato sack race or an obstacle course.

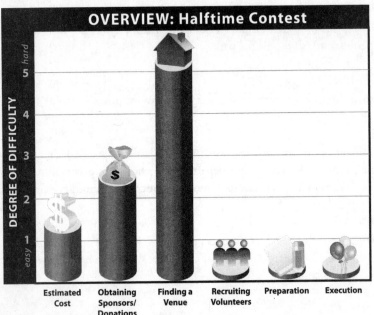

Special Materials/Equipment

- Sports equipment

Sponsors/Donations

- Set various sponsorship levels to attract both large and small sponsors. Offer to include sponsors' names on all advertising, banners, and fliers.

Possible Venue(s)

Sports facilities and fields used by professional, semi-pro, university, secondary and elementary school teams work well.

Recommended Volunteer

2 to 3 to set up and run contest

Preparation

Determine the timing of the event (like at the start of the game or between periods), as well as where it will be held (such as midfield or on the sidelines). Create signs to display where tickets are sold.

Execution

Sell tickets near the entrance or ticket office of the facility or field for maximum visibility. Draw a winning ticket from all entries. Provide the field announcer with a prepared script giving the name of the lucky player and details about what the contest entails. Award a cash or sports-themed prize to the winner.

Tip(s)

- To keep the crowd from leaving their seats during intermission and to gain maximum exposure for your organization, minimize set-up time by having all equipment as close to the sidelines as possible and have plenty of volunteers help you set up quickly while someone immediately announces what will be going on.

Variation(s)

- Offer your organization's services to professional and university sports teams to assist with tasks like taking tickets, selling food, or cleaning up in exchange for a cash donation.
- Throw a party tied to an annual event like March Madness or the Super Bowl. Charge a nominal fee to attend a big-screen TV party in your organization's headquarters, a gymnasium, or a restaurant, and charge for refreshments like hot dogs and soft drinks.

Polar Plunge

An event for the brave and perhaps the (fool)hardy, the Polar Plunge is a winter endurance activity. Participants slip into their swimsuits and take a dip in a frigid body of water. Dippers raise pledges based on their ability to take the plunge or other criteria, like staying in the water for a certain amount of time or submerging completely.

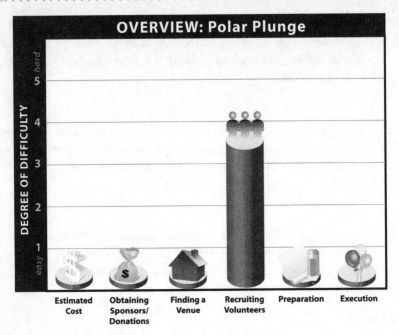

OVERVIEW: Polar Plunge

DEGREE OF DIFFICULTY

5 hard
4
3
2
1
easy

Estimated Cost | Obtaining Sponsors/ Donations | Finding a Venue | Recruiting Volunteers | Preparation | Execution

Sponsors/Donations

- Send letters to schools, civic organizations, clubs, and other groups to line up teams. Charge each team a small fee to participate.
- Contact local restaurants for donations of food and drinks that can be sold during the event.

Possible Venue(s)

Lightly iced-over lakes, channels, streams, outdoor pools, or the ocean is appropriate.

Recommended Volunteer

5 to 6 to collect entry fees (if any), run concessions, and cheer on the participants

Preparation

Set up a website to collect plunge registrations and up front donations. Create an e-mail template that participants can customize and send to friends and family to collect donations. Create a sign-up form that can be printed and given to teams and other participants to collect pledges (see sample form and rules in Appendices). Promote the event to the media through news releases. Invite a local celebrity to take the first plunge at the event.

Execution

Set up a refreshment stand with food and plenty of hot drinks, including hot chocolate. Have a countdown to the plunge to build excitement.

Tip(s)

- Offer a prize to the team that collects the most money.
- Have a microwave on site, and sell hot towels, gloves and socks. Also, sell hot beverages.
- Have participants sign waivers to participate at their own risk.
- Station a medical/first aid team on site in case of emergencies.

Putt-Putt Golf

Test the golfing skills of adults and kids alike by asking them to putt for a hole-in-one on a portable golfing green. This is an especially popular event during the winter, when hardcore and casual golfers alike are longing for the start of the spring golfing season.

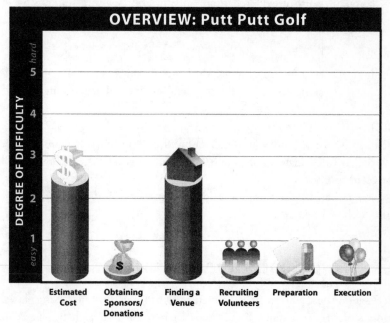

OVERVIEW: Putt Putt Golf

DEGREE OF DIFFICULTY — easy (1) to hard (5)

Estimated Cost | Obtaining Sponsors/ Donations | Finding a Venue | Recruiting Volunteers | Preparation | Execution

Special Materials/Equipment

- Putters
- Golf balls
- Portable putting green or putt return system (available at sporting goods stores or online)

Sponsors/Donations

- Golf equipment and other sporting goods stores might be willing to donate funds in exchange for publicity at the event. The parks and recreation department at your local municipality is another possibility.

- In addition, ask local businesses like restaurants to donate gift certificates that you can use as prizes.

Possible Venue(s)

City and church festivals, carnivals, school events, and parks work well. Also contact miniature golf courses, which may be willing to donate a part of the proceeds to your organization on the designated fundraising date.

Recommended Volunteer

2 to 3 to manage equipment and participants

Preparation

Contact one of the online companies that rent 18-hole portable putting greens. Some of these companies also provide charitable organizations with a fundraising website and access to PayPal for donation collection as part of the mini-golf package.

Execution

Have volunteers wear identical polo shirts, or T-shirts with the name of your organization. Set up the portable green in a centrally located area for high visibility.

Variation(s)

- Hold an 18- or 36-hole mini-golf event. Rent a mini-golf course or locate a course that will donate its "fairway." Charge admission, and sell both per-hole and scorecard sponsorships.
- Sponsor father/daughter or mother/son tournaments, and offer a trophy or other prize to the winning duo.

Stair Step Challenge

A great event for those who are fit and athletic, this fundraiser entails having participants repeatedly scale a set of stairs. Funds are raised by collecting pledges based on the number of times participants climb the stairs or the number of stairs climbed.

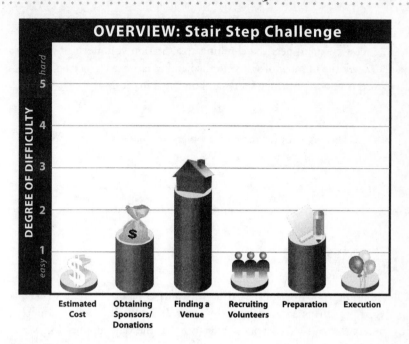

Sponsors/Donations

- Ask grocery stores, party stores, or water bottling companies for donations of bottled water that you can sell, as well as donations of sports drinks and energy bars.
- Sport shoe companies may be willing to make a cash donation for publicity at the event, which could be used for signs.

Possible Venue(s)

Sports arenas, school auditoriums, theaters, or municipal parks with outdoor staircases are good choices.

Recommended Volunteer

5+ to keep track of participants' accomplishments, collect pledges, and cheer on the steppers

Preparation

Set a price per staircase or stair based on your fundraising goals. Promote the event and your cause through ads in free community newspapers and on bulletin boards, and by sending news releases to the media. Let people register by phone or e-mail. Create a computer-generated pledge sheet and a tally sheet that can be used during the event. Prepare climbing event T-shirts to sell at the event.

Execution

Set up a concession stand near the climbing area. Station volunteers at the bottom of the stairs to track the number of stairs climbed and to cheer on the steppers. Designate other volunteers to accept pledge sheets and on site donations.

Tip(s)

• Check the venue's liability insurance policy to make sure the steppers will be covered in case of an accident.

Variation(s)

• Make this a team event and give a prize to the team that climbs the most steps.

Tailgate Party

Find the hopping spot for tailgate parties on college- or pro-football weekends, and set up everything fans need to kick off the game. In addition to selling munchies like nachos, beverages, and baked goods, offer other game day supplies like sunglasses, sunscreen, lip balm, hats, and other paraphernalia.

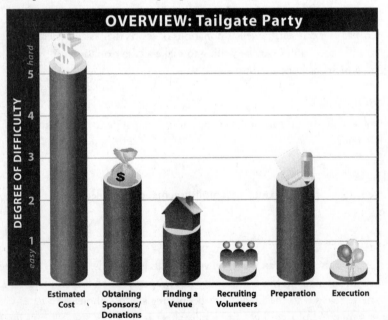

Special Materials/Equipment

- Barbecue grill
- Charcoal
- Lighter
- Coolers
- Tables
- Folding chairs
- Sport utility vehicle or truck with a tailgate
- Sound equipment (to broadcast the pregame show or play fight songs)

Sponsors/Donations

- Everyone loves football season, so it should be easy to land donations and financial sponsorships from grocery stores, convenience stores, sporting goods stores, and sports bars.

Possible Venue(s)

A parking lot near the sports event, open air market or community center, especially one with a big screen TV to broadcast the game for those with no tickets, works well.

Recommended Volunteer

5 to 6 to set up and run sales

Preparation

Check to see if a license is required to sell food and beer. Arrive early to stake out a good spot in a visible area. Start grilling early to put fans in the mood to party.

Execution

Keep the grill stoked up and the food coming, and the event will run itself.

Tip(s)

- Set up a TV and ask for donations from people without game tickets who want to watch the game.

Variation(s)

- Obtain permission to set up a tailgate party in the parking lot of a large company during lunch on the day before a big game. Charge employees for a chance to play in a friendly game of flag or touch football, and award a (donated) cash prize to the winning team.

Water Balloon Fight

Make a big splash for your charity by hosting a water balloon battle. It is a refreshing way to raise money during the dog days of summer, and cleaning up is fast.

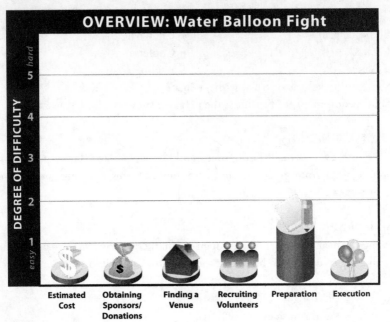

OVERVIEW: Water Balloon Fight

DEGREE OF DIFFICULTY — 5 hard, 4, 3, 2, 1 easy

Estimated Cost | Obtaining Sponsors/ Donations | Finding a Venue | Recruiting Volunteers | Preparation | Execution

Sponsors/Donations

- Ask a water-related company, such as a sprinkler company, car wash, auto detailer, or bottled water company, to sponsor the event. Besides footing the bill for the water, suggest that the company provide latex balloons preprinted with its name to increase the publicity value.

Possible Venue(s)

A large open area without obstacles is great, although an area with natural barriers like bushes and trees is even better so participants can hide and ambush their opponents. A nearby water source is a plus in case the balloon supply runs low.

Recommended Volunteer

5 to 8 or more to collect money, fill up balloons, monitor the fight, and clean up

Preparation

The day of the event, set up an assembly line of volunteers to fill balloons, tie them off, place them in a tub or other container, and trundle the container to the battlefield.

Execution

Decide whether to charge by the balloon (for example, three balloons for $5) or by the team. The latter is easier to keep track of, but you will go through plenty of balloons really fast. Assign volunteers to balloon-filling duty to keep up with demand, because you might need thousand of balloons to keep the combatants armed and happy.

Tip(s)

- Use a garden hose with a nozzle to fill balloons fast.
- Purchase or rent a water balloon launcher to crank up the fun.

Variation(s)

- Organize a dodge ball fundraiser using water balloons. Entice a local celebrity or public official to serve as a willing target so paying customers can lob water balloons at him or her.

Workplace Mini-Golf

Turn any workplace into a miniature golf course by setting up greens that snake through the office. Include ramps, water hazards, and sand traps to tee up extra excitement. Sign up twosomes, and award a prize to the pair with the lowest score.

Special Materials/Equipment

- Putting greens
- Golf balls
- Water and sand hazards (try Slip 'N Slides and sand-filled kiddie pools)

Sponsors/Donations
- Contact sporting goods stores for financial donations.
- Ask a municipal park and recreation department to lend equipment.
- Obtain gift certificates and other prizes from local businesses.

Possible Venue(s)
Make arrangements through the human resources department of businesses with many employees, including corporations, government entities, schools and universities, and medical facilities.

Recommended Volunteer
7+ to set up the course, register participants, and monitor the games

Preparation
Visit the venue to map out a challenging 9-hole course that will not excessively disrupt business. Measure aisles to make sure the golfing props and hazards will fit comfortably. Build or borrow mini-golf props like fake rocks or palm trees. Collect greens fees in advance.

Execution
Designate a specific tee time for each pair. Station a volunteer at each "hole" to keep score.

Tip(s)
- Schedule the event to coincide with a major golfing event, like the Masters or the U.S. Open. Have participants bring their own putters.
- Charge a participation fee based on the players' positions in the company. For instance, charge $25 for upper management pairs, $15 for middle management duos, and $10 for all other twosomes.
- Make sure the prize is significant enough to warrant the cost of the entry fee.
- Hold a 50/50 raffle to entice non-golfers to contribute to your cause.

Chapter 8

Themed Events

These events tie a fun theme with a good cause, providing family fun activities. The projects you will find in this chapter include:

- ◉ Dress Down Day
- ◉ Kids Sleepover
- ◉ Mini Luau
- ◉ Parents' Night Out
- ◉ Wild West Fundraiser

Dress Down Day

Give students or employees the option of wearing casual clothing like jeans or flip-flops outside of their normal dress code in exchange for a small cash donation (usually $1 to $5) for your organization. There are no overhead costs, so all money collected is pure profit for the organization.

OVERVIEW: Dress Down Day

DEGREE OF DIFFICULTY — easy to hard

Estimated Cost | Obtaining Sponsors/ Donations | Finding a Venue | Recruiting Volunteers | Preparation | Execution

Special Materials/Equipment
- Collection containers
- Roll of two-part tickets (to give to participants in exchange for their contribution)

Sponsors/Donations
- It is usually easy to convince a school or business to host a casual day fundraiser because there is little work and no out-of-pocket cost involved. Simply call the business office of a school or personnel office of a company and explain what organization you are with and what the funds will be used for.

Possible Venue(s)
Elementary or high schools, or businesses, especially those that require uniforms or have professional staff that normally wear formal business attire, work well.

Recommended Volunteer
3 to 4 to advertise and collect money

Execution

On the designated casual day, send volunteers to the school or business with collection canisters. Designate a central contribution point, or have volunteers go door to door.

Tip(s)

- Give participants buttons or stickers to wear that promote your organization on the event day.
- Collect money the day before the event and give contributors a ticket as proof that they have paid.

Variation(s)

- Hold a Dress Up Day fundraiser, during which students or workers can wear as much bling and makeup as they like, or wear whatever crazy costume they wish.
- Charge a dress-down fee for employees to wear team jerseys and T-shirts on the day before a big game.

Kids Sleepover

Host a pajama party or themed sleepover for children at your organization's headquarters or other location, complete with music, games, food, and fun.

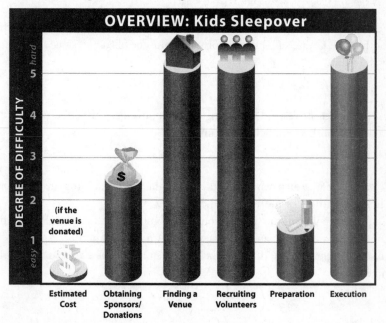

Special Materials/Equipment

- Board games
- Dress-up clothes (raid your closet)
- Age-appropriate films borrowed from the library
- Event tickets, which can be made up on a computer and printed on a copier machine to cut costs
- Karaoke
- Food (like pizza and soft drinks)

Sponsors/Donations

- Pizza restaurant or delivery company for food and drinks, discount stores or party supply companies for paper goods and utensils, toy stores for board games, thrift shop for unsalable clothing that can be used for dress-up.

Possible Venue(s)

Consider a school auditorium, gymnasium, large classroom, church gathering center, YMCA/YWCA, or your organization's meeting room.

Recommended Volunteer

1 for every 5 to 10 children is a good idea, and as many adults who can stay overnight as possible to oversee activities and promote a safe environment

Preparation

Promote the event in local media. Create a flier outlining what children should bring (including a sleeping bag or blanket and pillow, pajamas, stuffed animals, toothbrush and toothpaste). Create a permission form that must be filled out, signed, and returned before the event.

Execution

Have someone tell stories and lead a sing-along. If possible, settle children according to age group. Establish a firm lights-out time.

Tip(s)

- A parent or guardian who will stay overnight should accompany children who require nighttime or morning medication.
- Request details on the permission slip about allergies and relevant medical conditions, and obtain an emergency contact name and number.
- Inform parents as they drop off their children about the next morning's pick-up time.

Mini Luau

Bring the tropics to your town by hosting a luau, complete with Hawaiian music, a buffet of island cuisine, tropical drinks, hula dancing, and tiki torches. Sell island-inspired goods like leis, grass skirts, Hawaiian shirts, and macadamia nuts. Award prizes to attendees with the most colorful or authentic Hawaiian garb. Charge a general admission fee, and charge separately for the buffet.

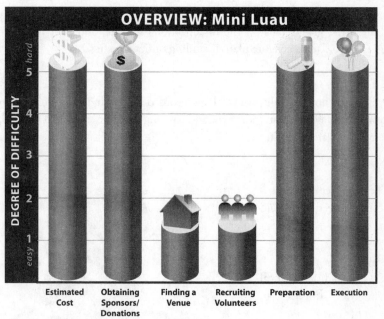

OVERVIEW: Mini Luau

Special Materials/Equipment
- Sound equipment (microphone, speakers)
- Hawaiian decorations (i.e. tiki torches)

Sponsors/Donations
- Line up a local band that can play island tunes to donate a few hours of play time.
- Locate restaurants that can prepare and donate Hawaiian-style pork, ribs, or barbecued chicken, or seek donations to purchase menu items.
- Contact party supply stores for donations of leis, grass skirts, and tiki torches.
- Ask a bar to donate bartending time and ingredients for mai tais, piña coladas, and non-alcoholic fruit drinks.
- Find a dance troupe to perform native dances.
- Ask local businesses for prizes.

Possible Venue(s)

A public beach, municipal park, fairground, or parking lot is a good option.

Recommended Volunteer

15+ depending on the number of activities offered

Preparation

Promote the event heavily in local media; advertise in free community papers. Distribute fliers, give details on the organization's website, and post notices on free bulletin boards. Create a venue plan, including buffet logistics.

Execution

Have volunteers don Hawaiian shirts. Play recorded Hawaiian music while selling food and souvenirs. Have live entertainment and dancing after the sun sets. Hold a drawing for the best Hawaiian outfit.

Tip(s)

- Check to see whether a license is needed to hold the event.

Variation(s)

- Serve a traditional meal luau-style around an open fire pit.

Parents' Night Out

Give parents a chance to enjoy a kid- and guilt-free evening out by offering babysitting services in a group setting. Offer activities for the kids like movies, arts and crafts, story-telling, and face painting. Charge a per-child fee, or set an hourly rate.

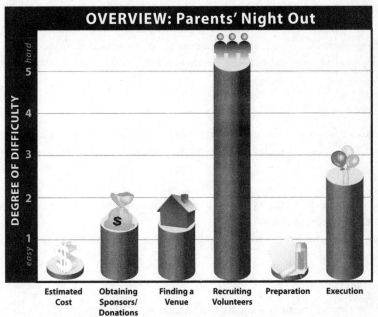

Special Materials/Equipment

- Arts and crafts materials
- Makeup for face painting, age-appropriate DVD
- DVD player
- Large monitor

Sponsors/Donations

- Seek a facility with a large gathering room and bathroom facilities, and ask for permission to host the gathering, show a film, and provide refreshments like popcorn and soft drinks.

Possible Venue(s)

Churches, municipality auditoriums, school gymnasiums, community centers, or mall activity centers work well.

Recommended Volunteer

Plan on having 1 adult or babysitter for every 3 children who are younger than 5 years old, or one adult or babysitter for every 8 to 10 children who are more than 5 years old. Contact a teen center, high school, or community college to gather volunteers.

Preparation

Make the donated room kid-friendly by removing anything with sharp edges and relocating breakable objects. Install child-proof covers on accessible outlets, and clear away tripping hazards, like exposed electrical cords. Establish a firm pick-up time for parents.

Execution

Keep exterior doors locked during the event to safeguard the children. Offer one activity at a time, and conclude with a movie to reduce the activity level before pick-up time.

Tip(s)

- Create a parental consent form, and include space for medical conditions and emergency contact information.
- Ask parents to bring a blanket and pillow for kids who might zonk out before pick-up time.

Variation(s)

- Time parents'-night-out events to coincide with the holiday season to take the stress out of holiday shopping.

Wild West Fundraiser

A family-friendly event that will put the "wild" in anyone west — or east — of the Mississippi. Offer Western-themed activities; sell refreshments, baked goods, and souvenirs. Hold a contest for the best Western attire and offer pony rides. Charge an entry fee, or charge to participate in activities.

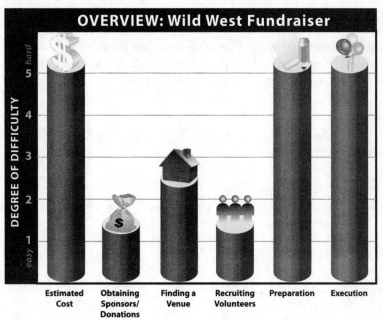

Special Materials/Equipment

- Kid games (i.e. lasso a stuffed animal)
- Adult games (i.e. horseshoes and darts)
- Pictures to color
- Face painting supplies
- Party favors (sheriff badges, toy horses)
- Plywood and paint (to build a fun Western town backdrop)

Sponsors/Donations

- Approach local civic groups known for supporting children's causes for sponsorships or donations.
- Ask a horse farm or stable to provide pony rides at a reduced cost.

Possible Venue(s)

Try a municipal park, school auditorium or gymnasium, stable, or farm.

Recommended Volunteer

10+ depending on the activities chosen

Preparation

Send out news releases, and advertise the event in local media. Post notices on open bulletin boards in stores and at day care centers. Map out the staging area to accommodate the various activities. Set up a saloon tent where adults can enjoy alcoholic beverages. Apply for a temporary liquor license for fundraising events from your municipality and a food license, if needed. Designate a clean-up committee.

Execution

Assign volunteers to take tickets, run games, do face painting, and run concessions. Offer Western-themed fare, like corn on the cob, baked beans, and chili, along with burgers and hot dogs. Play country music for dancing.

Tip(s)

- Make sure the person or company that provides pony rides is insured and can provide helmets for riders.

Variation(s)

- Hold a Native American powwow complete with native dancers, food, and crafts.

Chapter 9

Sales

These events provide quality products for your community while still being affordable for your organization. The projects you will find in this chapter include:

- Adopt a Tree
- Balloon Bouquets
- Collectible Coins
- Community Rummage Sale
- Custom T-shirt Sale
- DVD and Videotape Sale
- Electronics Drive
- Flower Sale
- Magazine Subscription Drive
- Silicone Bracelet Sale
- Spirit Doormat Sale

- Baby-Clothing Sale
- Candle Sale
- College Care Packages
- Custom Calendar Sale
- Customize a Brick
- Earplug Sale
- Flower Bulb Sale
- Fundraising Scratch Cards
- Reusable Bag Sale
- Special Delivery Telegrams
- Used Book Sale

Adopt a Tree

Teach kids and adults the importance of protecting and preserving the environment while encouraging them to be earth-friendly by inviting them to "sponsor" newly planted trees in their community. In addition to hosting a tree-planting event, give an informal talk on the benefits of planting trees (including decreasing the earth's carbon footprint, reducing groundwater pollution, and improving property values). Offer healthy snacks and soft drinks for sale to increase fundraising.

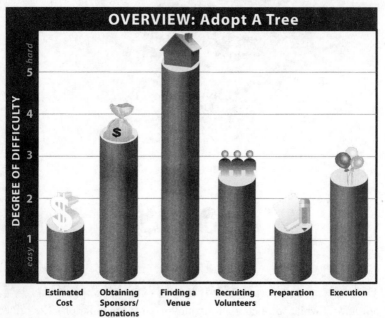

Special Materials/Equipment

- Trees or seedlings

Sponsors/Donations

- Speak to nurseries, tree farms, and other growers to solicit the donation of a tree that can be planted. Ask for the donation of seedlings that can be given to those who donate.
- Ask a sign company to donate a sign that gives information about the tree species, the dedication date, and who paid for it (such as, "Donated by the people of Chesterfield Township").

Possible Venue(s)

Municipal parks, schools, government buildings, churches, or anywhere else beautification efforts are spearheaded is appropriate.

Recommended Volunteer
5 to 10 with 1 to give an earth-friendly talk and others to assist with the planting

Preparation
Conduct a door-to-door "adopt-a-tree" campaign to solicit funds and invite people to a dedication ceremony. If possible, distribute donated seedlings to contributors as a thank-you gift.

Execution
Carefully select a location for the tree that gets good sun and has adequate rainfall or irrigation. The location also should be in a spot that will allow participants to gather around. Plant the tree during a brief ceremony conducted by your community's mayor or other official.

Tip(s)
- Distribute information pamphlets to participants that tell them how their efforts help the environment, thank them, and tell them how to donate more to your organization or get involved as a volunteer.

Variation(s)
- Sell tree and/or seed starter kits door to door.

Baby-Clothing Sale

Kids outgrow their clothes fast, so gently used baby clothes are always in demand. Organize a community collection effort, and resell the merchandise during a baby-clothing sale. Include shoes and accessories like socks and hats to ramp up sales, and sell refreshments like coffee and pastries to keep shoppers happy.

Special Materials/Equipment
- Sale day signs
- Cashbox and startup funds
- T-shirts (for volunteers working the event)
- Tables (to display merchandise)

Sponsors/Donations
- Ask baby clothing and department stores for donations of past-season merchandise.

Possible Venue(s)
A church or municipal community center, or parking lot in a highly visible location works well.

Recommended Volunteer
10+ to sort clothes, organize the sale area, handle cash, and promote the event

Preparation
Advertise for donations in free community newspapers, church bulletins, and school newsletters at least a few months in advance. Store incoming donations at a designated venue. Sort and price clothing as it arrives to minimize set-up time on sale day. Create a donation receipt. Advertise the event in free community newspapers, in classified ads, and on free bulletin boards. Send a news release to the local media. Create sale day signs.

Execution

Place sale signs in strategic locations near the venue. Set up your table and sell, sell, sell.

Tip(s)

- Be sure to specify size availability in all advertising.
- Curtain off a corner of the venue so older kids can try on clothes in private.
- List higher-priced designer clothes or new brand-name items on eBay to maximize your earnings.
- Dispose of remaining clothing by having a bag sale (such as $10 for a full bag of merchandise) in the last hour.

Variation(s)

- Have a Back-to-School Clothes Sale.

Balloon Bouquets

Attract attention and make everyone from small kids to the young at heart happy with a colorful balloon bouquet. Balloons can be sold anywhere people congregate, but are especially appropriate at kids' parties and events.

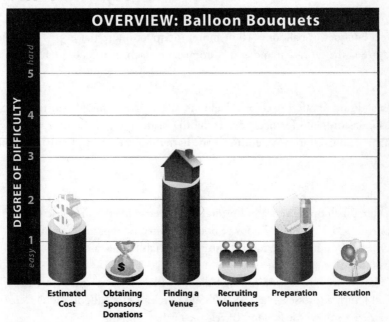

Special Materials/Equipment
- Tank of helium (purchased or rented from a party supply company)
- Balloon weights (especially for display purposes)
- Balloons (latex or Mylar)
- Colored string or ribbon

Sponsors/Donations
- Companies that cater to children, like kid-friendly hair salons, pizza parlors, water parks, skating rinks, and toy stores.
- Craft shows might also be a good place to set up a balloon booth.

Possible Venue(s)
City fairs, church festivals, or school events (i.e. sports games, dances) are great places.

Recommended Volunteer
2 to 3 to fill, tie, and sell balloons

Preparation
Gather all materials.

Execution
Inflate a bouquet of balloons (10 or more) to attract interest at events or for in-store displays. Sell them on-demand and customized to each customer's preferences.

Tip(s)
- In addition to offering colored balloons, always have a varied assortment of design balloons on hand for occasions including birthdays, graduations, weddings, new babies, anniversaries, Valentine's Day, Easter, Mother's Day, Christmas, and New Year's Day.

Variation(s)
- Offer a balloon service at a hospital in concert with the in-house florist or floral provider. Deliver the balloons or bouquets directly to patients' rooms.
- Offer add-on items like candy or stuffed animals to increase the price point of each balloon sale.
- Host a balloon release event. Tag balloons with a card listing the purchasers' names and return addresses. Have a ceremony to release the balloons, and award a prize to the person whose balloon travels the farthest.

Candle Sale

Easy to organize and simple to run, a candle sale can shine a new light on fundraising for your organization.

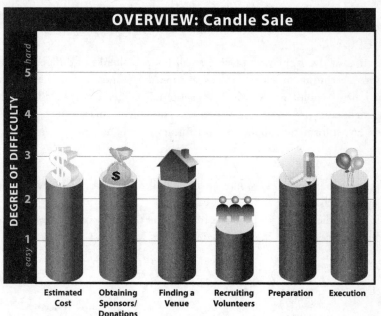

Special Materials/Equipment

- Sample candles
- Easel for signs
- Cashbox and startup funds (for making change)
- Tables

Sponsors/Donations

- Contact a candle company to propose a sponsorship arrangement.
- Work with a gift store to obtain donations of past-season product.
- Ask a mall or shopping center management office to sponsor the event.

Possible Venue(s)

Malls, shopping centers, grocery store lobbies, or community events like art or craft shows work well.

Recommended Volunteer

3 to 4 to obtain products and sponsorships, set up the event display, sell products, and collect cash

Preparation

Advertise the event in free community newspapers and on store bulletin boards. Send a news release to the community events editor at local papers. Price the merchandise or create signs indicating the prices. Work with a print or sign store to create a professional-looking sign.

Execution

Create an attractive display by placing small boxes or books of different sizes on the table and covering them with a tablecloth to create a landscape on which to arrange merchandise. If holding the sale in a shopping center or mall, ask the facility's management company to broadcast periodic announcements about the sale to attract buyers. Have information about your organization and business cards available.

Tip(s)

- Tie the sale in to holidays, like Thanksgiving, Christmas, Hanukkah, Valentine's Day, and Easter.
- Host a candle party with products from one of the many companies found online, which provide everything needed for a successful event.

Variation(s)

- Sell battery-powered candles.

Collectible Coins

Create a series of collectible coins for your organization. Sell them outright or award them to donors who contribute a certain amount of money to your organization during fundraising events.

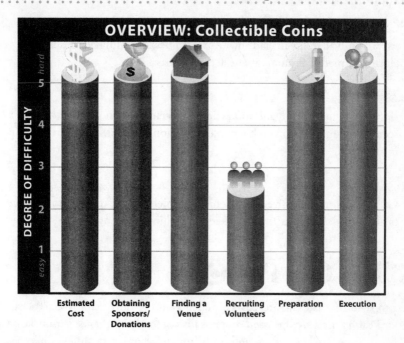

Sponsors/Donations
- Because this is a high-cost product, approach known entrepreneurs and philanthropists for donations.
- You also may be able to obtain a state or federal grant to help fund the project.

Possible Venue(s)
Gift shops, your organizations' website, coin shows, coin stores, coin magazines, or online auctions like eBay work well. Ask local utility companies to include a flier or message with their bills. Banks may be willing to sell the coins if they are struck in a certain type of metal.

Recommended Volunteer
5 to 10 to locate a mint, design the coin or create the template, market the final product, and fill orders

Preparation
Find a mint that is able to strike the coins. Work with its designers to create the design, or hold a contest to find the best design and award a prize to the winning artist. Limit the number of coins struck to keep extrinsic value high.

Set up a merchant account or a PayPal account to clear credit orders.

Execution

Advertise coin availability in paid and unpaid venues, including newspapers, magazines, and electronic media. Promote it as the first in a series.

Tip(s)

* Beside putting your organization's name and emblem on the coin, tie it to a local, recognizable facility, an architectural attraction, or another landmark to increase interest.

Variation(s)

* Create a commemorative wooden nickel, which is less expensive to produce.
* Strike a medal in a base metal to keep the selling price low.

College Care Packages

Offer to send care packages to college students during final exam week. Packages can include healthy snacks, coffee, and coupons for fast food restaurants; personal care items like facial tissue, hand sanitizer, and lip balm; and even exam supplies like pens and pencils, erasers, highlighters, self-stick notes, and exam blue books or Scantron forms.

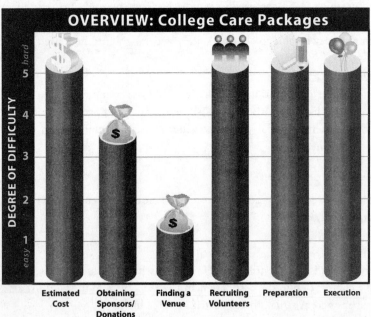

Special Materials/Equipment

* Boxes (to pack the goodies in)

- Labels identifying your organization as the purveyor
- Click-n-Ship labels (to mail via the U.S. Postal Service)

Sponsors/Donations

- Contact companies that supply trial-size products to request donations.
- Talk to grocery stores or farmers' markets to purchase produce at a discount.
- Hit up the university bookstore for a monetary sponsorship in exchange for an advertising plug.

Possible Venue(s)

University and college events where parents congregate are key. You can also purchase a mailing list and send a letter to solicit sales.

Recommended Volunteer

10+ to take advance orders and pack boxes

Preparation

If selling at an event, prepare a few sample care packages that can be displayed for prospective buyers.

Execution

If the campus is a metropolitan area, hand-deliver packages to dorms or to a central drop-off point designated by the university.

Tip(s)

- Include fun stress-busters like a Frisbee or stress ball.
- Avoid sending energy drinks.
- Be sure the target university or college does not already sell a final exam package of its own.

Variation(s)

- Offer customized packages. Have purchasers fill out a simple form that requests information about students' favorites in various categories. Price the package based on the number of items selected.
- Purchase premade final exam packages from an online company; sell them at a markup to generate funds.

Community Rummage Sale

Collect donated clothing, accessories, household goods, small appliances, CDs and DVDs, and other treasures, and resell them at a profit. Locate a no-cost venue and 100 percent of the profits will go to your organization.

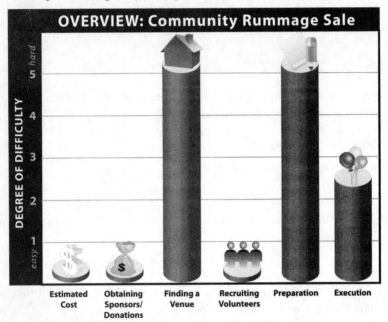

Special Materials/Equipment
- Cashbox and start-up funds
- T-shirts with your organization's name for volunteers
- Tables on which to display merchandise
- Signs (to advertise) the event

Sponsors/Donations
- The general public is the best source of donations.
- Contact retailers for donations of out-of-season or other unwanted merchandise you could sell.

Possible Venue(s)
Try a church or municipal community center, or a parking lot in a highly visible location.

Recommended Volunteer
10+ to solicit donations, sort merchandise, and promote the event

Preparation

Start requesting merchandise donations at least three months in advance through ads in free community papers and the media. Designate a central collection point, such as your organization's headquarters. Create a donation receipt. Sort through merchandise as it arrives to keep the job manageable. Price individual items using preprinted tags, or place similar items in a large box at one price. Advertise the sale dates in free community newspapers and on free bulletin boards. Send a news release to the local media.

Execution

Set up your merchandise and enjoy the rush of rummagers. Have volunteers sell refreshments like coffee and doughnuts to keep shoppers energized.

Tip(s)

- Time the sale for spring cleaning season or before the holidays, when people are looking for a last-minute charitable tax deduction.
- Donate leftover items to another organization, like the Salvation Army, to help it with its own charitable efforts.

Variation(s)

- Try setting up a trading post and charging participants an entry fee to come trade their unwanted items for someone else's treasures.

Custom Calendar Sale

Proudly draw attention to your city or regional area and make money for your organization with a custom calendar sale. Select 12 outstanding photographs, work with a company to print the calendars, and sell them directly or through an online company.

Sponsors/Donations

- Ask a youth group like the Girl Scouts to help sell calendars, either to earn merit badges or for a pizza party.
- Ask a pizzeria to donate the pies and pop.
- Contact local businesses for start-up seed money.

Possible Venue(s)

For on site sales, try shopping centers or malls and bank or grocery store lobbies. For consignment sales, approach bookstores, gift shops, and department stores. For online purchases, use an online company like Shutterfly.com, which creates each calendar on demand from the pictures you supply and ships them right to the purchasers.

Recommended Volunteer

3 to 5 depending on whether you are selling calendars personally or using an online company to sell for you

Preparation

Identify a calendar printer and provide 12 high-quality photographs. Advertise in free shopper papers, post notices on free bulletin boards, and send news releases to radio and cable stations. Put a link on your organization's website to an order form. To encourage online sales, offer PayPal as a payment option.

Execution

Sell from a table in a frequented location, or let an online company handle sales.

Tip(s)

- Obtain photos by holding a contest for the best pictures.

Variation(s)

- Have local heroes like firefighters or college athletes pose for a beefcake calendar. This works best if you can find a photographer willing to donate his or her services.

Custom T-shirt Sale

Americans are crazy for T-shirts with sports team names, sayings and pictures, which makes T-shirts the perfect fundraising item. They may be customized to sell for specific events or created on demand and delivered later.

Special Materials/Equipment

- Order forms
- Computer with Internet access for taking orders

Sponsors/Donations

- Because a customized T-shirt is a blank canvas, you can promise a potential donor space for its name and/or logo somewhere on the shirt.

Possible Venue(s)

Fun runs, marathons, sporting events, or schools (for custom spirit wear) are great.

Recommended Volunteer

3 to 5 including 1 who is Internet savvy and can create the custom shirt design online

Preparation

Preprinted shirts must be designed and ordered before the event. On-demand shirts require little more than a table and a computer with an Internet connection.

Be sure to advertise the event via news releases, fliers, and free ads in community newspapers.

Execution

There are a number of options for selling custom T-shirts. For one, you can order T-shirts appropriate for a particular event or facility, then set up a table and sell shirts to attendees. This requires an upfront financial commitment with funds recouped as you sell. Another option is to take special orders during an event, have the shirts printed, then deliver them to purchasers. This works especially well for school activities (like sporting events and pep rallies). Finally, you can work with an online create-on-demand company to design a custom shirt online and personalize it while the customer waits, then have it mailed directly to the purchaser. Generally, the organization will earn a commission on that type of sale rather than a set price.

Tip(s)

- Have a sample of each size on site so customers can make sure they will be satisfied with the fit of their T-shirts.

Variation(s)

- Sell custom sweatshirts, sweatpants, pajama pants, athletic shorts, and/or hats.

Customize a Brick

Sell laser-engraved bricks that can be installed in a prominent place, such as an entryway, walkway, patio, or wall. Because project areas tend to be large and the cost to buy a brick can be considerable, this fundraiser can raise a large amount of money for your organization.

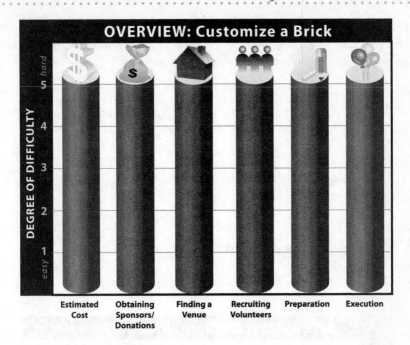

Sponsors/Donations
- Because of the longevity and permanence of brick installations, major businesses might be more willing to donate to your cause. Offer those that purchase a large quantity of bricks a prominent position in the installation. Also feature them in promotional materials.

Possible Venue(s)
Any company, municipality, building, or other venue, including your own, that is building, remodeling, or updating its grounds or facility works well. Because your organization will sell the bricks at a profit, then turn them over to the venue either for free or for an additional donation, it should be easy to persuade a company to agree to provide a "home" for the engraved brick pavers. Show them sample installation plans to pump up the excitement.

Recommended Volunteer
10 to 15 or more. This is best handled as an organization-wide fundraiser to sell as many bricks as possible.

Preparation
Locate a company that sells and laser-engraves bricks. Line up a venue where they will be installed. Create a promotional brochure showing how to buy bricks. Feature the promotion on your organization's website, and mail information to donors on your mailing list. Pitch the fundraiser to local media, and promote it to any publications the sponsoring venue may have.

Execution

Personally contact potentially large donors. Sell bricks at organization and community functions. Call in to radio programs to pitch the fundraiser.

Tip(s)

- If it is at a school, target parents of upcoming graduates and advertise it as a lasting graduation gift that can be visited for years to come.

Variation(s)

- Let customers paint their own bricks instead and display them indoors for a cheaper option.

DVD and Videotape Sale

Hold a drive to collect new and gently used DVDs and videotapes. Resell them to earn money for your charity.

Sponsors/Donations

- Contact libraries and video stores for donations of old or cast-off materials.
- Shop used bookstores for well-priced materials you can resell.
- Send out news releases to local media informing the public that donations are being accepted.
- Ask grocery stories to donate bags.

Possible Venue(s)

Your organization's meeting room, a church basement or meeting hall, or a donated party room at a restaurant is great.

Recommended Volunteer

10+ depending on the volume of donated materials

Preparation

Sort donated media into categories, such as action, adventure, romance, comedy, documentary, and fitness. Set aside well-used materials or DVDs with cracked cases and offer them at rock-bottom prices. Make sure the cash box contains a modest amount of start-up funds (both bills and coins) so you can make change.

Execution

Set up a DVD or VHS player, and run popular movies continuously to get people in the mood to buy. If there are too many videos to display all at once, assign someone to restock the tables as the supply dwindles. Re-sort materials that shoppers deposit in the wrong category.

Tip(s)

- List new movies or other videos that are still shrink-wrapped in an online auction like eBay, Half.com, or Amazon.com.
- Offer unsold items at a bag price at the end of the sale, or donate them to local libraries, which can resell them during their own book sales.

Variation(s)

- Hold a pre-sale event for which shoppers pay a small entrance fee for the privilege of shopping before the general public.

Earplug Sale

Inexpensive to buy and easy to sell, earplugs can be sold anywhere the ambient noise level is loud to earsplitting. Although corded earplugs are convenient, loose earplugs packed in plastic storage capsules have additional promotional value because they can be imprinted with your organization's name, phone number, and website address.

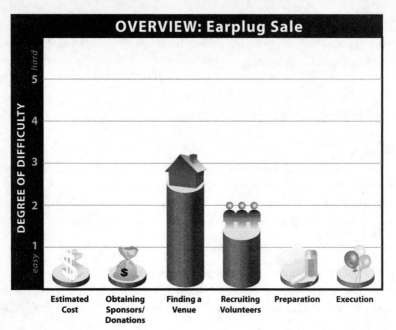

Sponsors/Donations
- Earplugs are inexpensive — usually from about $1.35 to $2 per pair — so you may be able to purchase them out of your organization's treasury.
- If your means are modest, solicit donations from local business owners to cover the cost.

Possible Venue(s)
Any place the decibel level is high, including arena and outdoor sporting events, NASCAR and other racing events, live concerts, and air shows, is appropriate.

Recommended Volunteer
3 to 4 to handle sales

Preparation
Prepare large signs for the chosen venue that feature both your organization's name and the names of your sponsors. Order product online, leaving extra time for orders that require personalization. Promote the event in your organization's newsletter and website, and in free community newspapers.

Execution
Have a central selling point near the entrance to the event or venue. Have volunteers wear a T-shirt imprinted with your organization's name, and if selling corded earplugs, have them drape a set around their necks.

Tip(s)
- You can charge more for each pair of earplugs if sponsors cover the upfront cost because your organization will not have any out-of-pocket costs.
- Do not spend money on advertising, because only those who attend an event will be tempted to buy.
- Order ear plugs in various colors, if possible, so purchasers can select their favorite.

Electronics Drive

Hold a community electronics recycling drive to collect old, outdated, and broken electronic equipment, including cell phones, laptops, MP3 players, digital cameras, calculators, gaming devices, external hard drives, and tablet e-readers. Then ship everything for free to a recycling site like YouRenew.com, which pays cash for equipment deemed to still have value.

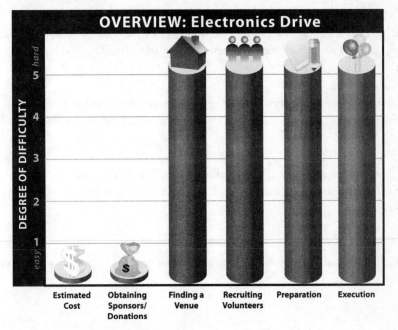

Special Materials/Equipment:
- Boxes (to ship the electronics to the recycler)
- Handcart (for moving the boxes)

Sponsors/Donations
- Everyone has outdated and broken electronic devices collecting dust, so start by appealing to the public for donations.
- Stores that sell electronic equipment, including mobile phone detailers and big box electronic stores, might also be willing to donate broken items.

Possible Venue(s)
Collection sites might include a parking lot, municipal or community center, church gathering room, or your organization's own building or meeting room. Ideally, the collection site should have storage space so you do not have to move the donations more than once before they are shipped.

Recommended Volunteer
10+ to collect, sort, and box the donated electronics for shipping

Preparation
Advertise the collection event in free community newspapers, on bulletin boards, and on your organization's website. Send news releases to the media.

Execution
Keep a running inventory of all donated items for your records, and immediately pack the electronics into boxes. Have tax deduction receipts available for those who request them.

Tip(s)
- To gain more attention, promote the event as a green recycling effort.
- Collect equipment on an ongoing basis to have a steady revenue stream for your organization.

Variation(s)
- Collect unfixable, unusable electronics and have people pay to enter a robot-making contest. Award prizes to winners.

Flower Bulb Sale

Late winter or early spring is the perfect time to cultivate a flower bulb fundraising effort. Your members will use colorful brochures provided by the bulb supplier to entice customers. The bulbs are shipped en masse directly to your organization so you can distribute orders to buyers.

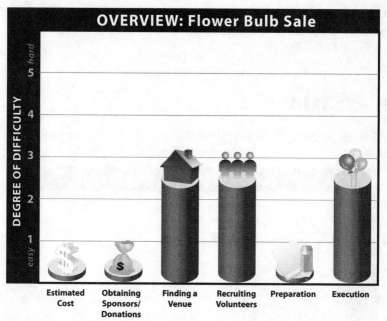

OVERVIEW: Flower Bulb Sale

Special Materials/Equipment
• T-shirts with the name of organization (for volunteers)

Possible Venue(s)
Community events, church fairs, shopping centers, or malls are good options.

Recommended Volunteer
3 to 5 to promote sales

Preparation
Find a bulb supplier online. Order brochures and order forms. Prepare signs to display on your table. Promote the sale in community newspapers and on bulletin boards. Send a news release to the lifestyle editor of local newspapers and broadcast stations, emphasizing what the funds will be used for.

Execution

Set up a table with signs. Place a potted plant or two on the table to put buyers in a floral frame of mind. Have volunteers greet passersby in a friendly way before hitting them up with a sales pitch. Help customers fill out order forms.

Tip(s)

- Offer home delivery of bulbs to customers for an extra charge. Priority Mail Flat Rate boxes cost as little as $4.95 to mail from the U.S. Postal Service and make it easy to send out orders.

Flower Sale

Sell single flowers, bouquets, or potted flowers and plants as beautiful ways to brighten someone's day.

Special Materials/Equipment

- Fresh flowers
- Plants
- Potted flowers

Sponsors/Donations

- Ask florists, flower markets, and wholesale flower suppliers for reduced rates or free products. Because freshly cut flowers have an expiration date, florists may be willing to donate products to your organization at no cost. Be sure the flowers are not too old, because you want your customers to be able to enjoy their purchase for a reasonable amount of time.
- Also ask for donations of flower food, cellophane, and ribbon for wrapping single stems. A craft store also may be willing to donate such materials.

Possible Venue(s)

Anywhere people congregate, including malls and shopping centers, public parks, boardwalks, tourist areas, business districts, office buildings, schools, works well.

Recommended Volunteer

2 to 3 to obtain flowers and handle sales

Preparation

After obtaining flowers and plants from florists or flower distributors, store them in a cool place until they are used. Cut flowers should be placed in a bucket of clean water into which fresh flower food has been mixed.

Execution

Have all volunteers dress alike, or provide them with T-shirts with the name of your organization. Set up a table or small stand in the venue of your choice. Wrap single stems in cellophane and tie with a ribbon for a pretty presentation. Tie a ribbon around flowers or plants that are in containers.

Tip(s)

- Be sure to keep cut flowers in water until they have been sold so they stay fresh.
- Time the fundraising event to coincide with a holiday like Valentine's Day or Mother's Day to increase sales.

Variation(s)

- Make fake flower arrangements and add glitter, ribbons, and other decorations. These could be holiday-themed or personalized by writing names on the ribbons tied around the pots.

Fundraising Scratch Cards

You can earn a 90 percent profit with this promotion. Sell fundraising scratch cards, which typically have 60 dots on them under which there are various amounts to donate, from zero to $2.50. The donor chooses and scratches off a dot to uncover the amount to be paid. Because the amounts are so low, buyers may choose to scratch off more than one dot. If all dots are scratched off, the card totals $100.

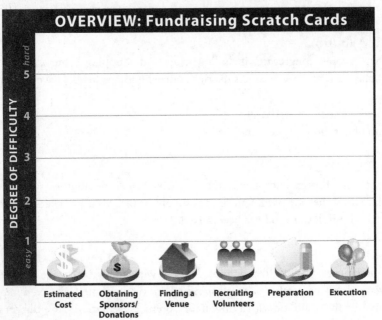

Special Materials/Equipment
- Fundraising scratch cards (available online and can be personalized for your organization)

Sponsors/Donations
- Scratch cards are inexpensive, so many organizations simply purchase them with funds from their operating budget. But if you solicit donors, offer them the opportunity to put their name and/or company logo on the cards.

Possible Venue(s)
Try this fundraiser at organization events, for door-to-door sales, outside retail stores, and in conjunction with other fundraising activities (such as candy bar sales).

Recommended Volunteer
15+ Every person in the organization should be recruited to help.

Preparation

Obtain a solicitation license if going from door to door. Obtain permission to set up outside a retail store.

Execution

Wear T-shirts or buttons that identify volunteers as members of your group. Have documentation available showing that your organization is a registered nonprofit.

Tip(s)

- Some scratch card providers include a sheet of national brand name coupons that can be given to donors as a token of thanks. The donation amounts on these cards typically run from zero to $2.50 for a 60-dot card, and from $1 to $5 for a 30-dot card.

Variation(s)

- Tie a scratch card promotion to your organization's goals. For instance, if your organization raises money for abandoned pets, hold your fundraiser during Prevention of Cruelty to Animals Month in April.

Magazine Subscription Drive

Sell new or renewal subscriptions at prices greatly discounted from the newsstand prices. Typically, customers choose from a list of hundreds of titles, and your organization earns about 40 percent of sales.

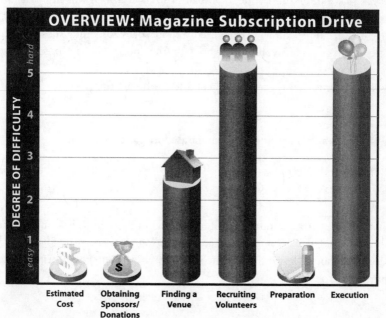

Special Materials/Equipment
- T-shirts (for volunteers)

Possible Venue(s)
Malls and shopping centers, bank and grocery store lobbies, and door to door in residential communities are effective.

Recommended Volunteer
10+ especially for door-to-door drives. Choose people with a gift of gab and an easy-going disposition.

Preparation
Search online for a subscription company. Download magazine price lists and order forms.

Execution
Approach prospects in a friendly way and stress how much money they can save by subscribing or renewing during the fundraising drive. Help customers fill out paperwork and collect payment.

Tip(s)
- Have volunteers wear something that identifies them with your organization because they are collecting money.
- Check to see if the subscription company you have chosen will allow customers to order subscriptions on its website. Alternatively, you can choose a company that helps your organization set up a personalized website solely for selling subscriptions.
- Offer a prize to the volunteer who sells the most subscriptions to encourage friendly competition.
- An adult should always accompany children who are fundraising.

Variation(s)
- Collect like-new magazines and have a used magazine sale.

Reusable Bag Sale

Demonstrate your group's commitment to the environment by selling environmentally friendly reusable bags. Have your organization's logo custom-printed on the bag to advertise your cause. Depending on the supplier, your group could earn profits of 40 percent or more per bag.

Special Materials/Equipment
- Custom-printed bags
- Signs (to advertise)

Sponsors/Donations
- Seek funding from retail stores that do not currently offer their own bags. Offer to include their logo on the bag in exchange for a donation.
- A recycling center or a municipality that recycles might also be willing to contribute funds.

Possible Venue(s)
Grocery stores, malls, shopping centers that do not offer reusable bags are good ideas.

Recommended Volunteer
2 to 3 to handle sales, if bags are sold outside of a retail store. Ask everyone in your organization to help promote the bags.

Preparation
Locate a reusable bag supplier on the Internet. Set up a website to handle online orders, or add a shopping cart to your current website. Set up a PayPal payment option.

Execution
Promote sales to the local media and in any organization materials, including newsletters and e-mails. Hold regular sales at tables in front of retail stores.

Tip(s)

- Include a flier about your organization with information about how to donate or volunteer in each bag.

Variation(s)

- Hold a design-a-bag contest. Offer a cash prize to the person who creates the best design. Contact youth organizations like the Boy Scouts, which might be willing to help sell the bags to earn merit badges.

Silicone Bracelet Sale

Custom silicone bracelets are popular with the public because they declare the wearers' support for a cause while making an eye-catching fashion statement. Come up with your own catchy slogan to put on low-cost silicone bracelet bands, or choose a custom shape or logo that represents your organization to have made into silicone rubber band bracelets (popular for trading).

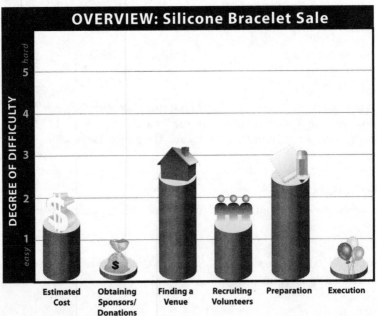

Sponsors/Donations

- Because silicone bracelets are quite inexpensive (often 15 cents or less each), you might be able to pay for them out of your organization's treasury. Otherwise, contact local business owners for financial support to place the order.

Possible Venue(s)

Try grocery store and bank lobbies, department stores, large home improvement stores, civic center entrances, or community or church fairs.

Recommended Volunteer

15+ including someone to order them and as many people as possible to sell the bracelets

Preparation

Prepare large signs for the chosen venue. Decide on a selling price ($1 or $2 each will usually generate the most sales). Promote the event in local media and on free bulletin boards. Sell the bracelets to your members first, because wearing the bracelets will be effective advertising for them.

Execution

Have all volunteers wear a bracelet and try to sell them to everyone who approaches the building you are stationed at. Alternatively, offer them to people as they exit the building, because they may feel freer to buy after they have made their primary purchases.

Tip(s)

- Order sample bracelets from several suppliers to judge the quality, thickness, width, and color before placing a full order, because returns are generally not allowed.

Variation(s)

- Offer bracelets with colored letters, glitter, or multi-color swirls, or in glow-in-the-dark or leather options. Note that these may increase the price point of each bracelet.

Special Delivery Telegrams

Deliver themed or congratulatory telegrams to mark special occasions. Possible events include birthday parties, graduation parties, bachelor or bachelorette parties, wedding receptions and showers, new baby arrivals, anniversary parties, retirement parties, going-away parties. Holidays like Valentine's Day, Mother's Day, Father's Day, and Christmas are also great times to promote telegrams.

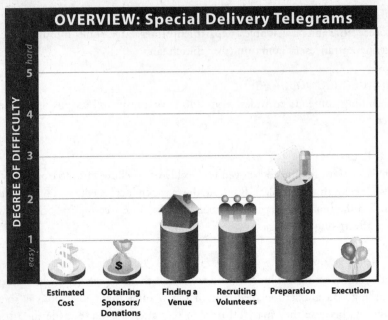

Special Materials/Equipment
- Work order forms (for scheduling deliveries)
- Floral or balloon bouquets (offered as add-on items to increase profit potential)

Sponsors/Donations
- You could seek monetary donations from companies whose names would appear in promotional materials in exchange for a contribution. Your organization would enjoy a 100 percent profit in return.

Possible Venue(s)
Deliver telegrams wherever the recipient is located (home, office, school).

Recommended Volunteer
2+ depending on the number of people who pay to have a telegram delivered

Preparation
Promote a "Telegram Day" or "Telegram Weekend" so you can offer deliveries for as many types of occasions as possible. Prepare a script for each type of event.

Execution
Send out a small contingent of people from your organization to deliver each telegram. Have someone take a digital photo of the recipient, and e-mail it as a value-added feature.

Tip(s)

• Wear attire related to your charitable organization when delivering the telegram.

Variation(s)

• Offer singing telegrams. This is especially appropriate for choirs or musical groups, but can be fun for anyone who has a pleasant singing voice — or the guts to belt it out in front of a group.

Spirit Doormat Sale

Step up school spirit by selling custom doormats in the colors of favorite high school sports teams. Either purchase a supply of mats to sell at school–related events or order a few samples to display, take orders on site, and deliver mats to purchasers later.

Special Materials/Equipment

• Signs that can be posted on site (to advertise the availability of mats)
• Order cards (if you are not selling on demand)

Sponsors/Donations

• Because it is usually best to have the mats available for sale on site, contact sports booster organizations, restaurants, or other businesses that sponsor sports teams, as well as stores that sell spirit gear like jerseys, to obtain enough funding to place your first order.

Possible Venue(s)

School pep rallies and athletic competitions (i.e. football, wrestling, baseball) are ideal. You can even set up a table in a school cafeteria or sell the mats in the principal's office.

Recommended Volunteer

4 to 5 to set up, take orders, and deliver mats

Preparation

Locate a company online that sells spirit mats. Contact the target school to obtain a logo and verify correct team colors.

Execution

Set up a table at a school event, and sell, sell, sell.

Tip(s)

- Do not play favorites – sell mats for competing teams at the same event and watch your profits soar.
- Add a shopping cart to your organization's website, and offer the mats for sale online. Set up a PayPal or merchant account.
- Do not sell National Collegiate Athletic Association (NCAA) themed products, because the NCAA owns exclusive rights.

Variation(s)

- Sell spirit sticks, buttons, necklaces, ribbons, stickers, or temporary tattoos as well.

Used Book Sale

You can enjoy 100 percent of your profits by collecting donated, gently used books and reselling them to the public. Beyond bringing great reading materials to people at an affordable cost, you will also help save trees and reduce the planet's carbon footprint by recycling.

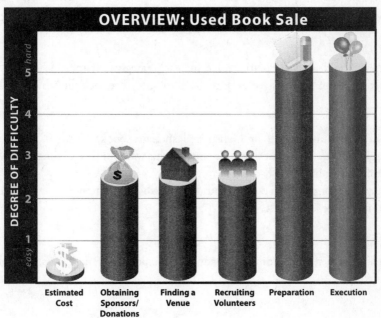

Special Materials/Equipment:

- Tables to display books
- Start-up money (singles and coins)
- Locking cashbox or aprons (to safeguard money and make change)
- Chairs for volunteers

Sponsors/Donations

- Contact local libraries and literacy groups for sponsorship/assistance. Ask libraries to donate cast-off books.
- Advertise for donations in church papers, free community newspapers, and free bulletin boards.
- Generate free publicity by sending news releases requesting donations and promoting attendance to local TV, cable, and radio stations.

Possible Venue(s)

Community halls, church gathering centers, libraries, and schools work well.

Recommended Volunteer
5+ to collect and sell books

Preparation
Designate a collection center. Sort books by type (for example, general fiction, romance, self-help, animals, business, popular authors, and so on). Establish a price schedule, such as 50 cents for paperbacks and $1 for hardcovers.

Execution
Designate a table or part of the table for each category. If more books have been acquired than can be displayed at once, have volunteers restock the tables regularly.

Tip(s)
- List rare, out-of-print, or high-priced specialty books (such as art books) on Amazon.com. You must pay to list and sell this way, but you might generate higher profits by doing so.
- Put a donation jar in a conspicuous location to collect money from browsers who do not make a purchase.

Variation(s)
- Sell other media, including DVDs and VHS tapes, CDs, magazines, and computer software.

Chapter 10

Miscellaneous

These events are easy to set-up and allow you to show off your creativity in a variety of ways. The projects you will find in this chapter include:

- Ballroom Dance Lessons
- Charity Buzz Cut
- Dollar Days
- Flamingo Flocking
- Fundraising by Blogging
- Massage-A-Thon
- "Please Do Not Come" Fundraiser
- Sacrifice Something You Love
- Speaker Forums
- Writing Letters for Support
- Cell Phone Collection
- Container Collection
- Fake Kidnapping
- Flier Delivery
- Lend a Helping Hand
- Peck for a Pig
- Pool Party
- Social Media and Networking Class
- Walking Billboard

Ballroom Dance Lessons

Supporters will leap at the chance to learn a new dance style or brush up on their foot skills. Ask a local dance instructor to donate a week of lessons for popular dances like salsa, waltz, swing, or tango, and charge participants a fee to attend.

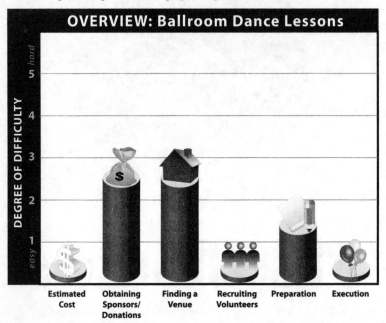

Sponsors/Donations
- Find a local dance instructor who is willing to donate a week of lessons. Appeal to the idea that supporters might pay to continue lessons with the instructor, bringing in business.
- Seek a venue that will donate space for lessons for a week.

Possible Venue(s)
A dance studio, gym room where fitness classes are held, or any large room with mirrors and a hard floor is best for dancing.

Recommended Volunteer
1 to schedule lessons with the instructor and sign people up

Preparation
Find an instructor. Agree on what kind of lessons will be given, where they will take place, and when they will occur. Advertise, sign people up, and collect payments.

Execution

Have the instructor give the lessons.

Tip(s)

- Collect payment in advance. That way, you make money even if someone doesn't show up for a lesson.
- Divide groups by experience level (beginner to advanced) or age group (children to adults).
- Hold this event around Valentine's Day to appeal to couples who might enjoy taking lessons together.

Variation(s)

- Have a small performance at the conclusion of the lessons. Invite family and friends to come watch, and charge an admission fee. You can also sell concessions and flowers at the show for additional fundraising.

Cell Phone Collection

Collect working, non-working, and obsolete cell phones, and send them to dealers or companies that refurbish and resell them. Your charity will receive cash for each phone sent in.

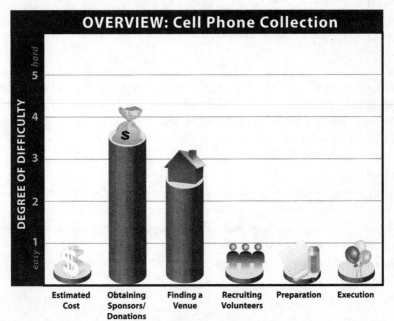

Special Materials/Equipment
- Locking bins or containers where phones can be deposited securely

Sponsors/Donations
- Ask individuals to donate cell phones.
- Contact large organizations that have sales staffs, because they are likely to update their electronic equipment regularly and might be willing to donate phones to your cause.
- Appeal to an organization or maintenance equipment store to donate locking bins.

Possible Venue(s)
Install collection bins in grocery stores, bank lobbies, libraries, and department stores.

Recommended Volunteer
1+ to set up a collection spot. Encourage everyone in your organization to collect phones for your organization as well as to donate their old phones.

Preparation
Obtain and install bins in selected locations. Send news releases to media to promote the event.

Execution
Set a collection deadline. Box up phones as they come in, and ship them to the selected dealer.

Tip(s)
- Emphasize how recycling old phones helps the environment by keeping them out of landfills.
- Promote how the funds will be used by your organization, especially if they will benefit the less fortunate.

Variation(s)
- Print postage-paid envelopes so donors can send phones directly to the organization. Ask mail order companies to include the envelopes in each package they send out.
- Select a recycling company that accepts inkjet cartridges along with phones to increase your organization's profit potential.
- Partner with an entertainment venue to offer discounted admission to patrons who donate a phone.

Charity Buzz Cut

Find a volunteer willing to have his or her head shaved for charity. Set a lofty monetary goal, and challenge the community to meet it. Once the goal has been met, hold an event in a public setting during which the volunteer loses his or her locks with plenty of fanfare.

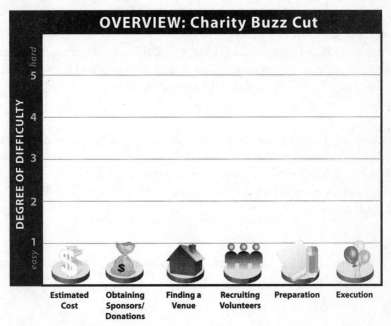

Special Materials/Equipment

- Stylist's cape
- Razor or sharp pair of shears

Sponsors/Donations

- Ask a stylist who has plenty of personal flair to donate his or her services for the big snip.
- Contact a local band to provide music during the event.

Possible Venue(s)

A community center, city park, city or church festival, or televised city council or borough meeting has potential.

Recommended Volunteer

5 to 10 or more to solicit funds

Preparation

Find a recognizable community leader, popular sports figure, or media personality who would be willing to make a big sacrifice for charity. Promote the event heavily to local media, playing up the charitable angle and the identity of the person who will be shorn and emphasizing how to donate. Take online donations through PayPal, which costs little to use.

Execution

Make the event into a community celebration, and invite the media to attend. Sell refreshments. Make an announcement concerning the amount of money raised; then have the person who will be shaved make a grand entrance.

Tip(s)

- Make a final pass with a collection canister among people in attendance to garner last minute donations.
- If the person being shaved has long hair, save the shorn hair so it can be donated to an organization like Locks of Love, which provides wigs for children with serious medical conditions.

Variation(s)

Make it a Charity Dye, for which someone agrees to dye his or her hair an outrageous color if the fund-raising goal is met.

Container Collection

A simple fundraiser that has the potential to raise big money with minimal effort. Just place labeled collection containers in prominent (and protected) locations, and wait for contributions to roll in.

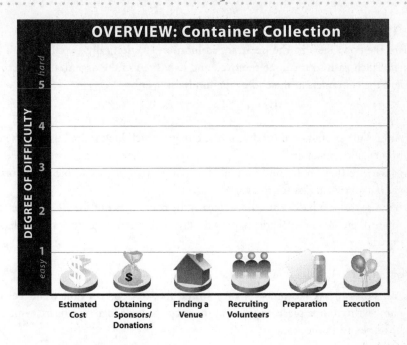

Special Materials/Equipment
- Labeled containers (inexpensive and readily available online)

Sponsors/Donations
- Though sponsors are not necessary for this low-cost fundraiser, your organization certainly can solicit a donation from any store or facility where the collection jars are placed.
- In addition, you could ask business owners to contribute to cover the cost of the collection containers.

Possible Venue(s)
Convenience stores, department stores, libraries, churches, or other service businesses like dry cleaners, pharmacies, and gas stations work well.

Recommended Volunteer
4 to 5 to place and regularly retrieve collection containers

Preparation
Order fundraising containers. Apply a label with your organization' name, phone number, and fundraiser name on each container. Contact businesses to request permission to place a container on their counter for a set amount of time.

Execution

Deliver the containers to the prearranged locations. Periodically check to see if they contain much cash so it can be removed and deposited in the organization's account. Retrieve the containers at the end of the fundraising effort.

Tip(s)

- Always use professional fundraiser containers, which look more businesslike than homemade containers.
- Make sure they are located in a safe location so they are accessible to donors but are not an easy target for thieves.
- Because this is a passive fundraiser, leave the containers out for a few weeks, then rotate them to new locations periodically to increase visibility and widen the donation range.

Variation(s)

- Ask stores to ask customers if they would like to donate a dollar and get their name written on a piece of paper in the shape of your logo or a heart, which will be displayed in the store.

Dollar Days

These days, it might seem like a dollar does not buy much, but it can do wonders for your organization. So this fundraiser encourages potential donors to contribute a dollar per day for a specified period of time, such as a week or two. If holding the fundraiser at a school, challenge parents to match their students' donations to double your organization's take.

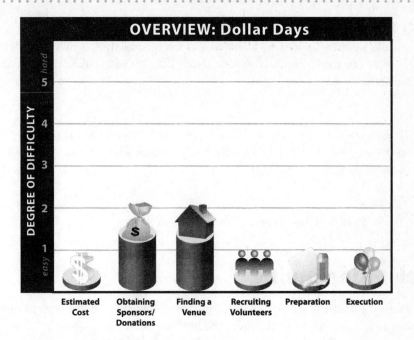

Special Materials/Equipment
- Canister or other collection container labeled with your organization's name and contact information (for picking up donations)

Sponsors/Donations
- Ask radio or TV stations to promote the fundraiser, especially during morning drive time when working adults are tuned in, and invite listeners or watchers to call in a pledge or visit your website to donate.

Possible Venue(s)
Schools are ideal venues because of the possibility of asking parents to match their children's donations. Other venues might include universities, small and large businesses, medical facilities, government offices, community events, churches, shopping centers, and malls.

Recommended Volunteer
3 to 4 to make announcements and collect money

Preparation
Contact the venue to obtain permission to solicit funds. Consider printing pledge cards donors can sign to agree to donate the specified amount of money, because this formalizes the pledge.

Execution

Unveil the fundraising idea to attendees during a regularly scheduled meeting or assembly, or at a special event. Distribute pledge cards. Send in volunteers each day of the fundraiser to collect donations.

Tip(s)

- To encourage 100 percent compliance at the target venue, offer an incentive, such as a cash prize that will be awarded to the person whose name is selected in a random drawing.

Variation(s)

- Try for $5 or $10 days to generate more donations.

Fake Kidnapping

"Kidnap" the leader of an organization, such as a minister or priest, elected official, sports coach, or other respected person, and hold him or her for "ransom" until enough funds are collected from the organization to meet a predetermined goal. Return the "kidnapped" person to his or her point of origin in a dramatic presentation.

Special Materials/Equipment

- Bandit costumes (masks, fake toy guns like squirt guns)

Sponsors/Donations

- Appeal to the public through radio public service announcements or the local TV news to help raise the ransom.

Possible Venue(s)

Churches, municipal meeting rooms, sporting events (after the big game), schools and universities, or community events are great options.

Recommended Volunteer

5 to 10 people to make a scene and whisk away the victim

Preparation

Contact local law enforcement and let them know what you are planning in order to head off any rescue attempts with actual loaded weapons.

Execution

Have the disguised "kidnappers" burst into the venue and storm the intended target. Announce that he or she is being kidnapped, and that the only way to get the person back is to donate money to your organization. Make it clear how long the person will be held and how much money is needed to win his or her release. Wave around a donation canister as the victim is escorted away.

Tip(s)

- Make it clear that this is a fake kidnapping.

- Pick someone with a sense of humor who will not mind being held "prisoner" for a short period of time.

- Get the participant's permission ahead of time to ensure that there are no problems, but do not tell the participant what day the kidnapping will occur in order to maintain the element of surprise.

Variation(s)

- Convey the "prisoner" to a fake jail and keep him or her there until enough money is raised to pay for a "Get out of Jail" card.

Flamingo Flocking

Plant a dozen pink flamingos on the front lawn of a residence or outside a business entrance. Hang a letter around the neck of the lead bird explaining that the recipient has been "flocked" for a good cause, and that the only way to get the flamingos to "fly away" is to pay or raise a certain amount of money, like $10 per flamingo. Once the money has been collected, the donor chooses the next recipient, and your volunteers relocate the flock to start the process all over.

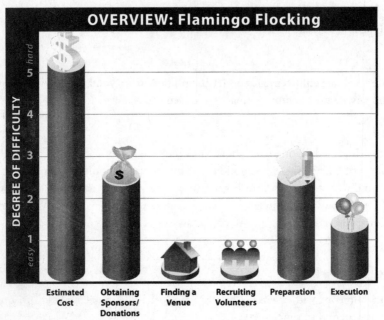

Special Materials/Equipment
- Several dozen pink flamingo lawn ornaments

Sponsors/Donations
- Approach lawn and garden stores, or discount stores with garden centers for donations of flamingos.

Possible Venue(s)
Pick the first "flocking" location, and let those who have been "flocked" decide where the next landing will be.

Recommended Volunteer
10+ depending on how many flocks are deployed

Preparation

Determine the recipients of the first flocks from a list of your previous donors. Write a short letter explaining how the fundraiser works, and give a phone number the recipient can call once the correct amount of money has been raised.

Execution

Try to set up the birds without being seen, because the element of surprise is part of the fun. Send volunteers to pick up and relocate the birds each time the donation amount has been raised.

Tip(s)

- Have up to six dozen flocks circulating to maximize donations.
- If you encounter someone who complains about being "flocked," collect the birds promptly, ask the previous recipient to designate another "victim," and relocate the flock.

Variation(s)

- Instead of flamingos, try a flag or an object related to your organization's mascot.
- Shower lawns with flower pinwheels instead.

Flier Delivery

Offer for your organizations' members to deliver advertising fliers for local businesses. Charge by the piece or by the hour. Because it can be pricey to mail printed pieces, business owners are likely to welcome the opportunity to use your members instead; plus the personal service is a big bonus.

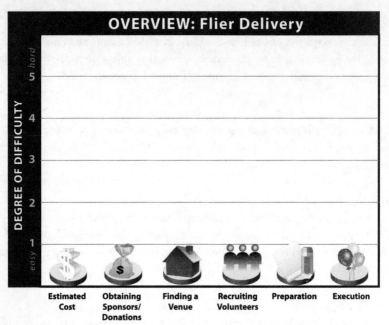

Special Materials/Equipment

- Messenger bag or other pouch, preferably emblazoned with your organization's name (to carry the fliers in)

Sponsors/Donations

- None needed, unless you would like to raise cash to pay for bags in which to carry the fliers. Any company that delivers, from restaurants to newspapers, might be interested in donating funds in exchange for a printed logo on the bag.

Possible Venue(s)

Pizza and other restaurants, hair and nail salons, home improvement companies, people running for public office, and others are good options.

Recommended Volunteer

10+ to deliver fliers

Preparation

Make sure the company you are delivering for has the necessary solicitation permits.

Execution

Pick up the fliers from the client or print shop, divide them among volunteers, drop them off door to door. Try threading them through the front door handle or inserting them securely into the seam of the door.

Tip(s)

- Have each volunteer carry a cell phone, both for safety and in case he or she runs out of fliers.
- Do not place fliers in mailboxes, which are considered federal property. The sponsoring organization could be fined if someone complains.

Variation(s)

- Sign up en masse to deliver telephone books from door to door, and turn over proceeds to your organization.

Fundraising by Blogging

Keeping potential donors and volunteers informed of your nonprofit's current activities is crucial, both to attract donations and to build goodwill among people who are genuinely interested in your cause. A blog can connect readers, build community by encouraging comments and discussions, and more. Use a blog to market the organization, give information about a capital campaign in progress, and provide up-to-date news about the good works the organization performs. For example, blog entries can profile individuals who have been helped by the organization as a way to show specifically how it is making a difference in people's lives. In addition, blog entries can offer readers useful information to help them personally so they feel like they are getting something valuable from your organization.

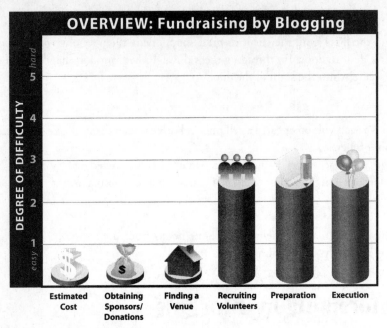

OVERVIEW: Fundraising by Blogging

Special Materials/Equipment
- Computer with Internet access, live website, blog publishing tool (like wordpress.com)

Sponsors/Donations
- Form an alliance with an affiliated or complementary organization where your blog can appear, in addition to on your own website. Include a donation button on the site to make it easy for blog readers to donate.

Possible Venue(s)
Your organization's own website or that of an affiliated or complementary organization that shares your values is effective.

Recommended Volunteer
1 to 2 or more who enjoy writing, can write grammatically and logically, and can meet deadlines regularly and reliably

Preparation
Read widely and follow developments in your field to get blogging ideas.

Execution

Establish a set schedule — say, once a week — to blog; then, meet it without fail. A blog that is not updated regularly will not induce readers to return to the website to find out what is new and exciting.

Tip(s)

- Offer PayPal and e-checks as payment options for donors.

Variation(s)

- Try podcasting valuable information and news that might be attractive to potential donors, and include updates about your organization.
- Keeping up a Twitter account for your organization is also a great way to get a following and make people aware of ways to participate and donate.
- Make a Facebook group for your organization and send out event invites for your fundraisers.

Lend a Helping Hand

Offer to do odd jobs and simple household tasks in the neighborhood for a fee. Tasks might include gardening, weeding, shoveling snow, raking leaves, painting, picking up dry cleaning, dog walking. Charge by the hour ($10 an hour is reasonable) or by the job.

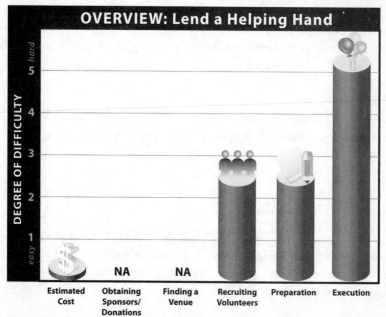

Sponsors/Donations
- Ask the homeowner to provide any necessary materials or equipment.

Possible Venue(s)
Virtually all work will be done at the homeowners' homes.

Recommended Volunteer
10+ so you have a large enough pool of people with varying skills to handle the tasks that will come up

Preparation
Advertise your organization's capabilities and availability with fliers and ads in free community newspapers and on bulletin boards. Contact local media, because they might be interested in doing a human-interest story on your group.

Execution
Deliver fliers door to door, and speak to the people who are home. Pass out business cards. Create a work schedule to make sure all jobs are handled promptly.

Tip(s)
- Check with the local municipality to determine whether you need a solicitation license.
- Offer both a phone number and an e-mail address at which interested parties can contact your organization.
- Put a link on your organization's website giving details about the services you offer.

Variation(s)
- If any of your members are proficient with a computer, offer simple computer services like hooking up peripherals and uploading or updating software and printer drivers.

Massage-A-Thon

Partner with a massage therapist or massage therapy studio to offer everything from chair massages to whole body treatments. Typically, a portion of the proceeds is donated to the charitable organization (usually 10 to 50 percent of the massage cost), while the balance goes to the masseur's/hosting studio.

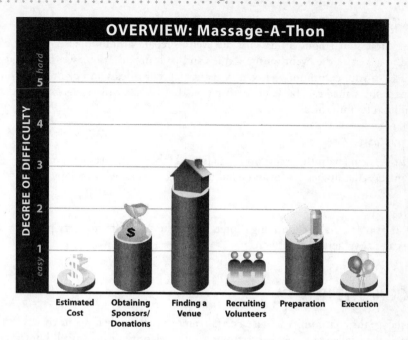

Special Materials/Equipment
- Massage tables or chairs

Sponsors/Donations
- In addition to locating masseurs who agree to offer their services, funds will be needed to provide refreshments, including snacks like cookies or fruit, and non-staining beverages like lemonade and bottled water.
- You can increase your organization's take by holding a raffle with cash prizes or goods solicited from local business owners.

Possible Venue(s)
A massage therapy studio, mall or other space with a large open area, community or church fair where a row of chairs can be accommodated, or even a home improvement, camping, boat, or other convention center show can work if the venue will provide space for free.

Recommended Volunteer
3 to 4 to find a massage therapist and schedule appointments with customers

Preparation

Have professional signs printed for the event. Prepare promotional copy that can be used to advertise the event on the venue's and your organization's website. Send news releases to your community's free newspapers, and broadcast and print media outlets. Prepare fliers that can be handed to passers-by. Check with your state concerning gaming rules for raffles.

Execution

Assist masseurs with the transport of chairs and tables to the venue, if necessary. Have volunteers chat up passers-by and hand out flyers to those who walk by.

Tip(s)

- If held at a mall or shopping center, have volunteers offer to carry packages to the car as a value-added service.

Peck for a Pig

Challenge the community to raise a certain amount of money for your charity. Promise that, if the challenge is met successfully, a local celebrity or other well-known person you have recruited for the cause will smooch a pig.

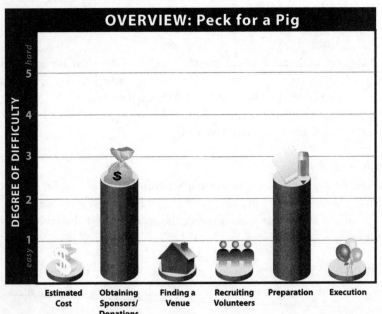

Special Materials/Equipment

- Pet pig
- Containers to collect cash

Sponsors/Donations
- Contact local businesses for donations, and offer them logo space on your publicity materials. Even if you are able to raise plenty of cash from sponsors, set the bar high for community donations to generate extra excitement.

Possible Venue(s)
This challenge is best held as part of another event, like a city or church festival or school activity. Collect money during sporting events so you can use the sports facility or playing field for the kiss.

Recommended Volunteer
2 to 3 to find the pig, the potential smoocher, and donors

Preparation
Create a poster or tally board featuring a picture of the pig. Publicize the event in as many free and low-cost publications as possible. Try to recruit a local celebrity like a TV anchor, DJ, sports star or coach, or elected official to do the deed. If you land a TV personality, be sure to give the station the exclusive story to report on.

Execution
Set up donation containers and coax people to come over and drop in their cash donations. Make a big production out of the pig kissing payoff after announcing that the donation goal has been met.

Tip(s)
- Keep an eye on the containers to deter theft, and remove cash from the containers regularly.

Variation(s)
- Substitute the local school's team mascot for the pig to encourage team spirit.

"Please Do Not Come" Fundraiser

This event invites supporters *not* to attend a lavish dinner with superb entertainment and fabulous door prizes — because there actually is no such event planned! Make it clear on the invitation that the event will not actually occur, but invite people to buy tickets anyway to support your cause. Invited guests will get a good laugh, and likely will be more than happy to support an event they do not have to attend.

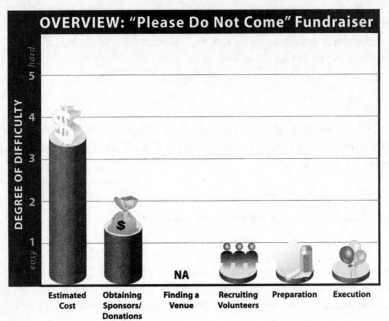

Special Materials/Equipment
- Fancy invitations
- Donation cards
- Postage
- Return envelopes
- Rented mailing list (to augment your organization's own mailing list and reach more potential donors)

Sponsors/Donations
- Ask a print shop to donate the cost of the invitations and other materials.
- Appeal to local merchants for the cost of postage.
- Mention donors' names prominently on the invitations.

Recommended Volunteer
5 to 10 to create and send out invitations

Preparation
Purchase a one-time use mailing list from a list rental company, which you can find online. Search the Web for a list of local and state politician names and addresses, as well as those of sports celebrities, media personalities, and so on, and invite them, too. Address each envelope by hand in a fancy script like calligraphy.

Execution
Literally, nothing needs to be done once the invitations go out, except to wait for donations to roll in.

Tip(s)

- Use stamps rather than a postage meter, because that gives the impression of personal rather than business mail.

Variation(s)

- Hold a "Do Not Come" sporting event with big name players, such as the New York Yankees versus the Boston Red Sox.
- Hold a Bakeless Bake Sale, inviting people not to do all the work that goes into it (bake, find a recipe, shop for ingredients, mix, cook, wash dishes, clean up your kitchen, deliver the product, or stand outside and try to sell anything). Instead, they can make a check out to your organization, stay home, and enjoy the free time as they wish.

Pool Party

This is fun summertime event for any age group. Admit kids free or for a small admission fee. Sell poolside food and snacks, and offer carnival-style games with prizes.

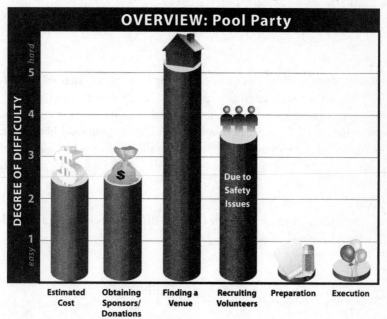

Special Materials/Equipment

- Pool toys
- Carnival games (rented or constructed)
- Tables or tent (for concession items)

Sponsors/Donations

- Approach toy stores for donations of stuffed animals or other toys that can be awarded as prizes.
- Offer signs and other publicity to pool owners who give permission to use their facility.
- If a membership facility like a fitness center gives you free pool time, offer to hand out membership applications to participants.
- Ask a party rental company to supply some beach chairs and a couple of beach umbrellas.

Possible Venue(s)

High schools, YMCA/YWCA, fitness facilities, community centers, and municipal pools work well.

Recommended Volunteer

10 to oversee carnival games, prepare and sell food, sell tickets, and lifeguard

Preparation

In addition to advertising the event and promoting it in the media, it will be necessary to make, purchase, or rent carnival games. These can include ring toss, baseball or basketball toss, wheel games, card games, and ticket games. It may be necessary in your state to have a food vendor license if you will be cooking food like hot dogs on site. You also might need a state license to hold a raffle. Search your state's website for information.

Execution

Set up the carnival activities and food area at a safe distance from the pool. Hold hourly raffle drawings. Keep a close eye on the pool to ensure that everyone is safe.

Tip(s)

- Fill a small plastic pool with ice to keep soft drinks cold.

Variation(s)

- Create your own water day with sprinklers, blow-up water slides, Slip 'n Slides, water balloon tosses, and other fun water games.

Sacrifice Something You Love

This simple fundraiser entails having a group of people, from students and groups of employees, to your organization's own members, give up something they truly love, and donate the cost of that special treat to charity instead. It can be a one-time donation or a donation made daily or weekly over a specified period of time. In either case, there is some sacrifice involved, which makes the donation even more valuable.

Sponsors/Donations
• Ask radio or TV stations to talk about the fundraiser, and invite listeners or watchers to donate.

Possible Venue(s)
Schools, universities, corporations and small-to-mid-sized companies, medical centers, government offices, community events, churches, shopping centers, or malls are great options.

Recommended Volunteer
4 to 5 to recruit participants, record pledges, and collect money

Preparation

Visit potential venues in person. Provide fliers explaining how the fundraiser works. For example, ask donors to sacrifice the cost of anything from a single latte or fast food meal, to the cost of a nail appointment, a movie ticket, a pizza, and so on. Stress that a contribution of any amount, no matter how small, is welcome. Inform the local media about the event and any particularly interesting sacrifices.

Execution

Assign volunteers to visit the target venue, and use the public address system to request donations. Make sure volunteers are visible throughout the day to remind people to make a donation. Have a collection container or box available that people can deposit donations into themselves.

Tip(s)

- Offer a prize to institutions like schools that have 100 percent compliance among the student body, or to one lucky participant in a random drawing.

Social Media and Networking Class

A timely and exciting event to introduce the parents and grandparents to the mysteries of social media and networking that are second nature to their kids. The class can touch on Facebook, MySpace, Twitter, Skype, and texting.

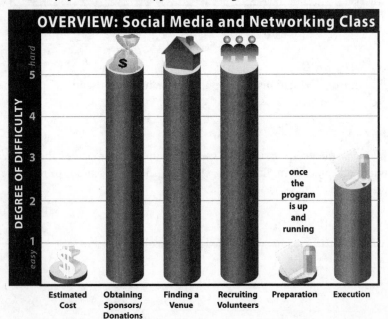

OVERVIEW: Social Media and Networking Class

Special Materials/Equipment
- Computer with Internet access
- LCD projector
- Handouts detailing what the class covers

Sponsors/Donations
- If no one in your organization is familiar enough with social media and networking to lead the class — or is not comfortable teaching — ask someone who teaches computer classes to donate his or her time.

- Alternately, contact the IT department of the local university or college and ask for a referral to a gifted student who would be willing to teach. Offer an honorarium if they need a monetary incentive.

Possible Venue(s)
High school or elementary school auditoriums or computer classrooms, adult education classrooms, or community centers work well.

Recommended Volunteer
3 to 4 including 1 to teach and 2 to 3 to set up equipment, collect fees, and pass out handouts

Preparation
Promote the class in community newspapers, in Parent-Teacher Association (PTA) newsletters, and on the venue's website. Initially, the instructor can create a curriculum for the class that can be taught over and over in the future.

Execution
Set up the equipment, dim the lights, and share your knowledge.

Tip(s)
- Create a second class to cover other types of electronic media like RSS feeds, YouTube, LinkedIn, and search engines.

Variation(s)
- Offer tips on how to download music and podcasts from iTunes and add them to an iPod.
- Demonstrate how to use Google tools like Gmail, Google Alerts, Google Earth, and others.

Speaker Forums

Invite the most interesting and articulate people in your community, from artists and musicians to authors and government officials, to kick off a series of fundraising speaker forums. Ask the orators to be keynote speakers at your organization's monthly luncheons or hold standalone events. Charge an admission fee, and give the audience an opportunity to ask questions at the conclusion of the talk.

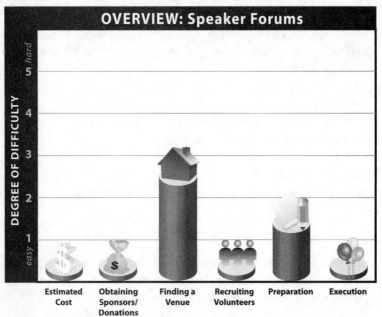

Special Materials/Equipment
- Sound equipment
- Podium
- Seating
- Microphone and stand (consider a miniature clip-on mic for the speaker's convenience and comfort)

Sponsors/Donations
- Approach local business owners to sponsor a talk or series of talks or to cover the cost of refreshments and an honorarium for the speaker. Match the sponsors to the speakers; for example, contact a bookstore to sponsor an author. Find a printer willing to print admission tickets.

Possible Venue(s)
A community center, church, or library meeting room, or your organization's headquarters is a great option.

Recommended Volunteer

3 to 5 to line up speakers, sell tickets, and serve refreshments

Preparation

Send personal invitations to interesting people in your community. Make up a schedule based on responses. Create an emergency plan in case a scheduled speaker drops out unexpectedly. Inform the media about the event, giving information both about the speaker and how to buy tickets. Prepare a bio of the speaker that will be read to introduce him or her.

Execution

Greet the speaker and audience members as they arrive. Serve refreshments after the talk. Place printed organization materials and membership applications in conspicuous places.

Tip(s)

- Provide the speaker with a drink during the speech.
- Present him or her with a certificate or plaque of appreciation.

Variation(s)

- Show interesting educational movies and hold movie forums.

Walking Billboard

Contact a wide variety of businesses and offer to have your members wear the shirt, hat, or other logoed item of their choice for an hour or two in a public place. In exchange, they give you a set donation amount per human billboard, like $25 or more.

Sponsors/Donations
- Any company is a potential candidate for this fundraiser, because virtually every company desires more advertising to increase business.
- You might find that small-to-medium size companies will be most interested in participating, because they tend to have small or nonexistent advertising budgets.

Possible Venue(s)
Malls and shopping centers, busy parks, the library, or anywhere else plenty of people congregate will maximize the publicity potential for the donor.

Recommended Volunteer
12+ to appeal to businesses regarding advertising exposure

Preparation
Send a news release to the local media to entice an editor to write an article about your event. Rent a mailing list of local businesses, then send an e-mail or flier offering to walk around advertising for them on a specific date. Call selected business owners in person. Create a schedule to keep track of the commitments.

Execution

Send logo-attired volunteers to predetermined locations to walk around and get noticed.

Tip(s)

- Because friendly dogs tend to attract plenty of attention, have volunteers bring along their leashed furry friends when walking outdoors.
- Make giant sandwich posters to wear or offer to get into the company's mascot outfit to attract extra attention.

Variation(s)

- Walk around in a sandwich sign or in your organization's mascot costume to attract additional attention.

Writing Letters for Support

Make a heartfelt plea for funds by writing a solicitation letter to potential donors. Start with your own friends and family before expanding into the community-at-large. Enclose a donation card indicating several levels of giving, such as $15, $25, $50, and $100. Include an "other" line where donors can fill in the amount of their choice.

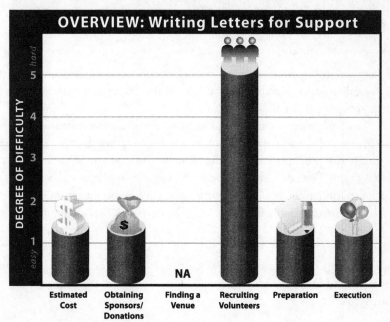

189

Special Materials/Equipment
- Stationery
- Stamps

Sponsors/Donations
- Solicit office supply stores or print shops for donations of stationery.

- Ask a professional fundraiser or another business communicator to help write the letter. Ask people sympathetic to your cause for funds to purchase stamps and rent a mailing list.

Possible Venue(s)
Put the mailings together at your office.

Recommended Volunteer
3 to 4 to fold and stuff letters and donation cards into envelopes, address envelopes or apply self-stick labels, affix postage, and deliver the envelopes to the post office

Preparation
Purchase or rent a prospect list from a mailing list company.

Execution
Print, stuff, and mail the letters.

Tip(s)
- If your organization does not have its own stationery, be sure to purchase high-quality paper. Résumé kits, which include paper and matching envelopes, are a professional but affordable choice.
- Affix nonprofit-rate postage stamps on the envelopes rather than using a postage meter to make the solicitations look like business rather than junk mail. Pay the cost of return postage to increase the response. Because you must cover the cost of postage even if you do not get a donation in return, apply for a U.S. Postal Service mailing permit account so you can imprint an indicia on the return envelope. That way, your organization will pay for only the envelopes that are returned to you.

Variation(s)
- Include a small gift, like stickers. When people receive something, they often feel more obliged to give.

Complex Events

Chapter 11

Auctions and Raffles

The events in this chapter require more planning and organization to put together, but can return great results. The projects you will find in this chapter include:

- Bachelor Auction
- Car Raffle
- Chair-ity Auction
- Dessert Auction
- Mall Auction
- Wine and Beer Auction
- Blind Gift Auction
- Celebrity Memorabilia Auction
- Decorated Tree Auction
- Hourly House Helper Auction
- Silent Auction

Bachelor Auction

Seek out single male firefighters, police officers, athletes, and other eligible bachelors to volunteer to impress female bidders with their style and charm. The highest bidders will have photos taken with the bachelors, as well as share a drink and dance with them. For additional profits, create a calendar of all the bachelors, and sell it by the entrance.

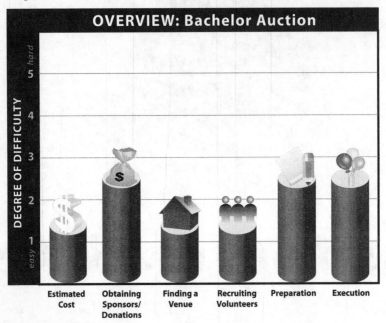

Sponsors/Donations

- Consider asking a major supporter to sponsor the entire event.
- You might consider sponsorship to cover the cost of the venue.
- You can also seek sponsors for tables. A sponsor might purchase a table that seats 10 for dinner. The sponsor might then give the tickets to employees, friends, or family.

Possible Venue(s)

Nice hotels are great places for such events because they will be able to offer large ballrooms that accommodate many people as well as offer catering. If your auction is going to be a live auction, a hotel can usually accommodate with an in-house sound system and lighting.

Recommended Volunteer

10+ including 5 to 7 or more to be committee heads for such tasks as venue, food, decorations, sponsors/donations, advertising, ticket sales, setup, and cleanup

Preparation

1. Start with a central committee of five to seven people who will serve as committee

heads for the venue, food, decorations, sponsors/donations, advertising, ticket sales, bachelors, setup, and cleanup.

2. Decide when to have the event. Before you settle on a date, find out what else is going on in your community and avoid conflicts.

3. Determine your budget. How much are you looking to raise, and what are you willing spend to raise that amount?

4. Start seeking sponsors and donations immediately.

5. Search for your perfect venue. If you have to change the date of your event to get the right venue, make sure, again, that you will have no competition from similar events that might be scheduled.

6. Identify bachelors from your community who you believe would bring in the most money. Approach them and request their participation. Be clear about what will be asked of them, such as to take a photo with the winner, have a drink together, and share a dance.

7. If you decide to serve food, plan your menu. Four months before the event, schedule a caterer, recruit people to cook, or ask restaurants or grocery stores to donate food.

8. Select what activities will occur at your event. You may want a live or silent auction, raffle, or band.

9. Determine whether your auction will be silent or live. Auctions such as this are better done live. A live auction is an entertainment in and of itself, especially when the items being auctioned off are alive and reacting to the bidding. If you go with a live auction, decide whether a professional auctioneer, a celebrity, or someone from your organization will be the auctioneer. A celebrity can help you market the event.

10. Three months prior to the event, advertise by sending e-mails and letters, posting fliers, putting a notice on your organization's website, and making an announcement in your newsletter. Send press releases to local media outlets like newspapers and magazines, and contact local TV news and radio stations to request coverage and publicity.

11. Use the event's theme in everything from marketing, to graphic design of tickets and programs, to venue decorations.

12. Have your various committees meet regularly and keep the lines of communication open.

13. Three months out from the event, print tickets and have everyone in your organization sell tickets. Offer an incentive to the individuals who sell the most tickets.

14. If you need any special equipment, such as seating, sound, light, or stage equipment, this is a good time to reserve these items. Do this as you think about how the venue will be set up for the event.

15. Do a walk-through of the venue a month before the event to check if all the venue systems work and ask when you can you get in to decorate.

16. Write a script to serve as your minute-by-minute flow of activities for the event. Plan a time to thank your sponsors and distribute information promoting your organization.

17. Hold a meeting with all event volunteers and go over the tasks and schedule. Be clear on what you expect every volunteer to do. Tell volunteers what to wear for the event. Get everyone's contact information (phone number and e-mail) in case you need to communicate any changes or reminders.

Execution

1. Come in early to decorate, set up equipment and food, and check the lighting and sound systems.
2. Have volunteers collect tickets as well as sell more tickets at the event.
3. Follow your script to carry out all planned activities.
4. Initiate cleanup at the designated end time.

Variation(s)

• Make it a Bachelorette Auction.

Blind Gift Auction

Have attendees bring a wrapped gift with them to this event. There are no limits to what could be inside, whether ugly, humorous, or valuable. Donors can be tricky by placing a brick in the box to make it appear heavier or have an extremely large box for a very small gift to disguise the actual contents inside the box. Before the auction, make an announcement that a certain amount of money is in at least one of the boxes. The amount will depend on your group's fundraising goals.

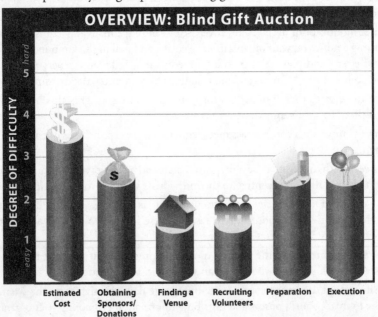

Sponsors/Donations

- Consider asking a major supporter to sponsor the entire event.
- Consider sponsorship to cover the cost of the venue.
- You can also seek sponsors for tables. A sponsor might purchase a table that seats 10 for dinner. The sponsor might then give the tickets to employees, friends, or family.

Possible Venue(s)

Nice hotels with large ballrooms are great because they can usually accommodate many people, handle catering, and provide a sound system and lighting.

Recommended Volunteer

10+ including 5 to 7 or more committee heads to handle such tasks as venue, food, decorations, donations (auction items), marketing (tickets), and entertainment. Have as many people as possible sell tickets.

Preparation

Prep Time: 6 months to 1 year

1. Start with a central committee of five to seven people who will serve as committee heads for the venue, food, decorations, sponsors/donations, advertising, sales, entertainment, setup, and cleanup.

2. Decide when to have the event. Before you settle on a date, find out what else is going on in your community, and avoid conflicts.

3. Determine your budget. How much are you looking to raise, and what are you willing to spend to raise that amount?

4. Start seeking sponsors and donations immediately.

5. Search for your perfect venue. If you have to change the date of your event to get the right venue, make sure, again, that you will have no competition from similar events that may be scheduled.

6. Determine whether your auction will be silent or live. Auctions such as this are better done live. A live auction is an entertainment in and of itself, especially when bidders are doing so blindly. If you go with a live auction, decide whether you will employ a professional auctioneer or if someone from your organization will be the auctioneer.

7. If you decide to serve food, plan your menu. Four months before the event, schedule a caterer, recruit people to cook, or ask restaurants or grocery stores to donate food.

8. Select what activities will occur at your event. You may want a live or silent auction, raffle, or band.

9. Pick an emcee — either an organization member or a local celebrity. A celebrity can help you market the event.

10. Advertise by sending e-mails and letters, posting fliers, putting a notice on your organization's website, and making an announcement in your newsletter. Send press releases to local media outlets like newspapers and magazines, and contact local TV news and radio stations to request coverage and publicity.

11. Use the event's theme in everything from marketing, to graphic design of tickets and programs, to venue decorations.

12. Have your various committees meet regularly and keep the lines of communication open.

13. Three months out from the event, print tickets and have everyone in your organization sell tickets. Offer an incentive to the individuals who sell the most tickets.

14. If you need any special equipment, such as seating, sound, light, or stage equipment, this is a good time to reserve these items. Do this as you think about how the venue will be set up for the event.

15. Do a walk-through of the venue a month before the event to check if all the venue systems work and ask when you can you get in to decorate.

16. Write a script to serve as your minute-by-minute flow of activities for the event. Plan a time to thank your sponsors and distribute information promoting your organization.

17. Hold a meeting with all event volunteers and go over the tasks and schedule. Be clear on what you expect every volunteer to do. Tell volunteers what to wear for the event. Get everyone's contact information (phone number and e-mail) in case you need to communicate any changes or reminders.

Execution

1. Come in early to decorate, set up equipment and food, and check the lighting and sound systems.

2. Have volunteers collect tickets as well as sell more tickets at the event.

3. Follow your script to carry out all planned activities.

4. Initiate cleanup at the designated end time.

Tip(s)

- Try to mix big-ticket items in with gag auction items to heighten the drama of the live auction.
- Do this event in spring to keep it out of the way of the winter holidays, when people might get burnt out from buying gifts or spending money.

Car Raffle

Who would not want to throw in a few bucks for a chance at winning some hot new wheels? Rev up your profits by raffling a car and several smaller cash prizes.

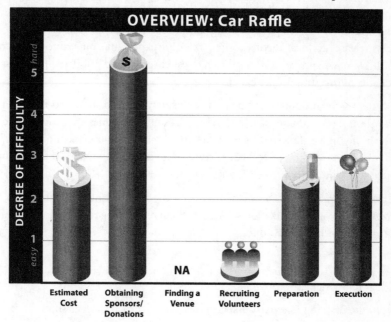

Sponsors/Donations

- The best sponsor donation you can get for a fundraiser like this is an automobile dealer — better yet a luxury car dealer — that will donate a vehicle or give you a great deal on a great car to be raffled.

Possible Venue(s)

The dealer's showroom is a great place to have your drawing. This is a win-win situation because it brings potential customers into the showroom for the dealer, too.

Recommended Volunteer

2 or more to organize and promote the raffle

Preparation

Prep Time: 3+ months

1. Establish a partnership with a car dealer. Work an arrangement out that benefits both of you. You want the dealer to give you a good deal on a nice luxury car, and you will bring the dealer recognition and potential customers into the showroom.

2. Because some people will not want the vehicle, plan to include a cash prize equivalent to the vehicle. Also, put aside $10,000 to $15,000 for additional prizes, and determine what they will be. Consider some high-end technology equipment or a weekend getaway and several smaller cash prizes.

3. Advertise by sending e-mails and letters, posting fliers, putting a notice on your organization's website, and making an announcement in your newsletter. Send press releases to local media outlets like newspapers and magazines, and contact local TV news and radio stations to request coverage and publicity. Emphasize the benefits of investing in the event.

4. Do the math to figure out how many tickets you need to sell to make a profit. You should sell enough tickets to rake in about three times the amount the car is worth. If you have a $50,000 car, you should sell $150,000 worth of tickets. So, if you price your tickets at $50 each, you should sell 3,000 tickets; if tickets are $20 each, you would need to sell 7,500 tickets.

5. Give your organization ample time to sell the required number of tickets. Have everyone in your organization sell tickets. Plan on holding the drawing two months after you announce the raffle.

Execution

1. Sell as many tickets as possible.

2. Hold the drawing in a party-like atmosphere in the car dealer's showroom.

3. Announce the winners, and send out a press release with the winners and prizes listed for further publicity.

Tip(s)

- Arrange to sell tickets at places that have a high amount of foot traffic such as malls and sports games.

- When bargaining for a car, you are doing well if you can get 25 percent off the list price.

- It is important that you offer a luxury car such as a Mercedes or Jaguar for raffle. It is easier to sell raffle tickets for a luxury car than for a cheap car.

Variation(s)

- This type of fundraiser can be done on an even larger scale by offering a house for raffle.

Celebrity Memorabilia Auction

Participants will go bonkers bidding for items previously owned by celebrities at a live auction, and your organization will rack in some A-list proceeds.

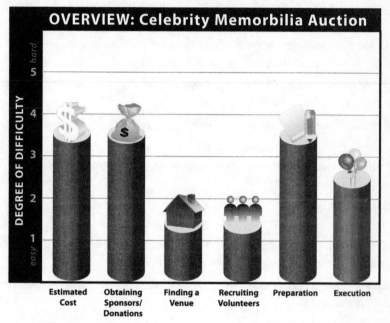

Sponsors/Donations

- Put together a list of contact information for the celebrities and mail out requests. In most cases, if you are soliciting items from actors, singers, or entertainment type celebrities, you will be approaching press agents.

Possible Venue(s)

A hotel will have a large meeting room or hall so people do not have to crowd to see the items you are offering for auction.

Recommended Volunteer

5 or more to soliciting for items to be auctioned, advertise, and monitor bidding

Preparation

Prep Time: 6 to 8 months

1. Start with a central committee of five to seven people who will serve as committee heads for the venue, sponsors/donations, and advertising, as well as to monitor bidding and collect bid sheets. Charge two or three people with researching and soliciting items from celebrities. Have one volunteer keep track of all auction items. As you receive items from celebrities, announce them on your organizational website to build excitement.

2. Decide when to have the event. Before you settle on a date, find out what else is going on in your community, and avoid conflicts.

3. Determine your budget. How much are you looking to raise, and what are you willing to spend to raise that amount?

4. Start seeking sponsors and auction items immediately.

5. Search for your perfect venue. If you have to change the date of your event to get the right venue, make sure, again, that you will have no competition from similar events that may be scheduled.

6. Pick an auctioneer — either an organization member or a local celebrity. A celebrity can help you market the event.

7. Determine the rules of the auction. Check online for ideas. Set times to open and close the bidding, and strictly enforce these times.

8. Make arrangements to receive payment in as many different ways as you can (cash, check, credit card).

9. Provide detailed descriptions for each item. Indicate an opening bid on each bid sheet from a staff member or volunteers, and plan for your emcee to provide pricing updates as well as time remaining reminders.

10. Consider creating an auction catalogue to distribute to those who might consider attending your event. Bundle small items together to make packages and baskets.

11. Advertise by sending e-mails and letters, posting fliers, putting a notice on your organization's website, and making an announcement in your newsletter. Send press releases to local media outlets like newspapers and magazines, and contact local TV news and radio stations to request coverage and publicity.

12. Have your various committees meet regularly and keep the lines of communication open.

13. If you need any special equipment, such as seating, sound, light, or stage equipment, this is a good time to reserve these items. Do this as you think about how the venue will be set up for the event.

14. Do a walk-through of the venue a month before the event to create a floor plan for the placement of your auctioned items. Give the big-ticket items a prominent placement at your venue. Arrange the space so that bidders can comfortably view the auction items.

15. Design bid sheets. The bid sheet should let the bidder know the actual value of the item and suggest a starting bid. You might also want to suggest minimum bid increases so you do not get a bid for $10.00 followed by a bid for $10.01. Below, the sheet should collect the name of the bidder and the amount they would like to bid. Some silent auctions will give those in attendance a number that they will use to bid on items rather than using their name.

16. Write a script to serve as your minute-by-minute flow of activities for the event. Plan a time to thank your sponsors and distribute information promoting your organization.

17. Hold a meeting with all event volunteers and go over the tasks and schedule. Be clear on what you expect every volunteer to do. Tell volunteers what to wear for the event. Get everyone's contact information (phone number and e-mail) in case you need to communicate any changes or reminders.

Execution

1. Come in early to set up.

2. Follow your script to run the auction. Have a few people in place to open, monitor, and close bidding and to collect bid sheets. Periodically announce the time left to bid, including the one-minute mark.

3. Once bidding has closed, collect all of the bid sheets and determine the highest bids. You can either announce the names or numbers of the winning bidders, or you can note them and place them where the bid sheets were. Have many volunteers in place to collect payment for items purchased.

4. Initiate cleanup at the designated end time.

Tip(s)

- To help patrons understand the extent of the items, prepare a catalogue that explains what is being auctioned and offers a good starting bid. The catalogue should also detail the rules of the auction process.
- The more specific you can be about what you are looking for, the easier it will be to solicit items. For example, request hats or clothing.
- Be sure to ask that the celebrity sign or authenticate the item in some manner.
- Also, keep in mind that rejection letters from celebrities can also bring in a few dollars, so do not throw those away. Think about what a rejection letter from the Queen of England might bring in. Maybe you can put all the rejection letters together in a book and auction that off.

Variation(s)

- Post the celebrity memorabilia on eBay.
- Ask celebrities to create doodles or other works of art for a celebrity art auction.
- Ask celebrities to create playlists for a celebrity iPod auction.
- Request culturally specific items from political leaders for a world leaders auction.

Chair-ity Auction

You will not want to sit this one out. Auction off new or used chairs that are uniquely presented with special decorations, accessories, and enhancements. Donations may include rocking chairs, kitchen chairs, children's chairs, computer chairs, recliners, car seats, and bar stools. Adorn each chair with its own theme of decorations.

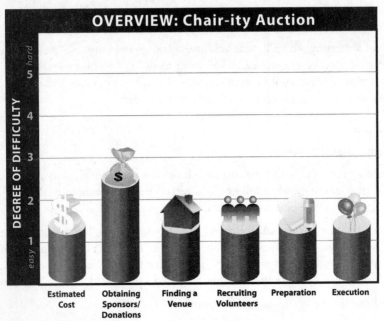

Special Materials/Equipment
- Chairs
- Decorations

Sponsors/Donations
- Ask a large number of people to decorate and donate chairs.
- Consider getting refreshments donated.
- Seek the donated services of a professional auctioneer.

Possible Venue(s)
Try having it at a club, restaurant, or bar, or in conjunction with a dinner. If your organization has its own space, such as a school or church, you can keep it on site.

Recommended Volunteer
5 to 10 or more to handle sponsors/donations, ticket sales, advertising, setup, and auction, including 3 to 5 people to run the auction (an auctioneer, someone on stage with the auctioneer to present the chairs, and people in the audience to identify bidders)

Preparation
Prep Time: 4 to 6 months

1. Start with a central committee of five to seven people who will serve as committee heads for the venue, food, decorations, sponsors/donations, advertising, ticket sales, entertainment, setup, and cleanup.

2. Designate 5 to 10 people to manage the auction, including an auctioneer, someone on stage with the auctioneer to present the chairs, and several people in the audience to identify bidders.

3. Decide when to have the event. Before you settle on a date, find out what else is going on in your community, and avoid conflicts.

4. Determine your budget. How much are you looking to raise, and what are you willing to spend to raise that amount?

5. Start seeking sponsors and chair donations immediately.

6. Book your venue.

7. Determine whether you will hold the event as a silent auction, a live auction, or a combination of the two. If you have a combination live/silent auction, hold the live auction before the close of bidding for the silent auction so you can continue to promote the silent auction items to those who did not win the live auction.

8. If you decide to serve food, plan your menu. Four months before the event, schedule a caterer, recruit people to cook, or ask restaurants or grocery stores to donate food.

9. Plan what additional entertainment will occur at your event, like live music.

10. Pick an auctioneer — either an organization member or a local celebrity. A celebrity can help you market the event.

11. Advertise by sending e-mails and letters, posting fliers, putting a notice on your organization's website, and making an announcement in your newsletter. Send press releases to local media outlets like newspapers and magazines, and contact local TV news and radio stations to request coverage and publicity.

12. Use the event's theme in everything from marketing, to graphic design of tickets and programs, to venue decorations.

13. Have your various committees meet regularly and keep the lines of communication open.

14. Three months out from the event, print tickets and have everyone in your organization sell tickets. Offer an incentive to the individuals who sell the most tickets.

15. If you need any special equipment, such as seating, sound, light, or stage equipment, this is a good time to reserve these items. Do this as you think about how the venue will be set up for the event.

16. Do a walk-through of the venue a month before the event to check if all the venue systems work and ask when you can you get in to decorate. Find a place to display the chairs on a stage or in a prominent place at the venue.

17. Write a script to serve as your minute-by-minute flow of activities for the event. Plan a time to thank your sponsors and distribute information promoting your organization.

18. Hold a meeting with all event volunteers and go over the tasks and schedule. Be clear on what you expect every volunteer to do. Tell volunteers what to wear for

the event. Get everyone's contact information (phone number and e-mail) in case you need to communicate any changes or reminders.

Execution

1. Come in early to decorate, set up equipment and food, and check the lighting and sound systems.
2. Have volunteers collect tickets as well as sell more tickets at the event.
3. Follow your script to carry out all planned activities.
4. Initiate cleanup at the designated end time.

Tip(s)

- Designate someone to seek "celebrity" chairs. Identify celebrities in your community or beyond who might design or decorate a chair for you.
- Hold the auction following a dinner.

Variation(s)

- Auction off decorated hats.
- Hold a Decorated Ties Auction.

Decorated Tree Auction

Auction off holiday trees decorated by florists and artists in the community. Make additional profits by auctioning miniature tree centerpieces and sets of unique ornaments. This is a great fundraiser for an arts organization.

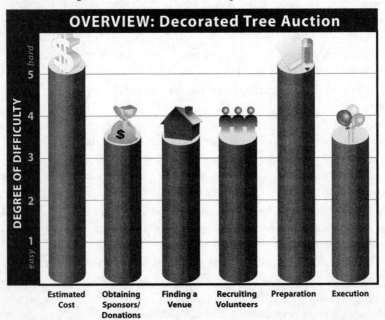

Special Materials/Equipment
- Trees (fake or real)
- Ornament-making materials
- Decorations

Sponsors/Donations
- Tree farmers are good sponsors for events such as this.
- Large retailers that handle a wide variety of holiday trimmings can be a great help.
- Identify artists in your community that would be willing to donate their decoration services.

Possible Venue(s)
A parking lot or other outdoor space large enough to display the trees would be appropriate.

Recommended Volunteer
7 to 10 or more including artists committed to making ornaments and decorating the trees, and other volunteers who will run the auction and deliver the trees

Preparation
Prep Time: 5 to 6 months

1. Start with a central committee of five to seven people who will serve as committee heads for the venue, sponsors/donations, artist, advertising, bid monitoring, and delivery.

2. Decide when to have the event. Before you settle on a date, find out what else is going on in your community, and avoid conflicts.

3. Determine your budget. How much are you looking to raise, and what are you willing to spend to raise that amount?

4. Start seeking sponsors, tree donations, and artists immediately. If artists prefer to work together or in a central meeting place, have a tree-decorating party.

5. Search for your perfect venue. If you have to change the date of your event to get the right venue, make sure, again, that you will have no competition from similar events that may be scheduled.

6. Pick an auctioneer — either an organization member or a local celebrity. A celebrity can help you market the event.

7. Determine the rules of the auction. Check online for ideas. Set times to open and close the bidding, and strictly enforce these times.

8. Make arrangements to receive payment in as many different ways as you can (cash, check, credit card).

9. Provide detailed descriptions for each item. Indicate an opening bid on each bid sheet from a staff member or volunteers, and plan for your auctioneer to provide pricing updates as well as time remaining reminders.

10. Consider creating an auction catalogue to distribute to those who might consider attending your event.

11. Advertise by sending e-mails and letters, posting fliers, putting a notice on your organization's website, and making an announcement in your newsletter. Send press releases to local media outlets like newspapers and magazines, and contact local TV news and radio stations to request coverage and publicity.

12. Have your various committees meet regularly and keep the lines of communication open.

13. If you need any special equipment, such as seating, sound, light, or stage equipment, this is a good time to reserve these items. Do this as you think about how the venue will be set up for the event.

14. Do a walk-through of the venue a month before the event to create a floor plan for the placement of your auctioned items. Arrange the space so that bidders can comfortably view the auction items.

15. Design bid sheets. The bid sheet should let the bidder know the actual value of the item and suggest a starting bid. You might also want to suggest minimum bid increases so you do not get a bid for $100 followed by a bid for $101. Below, the sheet should collect the name of the bidder and the amount they would like to bid. Some silent auctions will give those in attendance a number that they will use to bid on items rather than using their name.

16. Write a script to serve as your minute-by-minute flow of activities for the event. Plan a time to thank your sponsors and distribute information promoting your organization.

17. Hold a meeting with all event volunteers and go over the tasks and schedule. Be clear on what you expect every volunteer to do. Tell volunteers what to wear for the event. Get everyone's contact information (phone number and e-mail) in case you need to communicate any changes or reminders.

Execution

1. Come in early to set up.

2. Follow your script to run the auction. Have a few people in place to open, monitor, and close bidding and to collect bid sheets. Periodically announce the time left to bid, including the one-minute mark.

3. Once bidding has closed, collect all of the bid sheets and determine the highest bids. You can either announce the names or numbers of the winning bidders, or you can note them and place them where the bid sheets were. Have many volunteers in place to collect payment for items purchased.

4. Initiate cleanup at the designated end time.

Dessert Auction

Auction off gourmet desserts with a Chinese auction. Chinese auctions are a combination of silent auctions and raffles. Supporters purchase tickets for a set price and use the tickets to bid on the items by dropping them into a container next to the item. The more tickets a supporter drops into a container, the better chance the chance of winning. At the close of the auction, a ticket is drawn from each container identifying the auction winner.

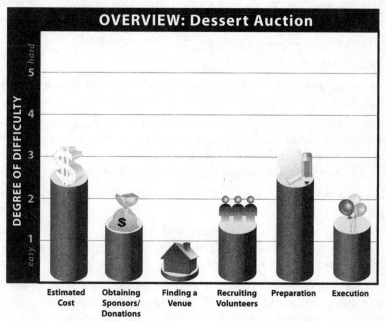

Special Materials/Equipment
- Display tables
- Gourmet desserts

Sponsors/Donations
- Seek bakers or volunteers with a knack for baking to donate specialty sweets.

Possible Venue(s)
A hotel banquet room works well because the hotel can provide catering, lighting, a sound system, tables, and seating.

Recommended Volunteer
10+ including 5 to 7 committee heads to handle the venue, food, decorations, sponsors/donations, advertising, ticket sales, auction, setup, and cleanup.

Preparation
Prep Time: 6 months

1. Start with a central committee of five to seven people who will serve as committee heads for the venue, sponsors/donations, and advertising, as well as to run the Chinese auction.

2. Decide when to have the event. Before you settle on a date, find out what else is going on in your community, and avoid conflicts.

3. Determine your budget. How much are you looking to raise, and what are you willing to spend to raise that amount?

4. Start seeking sponsors and dessert auction items immediately.

5. Book an appropriate venue.

6. Make arrangements to receive payment in as many different ways as you can (cash, check, credit card) for purchase of auction tickets.

7. Advertise by sending e-mails and letters, posting fliers, putting a notice on your organization's website, and making an announcement in your newsletter. Send press releases to local media outlets like newspapers and magazines, and contact local TV news and radio stations to request coverage and publicity.

8. Have your various committees meet regularly and keep the lines of communication open.

9. If you need any special equipment, such as seating, sound, light, or stage equipment, this is a good time to reserve these items. Do this as you think about how the venue will be set up for the event.

10. Do a walk-through of the venue a month before the event to create a floor plan for the placement of your auctioned items. Give the big-ticket items a prominent placement at your venue. Arrange the space so that bidders can comfortably view the auction items.

11. Write a script to serve as your minute-by-minute flow of activities for the event. Plan a time to thank your sponsors and distribute information promoting your organization.

12. Hold a meeting with all event volunteers and go over the tasks and schedule. Be clear on what you expect every volunteer to do. Tell volunteers what to wear for the event. Get everyone's contact information (phone number and e-mail) in case you need to communicate any changes or reminders.

Execution

1. Come in early to set up.

2. Follow your script to run the Chinese auction. Periodically announce the time left to enter the auction, including the one-minute mark.

3. Announce the winners and present them with their desserts.

4. Initiate cleanup at the designated end time.

Tip(s)

- Have many volunteers available to sell Chinese Auction tickets throughout your event.

Variation(s)

- Have a Chinese auction for a variety of items, like bath products, travel packages, gift cards, art, or jewelry.

Hourly House Helper Auction

In this funny fundraiser, male firefighters, police officers, athletes or college students who volunteer for the event are auctioned off to help with household chores for one hour. Charge an admission fee and then auction away.

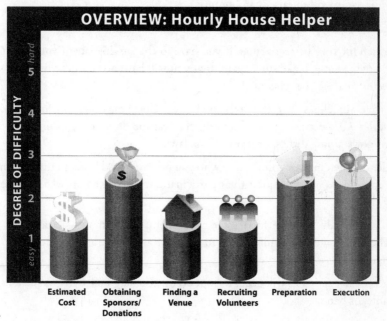

Sponsors/Donations

- Consider asking a major supporter to sponsor the entire event.
- You might consider sponsorship to cover the cost of the venue.
- You can also seek sponsors for tables. A sponsor might purchase a table that seat 10 for dinner. The sponsor might then give the tickets to employees, friends, or family.

Possible Venue(s)

Hotels with large ballrooms can accommodate a large group and handle the catering, sound system and lighting.

Recommended Volunteer

10+ including 5 to 7 committee heads to handle such tasks as venue, food, decorations, sponsors/donations, advertising, ticket sales, bachelors, setup, and cleanup

Preparation

Prep Time: 6 months to 1 year

1. Start with a central committee of five to seven people who will serve as committee heads for the venue, food, decorations, sponsors/donations, advertising, ticket sales, bachelors, setup, and cleanup.

2. Decide when to have the event. Before you settle on a date, find out what else is going on in your community, and avoid conflicts.

3. Determine your budget. How much are you looking to raise, and what are you willing to spend to raise that amount?

4. Start seeking sponsors and donations immediately.

5. Search for your perfect venue. If you have to change the date of your event to get the right venue, make sure, again, that you will have no competition from similar events that may be scheduled.

6. Create guidelines as to the tasks the house helpers may perform for the winning bidder. Create a list of possible tasks that can be done in an hour, like washing windows, doing dishes, or mowing the lawn.

7. Identify men in your community who you believe would bring in the most money. Approach them and request their participation. Be clear about what will be asked of them.

8. If you decide to serve food, plan your menu. Four months before the event, schedule a caterer, recruit people to cook, or ask restaurants or grocery stores to donate food.

9. Select what activities will occur at your event. You may want a live or silent auction, raffle, or band.

10. Determine whether your auction will be silent or live. Auctions such as this are better done live. A live auction is an entertainment in and of itself, especially when the items being auctioned off are alive and reacting to the bidding. If you go with a live auction, decide whether a professional auctioneer, a celebrity, or someone from your organization will be the auctioneer. A celebrity can help you market the event.

11. Three months prior to the event, advertise by sending e-mails and letters, posting fliers, putting a notice on your organization's website, and making an announcement in your newsletter. Send press releases to local media outlets like newspapers and magazines, and contact local TV news and radio stations to request coverage and publicity.

12. Use the event's theme in everything from marketing, to graphic design of tickets and programs, to venue decorations.

13. Have your various committees meet regularly and keep the lines of communication open.

14. Three months out from the event, print tickets and have everyone in your organization sell tickets. Offer an incentive to the individuals who sell the most tickets.

15. If you need any special equipment, such as seating, sound, light, or stage equipment, this is a good time to reserve these items. Do this as you think about how the venue will be set up for the event.

16. Do a walk-through of the venue a month before the event to check if all the venue systems work and ask when you can get in to decorate.

17. Write a script to serve as your minute-by-minute flow of activities for the event. Plan a time to thank your sponsors and distribute information promoting your organization.

18. Hold a meeting with all event volunteers and go over the tasks and schedule. Be clear on what you expect every volunteer to do. Tell volunteers what to wear for the event. Get everyone's contact information (phone number and e-mail) in case you need to communicate any changes or reminders.

Execution

1. Come in early to decorate, set up equipment and food, and check the lighting and sound systems.

2. Have volunteers collect tickets as well as sell more tickets at the event.

3. Follow your script to carry out all planned activities.

4. Initiate cleanup at the designated end time.

Mall Auction

Have every store in the mall donate items to be auctioned in a closed bidding. After a pre-determined time frame, the highest bidder on each item gets to purchase the item. Some or all profits generated can go toward your organization's cause.

Special Materials/Equipment
- Cases, tables or other ways to display the auction items

Sponsors/Donations
- Ask every store in the mall to donate items. When you make arrangements with the stores that will be donating auction items, ask if they will assist in marketing with fliers, posters, or in their print advertising.

Possible Venue(s)
Work with a mall for this event.

Recommended Volunteer
5 to collect store donations, market the event, and handle the silent auction

Preparation
Prep Time: 4 months

1. Decide when to have the event. Before you settle on a date, find out what else is going on in your community, and avoid conflicts.

2. Determine your budget. How much are you looking to raise, and what are you willing to spend to raise that amount?

3. Search for your perfect venue. If you have to change the date of your event to get the right venue, make sure, again, that you will have no competition from similar events that might be scheduled.

4. Give yourself a couple of months to "shop" for auction items. As you seek items for auction, remember to offer a way that the business or individual donating the item is recognized unless they ask not to be. Example: "London Theatre Vacation generously donated by XYZ Travel." Approach each store at the mall to discuss items for auction. Begin your approach by sending the store a letter that briefly describes your organization and what it is you are doing at the mall. Follow your letter up with a phone call to set an appointment to come in and speak with store management about your plans. When you meet with store management, be prepared to explain how your program can be a win/win proposition for both your organization and the stores of the mall. You will be promoting the stores as you promote your cause. The stores will be seen as community-friendly. The mall management will instruct you as to how to best work with the stores at the mall.

5. Decide early on if you will hold any additional activities at the mall to coincide with your silent auction. You may offer some kind of entertainment. You may want someone from your organization to speak about your cause.

6. Determine the rules of the auction. Set a time to begin taking bids and set a time when bidding will close, and strictly enforce these times.

7. Once you have collected your auction items, set suggested opening bids, and set your rules, publicize them. Also, let people know how payment can be made for purchased items. Plan to receive payment in as many different ways as you can (cash, check, credit card). If you have an organizational website, devote a page or two to your event. Consider putting together an auction catalogue to distribute to those who might consider attending your event.

8. Create a floor plan for the placement of your auctioned items. Plan on setting up in a central mall location. Give the big-ticket items a prominent placement at your venue. Arrange the space so that bidders can comfortably view the auction items.

9. Design bid sheets. The bid sheet should let the bidder know the actual value of the item. The bid sheet should also identify a suggested starting bid. You might also want to suggest minimum bid increases so you don't get a bid for $10.00 followed by a bid for $10.01. Below, the sheet should collect the name of the bidder and the amount they would like to bid. Some silent auctions will give those in attendance a number that they will use to bid on items rather than using their name. Every bid sheet should remind people to write legibly. You can help people to do this by taping or securing the bid sheets to the table in some manner.

10. Three months out from the event, print tickets and have everyone in your organization sell tickets. Offer an incentive to the individuals who sell the most tickets.

11. Three months prior to the event, advertise by sending e-mails and letters, posting fliers in mall stores, putting a notice on your organization's website, and making an announcement in your newsletter. Send press releases to local media outlets like newspapers and magazines, and contact local TV news and radio stations to request coverage and publicity.

12. Do a walk-through of the venue a month before the event to check if all the venue systems work and ask when you can you get in to decorate.

13. Write a script to serve as your minute-by-minute flow of activities for the event. Plan a time to thank your sponsors and distribute information promoting your organization.

14. Hold a meeting with all event volunteers and go over the tasks and schedule. Be clear on what you expect every volunteer to do. Tell volunteers what to wear for the event. Get everyone's contact information (phone number and e-mail) in case you need to communicate any changes or reminders.

Execution

1. Come in early to set up equipment and check the lighting and sound systems.

2. Have volunteers distribute bid sheets. Periodically announce the time left to bid. Remind people when they have one minute left.

3. Once bidding has closed, collect all of the bid sheets and determine the high bid. You can either announce the names or numbers of the high bidders, or you can note them and place them where the bid sheets were.

4. Have people in place to collect payment for items purchased. This is another good time to have many volunteers in place to finalize the transactions. Plan to take payment in as many different ways as you can.

5. Follow your script to carry out all planned activities.

6. Initiate cleanup at the designated end time.

Tip(s)

- When choosing a mall, take into account that the larger the mall, the more money you can earn, but also the more legwork and negotiations you will have.

- Some stores may be asked to donate big-ticket items such as electronics, while other store may be asked to donate packages of small items such as soaps or scarves. It is in your best interest to get a wide variety of items that cover a wide variety of prices.

- Do not advertise any item for auction until you have the item in your possession. Get started putting your auction items together as soon as possible so you can use them in your marketing. Ideally, you want to have all auction items collected before you start marketing your event. That is not always feasible, and you will always receive additional items after your marketing starts, but your big-ticket items should be locked in early.

- If you have received a number of smaller items, consider bundling them together in packages or baskets, like a home spa basket of donated soaps, shampoos, and bath oils.
- Be cautious about selling food as you may take business away from the mall food court.

Silent Auction

Talk up some incredible gift baskets, trips, spa days, pieces of art, or jewelry for a successful silent auction.

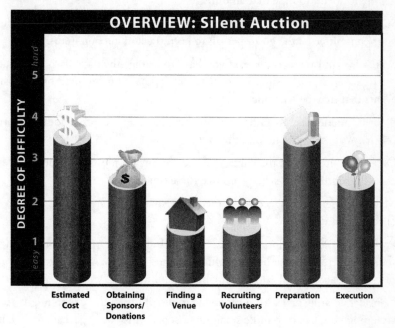

Sponsors/Donations
- Seek sponsor donations for big-ticket items to auction. Vacations, adventure trips (like African safaris), and other experience gifts are great. Also try to find sponsors to donate large home electronics.

Possible Venue(s)
A hotel meeting room or hall works well.

Recommended Volunteer
10+ including 5 to 7 to serve as committee heads for the venue, decorations, sponsors/donations, advertising, ticket sales, setup, and cleanup, as well as to monitor bidding and collect bid sheets

Preparation
Prep Time: 3 to 4 months or more

1. Start with a central committee of five to seven people who will serve as committee heads for the venue, decorations, sponsors/donations, advertising, ticket sales, setup, and cleanup, as well as to monitor bidding and collect bid sheets.

2. Decide when to have the event. Before you settle on a date, find out what else is going on in your community, and avoid conflicts.

3. Determine your budget. How much are you looking to raise, and what are you willing to spend to raise that amount?

4. Start seeking sponsors and auction items immediately. Have one individual on your committee be the go-to person to keep track of auction items.

5. Search for your perfect venue. If you have to change the date of your event to get the right venue, make sure, again, that you will have no competition from similar events that may be scheduled.

6. Pick an auctioneer — either an organization member or a local celebrity. A celebrity can help you market the event.

7. Determine the rules of the auction. Check online for ideas. Set times to open and close the bidding, and strictly enforce these times.

8. Make arrangements to receive payment in as many different ways as you can (cash, check, credit card).

9. Provide detailed descriptions for each item. Indicate an opening bid on each bid sheet from a staff member or volunteers, and plan for your emcee to provide pricing updates as well as time remaining reminders.

10. Consider creating an auction catalogue to distribute to those who might consider attending your event. Bundle small items together to make packages and baskets.

11. Advertise by sending e-mails and letters, posting fliers, putting a notice on your organization's website, and making an announcement in your newsletter. Send press releases to local media outlets like newspapers and magazines, and contact local TV news and radio stations to request coverage and publicity.

12. Have your various committees meet regularly and keep the lines of communication open.

13. Three months out from the event, print tickets and have everyone in your organization sell tickets. Offer an incentive to the individuals who sell the most tickets.

14. If you need any special equipment, such as seating, sound, light, or stage equipment, this is a good time to reserve these items. Do this as you think about how the venue will be set up for the event.

15. Do a walk-through of the venue a month before the event to create a floor plan for the placement of your auctioned items. Give the big-ticket items a prominent placement at your venue. Arrange the space so that bidders can comfortably view the auction items.

16. Design bid sheets. The bid sheet should let the bidder know the actual value of the item and suggest a starting bid. You might also want to suggest minimum bid increases so you do not get a bid for $10.00 followed by a bid for $10.01. Below, the sheet should collect the name of the bidder and the amount they would like to bid. Some silent auctions will give those in attendance a number that they will use to bid on items rather than using their name.

17. Write a script to serve as your minute-by-minute flow of activities for the event. Plan a time to thank your sponsors and distribute information promoting your organization.

18. Hold a meeting with all event volunteers and go over the tasks and schedule. Be clear on what you expect every volunteer to do. Tell volunteers what to wear for the event. Get everyone's contact information (phone number and e-mail) in case you need to communicate any changes or reminders.

Execution

1. Come in early to set up.

2. Have volunteers collect tickets as well as sell more tickets at the event.

3. Follow your script.

4. Have a few people in place to open, monitor, and close bidding and to collect bid sheets. Periodically announce the time left to bid. Remind people at the one-minute mark.

5. Once bidding has closed, collect all of the bid sheets and determine the highest bids. You can either announce the names or numbers of the winning bidders, or you can note them and place them where the bid sheets were. Have many volunteers in place to collect payment for items purchased.

6. Initiate cleanup at the designated end time.

Tip(s)

- As you seek items for auction, offer a way that the business or individual donating the item is recognized unless they ask not to be. For example, "London Theater Vacation generously donated by XYZ Travel."
- Ideally, you want to have all auction items collected before you start selling tickets to your event. Although that is not always feasible, your big-ticket items should be locked in early in order to generate excitement during ticket sales.

Variation(s)

• Hold the auction in conjunction with a fundraising dinner.

Wine and Beer Auction

Find a large venue and ask local liquor stores, pubs, and clubs to donate fine wine and high-quality beer. Charge an entry fee, and auction off the alcoholic beverages.

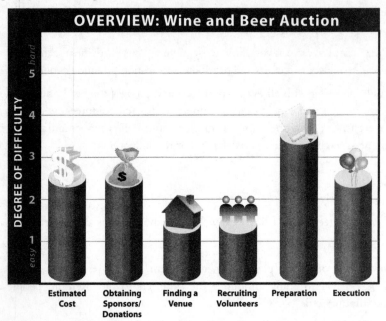

Special Materials/Equipment

• Displays for auction items

Sponsors/Donations

• Ask local liquor stores, pubs, and clubs to donate fine wine and high-quality beer.
• Seek a local alcohol distributor to sponsor the event.

Possible Venue(s)

The venue should be a location that is comfortably large so people do not have to crowd to see the items up for auction. Many auction events such as this are held in conjunction with fundraising dinners, so you might consider a large hotel meeting room or hall that offers catering.

Recommended Volunteer

10+ including 5 to 7 committee heads to handle venue, auction items, advertising, setup, and bidding

Preparation

Prep Time: 6 to 8 months

1. Start with a central committee of five to seven people who will serve as committee heads for the venue, decorations, sponsors/donations, advertising, ticket sales, bidding, entertainment, setup, and cleanup.

2. Decide when to have the event. Before you settle on a date, find out what else is going on in your community, and avoid conflicts.

3. Determine your budget. How much are you looking to raise, and what are you willing to spend to raise that amount?

4. Start seeking sponsors and donations from liquor stores and distributors immediately. As you collect your donated wine and beer, keep a detailed account of what you are gathering. A comprehensive catalogue of auction items will be a valuable tool in your marketing. You can sell ads in the catalogue to cover the printing cost.

5. Search for your perfect venue. If you have to change the date of your event to get the right venue, make sure, again, that you will have no competition from similar events that may be scheduled.

6. If you decide to serve food, plan your menu. Four months before the event, schedule a caterer, recruit people to cook, or ask restaurants or grocery stores to donate food.

7. Decide what other entertainment to have, such as a band.

8. Choose whether you will have a live or silent auction. If you decide on a live auction, pick an auctioneer — either an organization member or a local celebrity. A celebrity can help you market the event.

9. Create a floor plan for the placement of your auctioned items. Give the items that might generate a good deal of interest a prominent placement at your venue. Arrange the space so that bidders can comfortably view the auction items.

10. Determine the rules of the auction. Set opening bids. Let people know how payment can be made for purchased items. Plan to receive payment in as many different ways as you can (cash, check, credit card).

11. About two or three months before your event, start advertising by sending e-mails and letters, posting fliers, putting a notice on your organization's website, and making an announcement in your newsletter. Send press releases to local media outlets like newspapers and magazines, and contact local TV news and radio stations to request coverage and publicity. As you receive items for auction, let out little items on your organizational website or by using a social networking tool.

12. Use the event's theme in everything from marketing, to graphic design of tickets and programs, to venue decorations.

13. Have your various committees meet regularly and keep the lines of communication open.

14. Three months out from the event, print tickets and have everyone in your organization sell tickets. Offer an incentive to the individuals who sell the most tickets.

15. If you need any special equipment, such as seating, sound, light, or stage equipment, this is a good time to reserve these items. Do this as you think about how the venue will be set up for the event.

16. Do a walk-through of the venue a month before the event to check if all the venue systems work and ask when you can you get in to decorate.

17. Write a script to serve as your minute-by-minute flow of activities for the event. Plan a time to thank your sponsors and distribute information promoting your organization.

18. Hold a meeting with all event volunteers and go over the tasks and schedule. Be clear on what you expect every volunteer to do. Tell volunteers what to wear for the event. Get everyone's contact information (phone number and e-mail) in case you need to communicate any changes or reminders.

Execution

1. Come in early to decorate, set up equipment and food, and check the lighting and sound systems.

2. Have volunteers collect tickets as well as sell more tickets at the event.

3. Follow your script to carry out all planned activities.

4. Initiate cleanup at the designated end time.

You must pay extra attention to fundraisers that involve alcoholic beverages. Most states have specific laws to encourage nonprofit organizations to obtain a one day special alcoholic liquor license. You must allocate sufficient time for the application of this license. In addition you will need to comply with all state laws governing the sale and dispensing of alcoholic beverages. The organization will also be required in most cases to carry an insurance rider for the sale of alcoholic beverages, this insurance will protect the organization should someone be over served, or involved in an accident of some kind. Again allow sufficient time to speak with your insurance agent and do not even try to hold the event with out the proper licensing and insurance.

Chapter 12

Dances

These events combine a good cause with a good time, providing a night of dancing and donation. The projects you will find in this chapter include:

- ◎ Canine Ball
- ◎ Dance 'Til You Drop
- ◎ Dinner Dance Cruise
- ◎ Masquerade Ball
- ◎ Second-Chance Prom
- ◎ '60s Dance Party

Canine Ball

Have dog owners dress up and enjoy a gourmet dinner date with their furry friends. Sell tickets for admission to the event, and offer fun dog games, like bobbing for bones. Raise additional profits by setting up a gift shop with doggy treats and accessories.

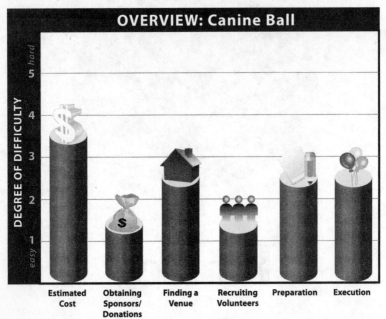

Special Materials/Equipment

- Dog beds/seats
- Dog treats
- Water and food bowls for dogs
- Game supplies

Sponsors/Donations

- Pet stores or pet supply companies are natural choices for sponsors.

Possible Venue(s)

A pet-friendly, upscale hotel would be ideal. A convention center or a local social club with a banquet room will also work well.

Recommended Volunteer

15+ including 5 to 7 committee heads to handle such tasks as for the venue, food, decorations, sponsors/donations, advertising, ticket sales, entertainment, setup, and cleanup.

Preparation

Prep Time: 6 months to 1 year

1. Start with a central committee of five to seven people who will serve as committee heads for the venue, food, decorations, sponsors/donations, advertising, ticket sales, entertainment, setup and cleanup.

2. Decide when to have the event. Before you settle on a date, find out what else is going on in your community, and avoid conflicts.

3. Determine your budget. How much are you looking to raise, and what are you willing to spend to raise that amount?

4. Start seeking sponsors and donations immediately.

5. Search for your perfect venue. If you have to change the date of your event to get the right venue, make sure, again, that you will have no competition from similar events that may be scheduled.

6. Four months before the event, choose your menu and schedule the caterer. You may require two caterers — one for human food and another for doggie food.

7. Select which activities will occur at your event. You may want a live or silent auction, raffle, or band. You may consider a dog show of sorts. If the dogs are dressed up, you can consider having a dog and owner fashion walk.

8. Pick an emcee — either an organization member or a local celebrity. A celebrity can help you market the event.

9. Advertise by sending e-mails and letters, posting fliers, putting a notice on your organization's website, and making an announcement in your newsletter. Send press releases to local media outlets like newspapers and magazines, and contact local TV news and radio stations to request coverage and publicity.

10. Use the event's theme in everything from marketing, to graphic design of tickets and programs, to venue decorations.

11. Have your various committees meet regularly and keep the lines of communication open.

12. Three months out from the event, print tickets and have everyone in your organization sell tickets. Offer an incentive to the individuals who sell the most tickets.

13. If you need any special equipment, such as seating, sound, light, or stage equipment, this is a good time to reserve these items. Do this as you think about how the venue will be set up for the event.

14. Do a walk-through of the venue a month before the event to check if all the venue systems work and ask when you can you get in to decorate.

15. Write a script to serve as your minute-by-minute flow of activities for the event. Plan a

time to thank your sponsors and distribute information promoting your organization.

16. Hold a meeting with all event volunteers and go over the tasks and schedule. Be clear on what you expect every volunteer to do. Tell volunteers what to wear for the event. Get everyone's contact information (phone number and e-mail) in case you need to communicate any changes or reminders.

Execution

1. Come in early to decorate, set up equipment and food, and check the lighting and sound systems.

2. Have volunteers collect tickets as well as sell more tickets at the event.

3. Follow your script to carry out all planned activities.

4. Initiate cleanup at the designated end time.

Tip(s)

- Offer dog-decorated doggie bags in which people can take home leftovers.

Variation(s)

- Have a Kitty Cat Ball.

Dance 'Til You Drop

Have supporters get sponsored to dance the day away. Choose a fun theme such as a disco, a tango, or an elegant ball. Sponsors will donate money to your organization for each hour the participants remain on the dance floor.

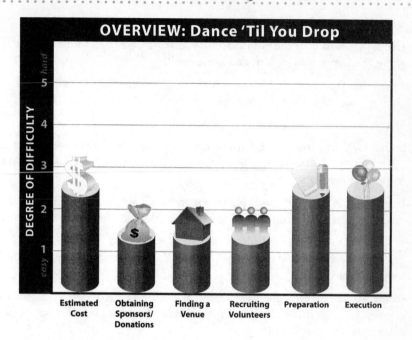

Special Materials/Equipment
- Sound system (microphone, speakers)
- Dance floor
- Music
- Fun lighting

Sponsors/Donations
- Have dancers seek sponsors to support each hour they sign up to dance in the same manner that they would for a walk-a-thon (see sample form and rules in Appendices), or charge a fee for participants to dance.
- Get a grand prize donated for the person who dances the longest. Try getting dance lessons donated by a local studio, or ask a theater to donate tickets to a professional dance show.

Possible Venue(s)
A school gym or a large social hall is ideal.

Recommended Volunteer
10+ including 5 to take care of the venue, the dancers, hospitality, and advertising

Preparation
Prep Time: 4 to 6 months

1. Start with a central committee of five to seven people who will serve as committee heads for the venue, food, decorations, sponsors/donations, advertising, ticket

sales, entertainment, setup, and cleanup.

2. Decide when to have the event. Before you settle on a date, find out what else is going on in your community, and avoid conflicts.

3. Determine your budget. How much are you looking to raise, and what are you willing to spend to raise that amount?

4. Start seeking sponsors and donations immediately.

5. Search for your perfect venue. If you have to change the date of your event to get the right venue, make sure, again, that you will have no competition from similar events that may be scheduled.

6. If you decide to serve food, plan your menu. Four months before the event, schedule a caterer, recruit people to cook, or ask restaurants or grocery stores to donate food.

7. Select what activities will occur at your event. You may want a live or silent auction, raffle, or band.

8. Come up with a prize for the person (or couple, if the theme is conducive to couples dancing) that dances the longest. Make the prize big to encourage people to dance as long as possible.

9. Pick an emcee — either an organization member or a local celebrity. A celebrity can help you market the event.

10. Advertise by sending e-mails and letters, posting fliers, putting a notice on your organization's website, and making an announcement in your newsletter. Send press releases to local media outlets like newspapers and magazines, and contact local TV news and radio stations to request coverage and publicity.

11. Use the event's theme in everything from marketing, to graphic design of tickets and programs, to venue decorations.

12. Have your various committees meet regularly and keep the lines of communication open.

13. Three months out from the event, print tickets and have everyone in your organization sell tickets. Offer an incentive to the individuals who sell the most tickets.

14. If you need any special equipment, such as seating, sound, light, or stage equipment, this is a good time to reserve these items. Do this as you think about how the venue will be set up for the event.

15. Do a walk-through of the venue a month before the event to check if all the venue systems work and ask when you can get in to decorate.

16. Write a script to serve as your minute-by-minute flow of activities for the event. Plan a time to thank your sponsors and distribute information promoting your organization.

17. Hold a meeting with all event volunteers and go over the tasks and schedule. Be

clear on what you expect every volunteer to do. Tell volunteers what to wear for the event. Get everyone's contact information (phone number and e-mail) in case you need to communicate any changes or reminders.

Execution

1. Come in early to decorate, set up equipment and food, and check the lighting and sound systems.

2. Have volunteers collect tickets as well as sell more tickets at the event.

3. Follow your script to carry out all planned activities.

4. Initiate cleanup at the designated end time.

Tip(s)

- To appeal to different crowds, play a wide variety of dance music from hip-hop to classical waltz.

Variation(s)

- Host a Zumba dance party, and attract people of all ages to enjoy the fast-paced Latin and International fusion dance class for a fee.

Dinner Dance Cruise

Fundraising will be smooth sailing with this delightful evening of dinner and dancing on the water. Sell tickets and cruise away.

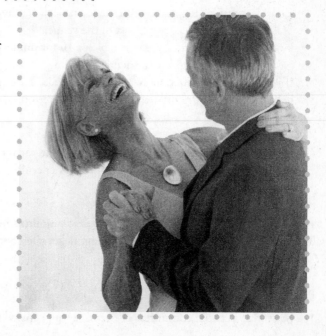

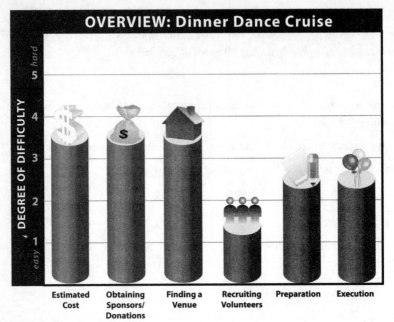

Special Materials/Equipment

- Cruise ship, yacht, or boat

Sponsors/Donations

- Consider asking a major supporter to sponsor the entire event.
- Seek sponsorship to cover the cost of the venue.
- Find sponsors to purchase, say, a table of 10 for dinner. The sponsor might then give the tickets to employees, friends, or family.
- If you have a silent auction or raffle, you can also have sponsors donate big-ticket items to auction or raffle such as trips, large electronics, or jewelry.

Possible Venue(s)

A cruise ship is perfect for a large group, and a private yacht is a nice option for smaller cruises. Many areas also have boats that offer dinner cruises on lakes or on the ocean.

Recommended Volunteer

10 to 15+ including 5 to 7 who will serve as committee heads for the venue, food, decorations, sponsors/donations, advertising, ticket sales, and entertainment

Preparation

Prep Time: 6 months+

1. Start with a central committee of five to seven people who will serve as committee

heads for the venue, food, decorations, sponsors/donations, advertising, ticket sales, and entertainment.

2. Decide when to have the event. Before you settle on a date, find out what else is going on in your community, and avoid conflicts.

3. Determine your budget. How much are you looking to raise, and what are you willing to spend to raise that amount?

4. Start seeking sponsors and donations immediately.

5. Search for your perfect venue. If you have to change the date of your event to get the right venue, make sure, again, that you will have no competition from similar events that may be scheduled.

6. If you decide to serve food, plan your menu. Four months before the event, schedule a caterer, recruit people to cook, or ask restaurants or grocery stores to donate food.

7. Plan what additional fundraisers and entertainment will occur at your event. You may want a live or silent auction, or a raffle.

8. Pick an emcee — either an organization member or a local celebrity. A celebrity can help you market the event.

9. Advertise by sending e-mails and letters, posting fliers, putting a notice on your organization's website, and making an announcement in your newsletter. Send press releases to local media outlets like newspapers and magazines, and contact local TV news and radio stations to request coverage and publicity.

10. Use the event's theme in everything from marketing, to graphic design of tickets and programs, to venue decorations.

11. Have your committees meet regularly and keep the lines of communication open.

12. Three months out from the event, print tickets and have everyone in your organization sell tickets. Offer an incentive to the individuals who sell the most tickets.

13. If you need any special equipment, such as seating, sound, light, or stage equipment, this is a good time to reserve these items. Do this as you think about how the venue will be set up for the event.

14. Do a walk-through of the venue a month before the event to check if all the venue systems work and ask when you can get in to decorate.

15. Write a script to serve as your minute-by-minute flow of activities for the event. Plan a time to thank your sponsors and distribute information promoting your organization.

16. Hold a meeting with all event volunteers and go over the tasks and schedule. Be clear on what you expect every volunteer to do. Tell volunteers what to wear for the event. Get everyone's contact information (phone number and e-mail) in case you need to communicate any changes or reminders.

Execution

1. Come in early to decorate, set up equipment and food, and check the lighting and sound systems.

2. Have volunteers collect tickets as well as sell more tickets at the event.

3. Follow your script to carry out all planned activities.

4. Initiate cleanup at the designated end time.

Masquerade Ball

During this formal ball, participants get to wear elaborate costumes and fancy face masks.

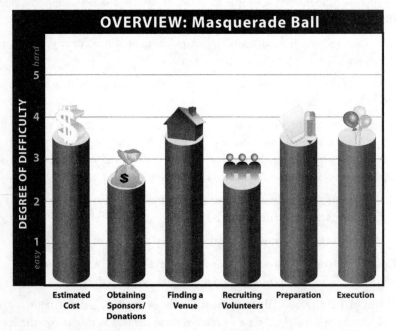

Special Materials/Equipment

-   Masquerade decorations
-   Tables and chairs
-   Dance floor
-   Sound system (microphone, speakers)

Sponsors/Donations

-   Ask a major supporter to sponsor the entire event. Consider sponsorship to cover the cost of the venue. Seek sponsors for say, tables of 10 for dinner. The sponsor might then give the tickets to employees, friends, or family.

- If you have a silent auction or raffle, you can also have sponsors donate big-ticket items to auction or raffle such as trips, large electronics, or jewelry.

Possible Venue(s)

A hotel with a large ballroom can take care of the catering, sound system, and lighting. An unusual location, like a large, old house or inn, is also a good choice.

Recommended Volunteer

15+ including 5 to 7 to serve as committee heads for the venue, food, decorations, sponsors/donations, advertising, ticket sales, entertainment, setup, and cleanup

Preparation

Prep Time: 6 months to 1 year

1. Start with a central committee of five to seven people who will serve as committee heads for the venue, food, decorations, sponsors/donations, advertising, ticket sales, entertainment, setup, and cleanup.

2. Decide when to have the event. Before you settle on a date, find out what else is going on in your community, and avoid conflicts.

3. Determine your budget. How much are you looking to raise, and what are you willing to spend to raise that amount?

4. Start seeking sponsors and donations immediately.

5. Search for your perfect venue. If you have to change the date of your event to get the right venue, make sure, again, that you will have no competition from similar events that might be scheduled.

6. If you decide to serve food, plan your menu. Four months before the event, schedule a caterer, recruit people to cook, or ask restaurants or grocery stores to donate food.

7. Plan what additional fundraisers and entertainment will occur at your event. You may want a live or silent auction, raffle, or band.

8. Pick an emcee — either an organization member or a local celebrity. A celebrity can help you market the event.

9. Advertise by sending e-mails and letters, posting fliers, putting a notice on your organization's website, and making an announcement in your newsletter. Send press releases to local media outlets like newspapers and magazines, and contact local TV news and radio stations to request coverage and publicity.

10. Use the event's theme in everything from marketing, to graphic design of tickets and programs, to venue decorations.

11. Have your various committees meet regularly and keep the lines of communication open.

12. Three months out from the event, print tickets and have everyone in your organization sell tickets. Offer an incentive to the individuals who sell the most tickets.

13. If you need any special equipment, such as seating, sound, light, or stage equipment, this is a good time to reserve these items. Do this as you think about how the venue will be set up for the event.

14. Do a walk-through of the venue a month before the event to check if all the venue systems work and ask when you can get in to decorate.

15. Write a script to serve as your minute-by-minute flow of activities for the event. Plan a time to thank your sponsors and distribute information promoting your organization.

16. Hold a meeting with all event volunteers and go over the tasks and schedule. Be clear on what you expect every volunteer to do. Tell volunteers what to wear for the event. Get everyone's contact information (phone number and e-mail) in case you need to communicate any changes or reminders.

Execution

1. Come in early to decorate, set up equipment and food, and check the lighting and sound systems.

2. Have volunteers collect tickets as well as sell more tickets at the event.

3. Follow your script to carry out all planned activities.

4. Initiate cleanup at the designated end time.

Variation(s)

- Have a themed masquerade event such as a Monster Mash.

Second-Chance Prom

Adults can do up prom a second time around by bringing dates and wearing their formal best, much like their high school proms from "back in the day." This adult-only event is ideal for Parent-Teacher Association (PTA) groups and will be talked about for years to come.

OVERVIEW: Second-Chance Prom

DEGREE OF DIFFICULTY — hard / easy

| Estimated Cost | Obtaining Sponsors/ Donations | Finding a Venue | Recruiting Volunteers | Preparation | Execution |

Special Materials/Equipment
- Decorations
- Music
- Sound equipment (microphone, speakers)
- Dance floor

Sponsors/Donations
- Ask community venues to donate a ballroom.
- Ask catering companies to donate food.

Possible Venue(s)
A hotel, venue with a ballroom, or school gymnasium will do the trick.

Recommended Volunteer
15+ including 5 to 7 committee heads to handle the venue, food, decorations, sponsors/ donations, advertising, ticket sales, entertainment, setup, and cleanup

Preparation
Prep Time: 6 months

1. Start with a central committee of five to seven people who will serve as committee heads for the venue, food, decorations, sponsors/donations, advertising, ticket sales, entertainment, setup, and cleanup.

2. Decide when to have the event. Before you settle on a date, find out what else is going on in your community, and avoid conflicts.

3. Determine your budget. How much are you looking to raise, and what are you willing to spend to raise that amount?

4. Start seeking sponsors and donations immediately.

5. Search for your perfect venue. If you have to change the date of your event to get the right venue, make sure, again, that you will have no competition from similar events that may be scheduled.

6. If you decide to serve food, plan your menu. Four months before the event, schedule a caterer, recruit people to cook, or ask restaurants or grocery stores to donate food.

7. Select what activities will occur at your event. You may want a live or silent auction, raffle, or band.

8. Pick an emcee — either an organization member or a local celebrity. A celebrity can help you market the event.

9. Advertise by sending e-mails and letters, posting fliers, putting a notice on your organization's website, and making an announcement in your newsletter. Send press releases to local media outlets like newspapers and magazines, and contact local TV news and radio stations to request coverage and publicity.

10. Use the event's theme in everything from marketing, to graphic design of tickets and programs, to venue decorations.

11. Have your various committees meet regularly and keep the lines of communication open.

12. Three months out from the event, print tickets and have everyone in your organization sell tickets. Offer an incentive to the individuals who sell the most tickets.

13. If you need any special equipment, such as seating, sound, light, or stage equipment, this is a good time to reserve these items. Do this as you think about how the venue will be set up for the event.

14. Do a walk-through of the venue a month before the event to check if all the venue systems work and ask when you can get in to decorate.

15. Write a script to serve as your minute-by-minute flow of activities for the event. Plan a

time to thank your sponsors and distribute information promoting your organization.

16. Hold a meeting with all event volunteers and go over the tasks and schedule. Be clear on what you expect every volunteer to do. Tell volunteers what to wear for the event. Get everyone's contact information (phone number and e-mail) in case you need to communicate any changes or reminders.

Execution

1. Come in early to decorate, set up equipment and food, and check the lighting and sound systems.

2. Have volunteers collect tickets as well as sell more tickets at the event.

3. Follow your script to carry out all planned activities.

4. Initiate cleanup at the designated end time.

Tip(s)

- To make this an authentic prom, consider casting adult volunteers in the roles of parent and teacher chaperones.
- Make the event kid-friendly by letting participants' children pretend to chaperone.
- Negotiate deals with a limo company, or have the parents' children act as chauffeurs or photographers.
- Sell corsages. Also, set up a photo booth and charge for photo packages and key chains.

Variation(s)

- Come up with a creative after-prom event, like drinks at a local bar or a late-night dance on the beach.

'60s Dance Party

Teach all the popular '60s dances, such as The Twist, The Ska, The Monkey, The Bird, and The Tighten Up at a party focused on that era. Buy a dance video demonstrating the moves for each dance so guests can follow along. With an entry fee, guests can participate in all the dancing delight, along with other activities geared toward the era, such as face painting '60s symbols like smiley faces, flowers, or peace signs.

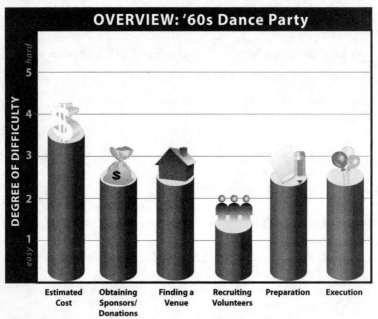

Special Materials/Equipment

- '60s decorations
- Sound system (speakers, microphone)
- Face paint
- '60s music
- Dance floor

Sponsors/Donations

- A local historical society might be a good place to begin looking for sponsorships and/or donations to use for the evening.

Possible Venue(s)

If there is a 1960s era hotel or social building in your community, this might be the perfect venue for an event such as this. Even better might be a '60s-era restaurant.

Recommended Volunteer

15+ including 5 to 7 to serve as committee heads for the venue, food, decorations, sponsors/donations, advertising, ticket sales, entertainment, setup, and cleanup

Preparation

Prep Time: 6 months to 1 year

1. Start with a central committee of five to seven people who will serve as committee heads for the venue, food, decorations, sponsors/donations, advertising, ticket sales, entertainment, setup and cleanup.

2. Decide when to have the event. Before you settle on a date, find out what else is going on in your community, and avoid conflicts.

3. Determine your budget. How much are you looking to raise, and what are you willing to spend to raise that amount?

4. Search for your perfect venue. If you have to change the date of your event to get the right venue, make sure, again, that you will have no competition from similar events that may be scheduled.

5. Select what activities will occur at your event. You may want a live or silent auction, raffle, or band. The 1960s are famous for having great classic rock music. If you plan to have live music at your party, be sure to book your band at least six months in advance.

6. If you decide to serve food, plan your menu. Four months before the event, schedule a caterer, recruit people to cook, or ask restaurants or grocery stores to donate food.

7. Pick an emcee — either an organization member or a local celebrity. A celebrity can help you market the event.

8. Advertise by sending e-mails and letters, posting fliers, putting a notice on your organization's website, and making an announcement in your newsletter. Send press releases to local media outlets like newspapers and magazines, and contact local TV news and radio stations to request coverage and publicity.

9. Use the event's theme in everything from marketing, to graphic design of tickets and programs, to venue decorations.

10. Have your various committees meet regularly and keep the lines of communication open.

11. Three months out from the event, print tickets and have everyone in your organization sell tickets. Offer an incentive to the individuals who sell the most tickets.

12. If you need any special equipment such as sound, lights, staging, or seating, this is a good time to reserve these items. Do this as you think about how the venue will be set up for the event.

13. Do a walk-through of the venue a month before the event to check if all the venue systems work and ask when you can get in to decorate.

14. Write a script to serve as your minute-by-minute flow of activities for the event. Plan a time to thank your sponsors and distribute information promoting your organization.

15. Hold a meeting with all event volunteers and go over the tasks and schedule. Be clear on what you expect every volunteer to do. Tell volunteers what to wear for the event. Get everyone's contact information (phone number and e-mail) in case you need to communicate any changes or reminders.

Execution

1. Come in early to decorate, set up equipment and food, and check the lighting and sound systems.

2. Have volunteers collect tickets as well as sell more tickets at the event.

3. Follow your script to carry out all planned activities.

4. Initiate cleanup at the designated end time.

Variation(s)

- Any era that has a specific style associated with it, such as the '50s, is a fun variation for a party.

Chapter 13

Food and Drinks

These events combine culinary treats with charitable events, on a larger scale than the events found in the first section of the book. The projects you will find in this chapter include:

- ◎ Breakfast and Book Signing with Author
- ◎ Celebrity Cookout
- ◎ Chef Competition
- ◎ Chocolate Tasting Party
- ◎ Cooking Demonstrations
- ◎ Dining with the Stars
- ◎ Exotic Meat Barbecue
- ◎ Martini Mingle
- ◎ Taste of the Town
- ◎ Thrilling Theater Dinner
- ◎ Wine Tasting

Breakfast and Book Signing with Author

Have a popular local author sign books and pose for photographs during a breakfast, and charge a fee for admission.

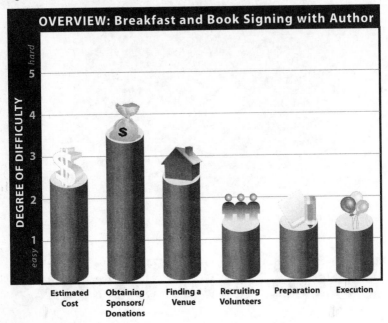

OVERVIEW: Breakfast and Book Signing with Author

DEGREE OF DIFFICULTY (easy → hard, scale 1 to 5)

Estimated Cost | Obtaining Sponsors/Donations | Finding a Venue | Recruiting Volunteers | Preparation | Execution

Sponsors/Donations

- Ask a local restaurant to donate the venue and food, or ask a local independent bookstore to host the event.
- Find an author to donate his/her time as the featured guest.

Possible Venue(s)

Consider holding this event at a restaurant, bookstore, school, church, or any venue that can accommodate the number of people you would like to attract and has the ability to handle catering.

Recommended Volunteer

5+ to handle the venue, food, advertising, ticket sales, and sponsor/donations

Preparation

Prep Time: 4 to 6 months or more

1. Start with a central committee of five to seven people who will serve as committee heads for the venue, food, decorations, author, advertising, ticket sales, entertainment, setup, and cleanup.

2. Decide when to have the event. Before you settle on a date, find out what else is going on in your community, and avoid conflicts.

3. Determine your budget. How much are you looking to raise, and what are you willing to spend to raise that amount?

4. Start seeking an author and donations immediately. When you identify the author who will join your organization for breakfast, set the ground rules for audience interaction. Determine if your ticket-buyers can ask for autographs and pictures. Decide whether to sell books, and if so, whether the book sales will benefit your organization in any way.

5. Search for your perfect venue. If you have to change the date of your event to get the right venue, make sure, again, that you will have no competition from similar events that might be scheduled.

6. If you decide to serve food, plan your menu. Four months before the event, schedule a caterer, recruit people to cook, or ask restaurants or grocery stores to donate food.

7. Plan what additional fundraisers and entertainment will occur at your event. You may want a live or silent auction, raffle, or band.

8. Pick an emcee — either an organization member or a local celebrity. A celebrity can help you market the event.

9. Advertise by sending e-mails and letters, posting fliers, putting a notice on your organization's website, and making an announcement in your newsletter. Send press releases to local media outlets like newspapers and magazines, and contact local TV news and radio stations to request coverage and publicity.

10. Use the event's theme in everything from marketing, to graphic design of tickets and programs, to venue decorations.

11. Have your various committees meet regularly and keep the lines of communication open.

12. A couple months before the event, print tickets and have everyone in your organization sell tickets. Offer an incentive to the individuals who sell the most tickets.

13. If you need any special equipment, such as seating, sound, light, or stage equipment, this is a good time to reserve these items. Do this as you think about how the venue will be set up for the event.

14. Do a walk-through of the venue a month before the event to check if all the venue systems work and ask when you can get in to decorate.

15. Write a script to serve as your minute-by-minute flow of activities for the event. Plan a time to thank your sponsors and distribute information promoting your organization.

16. Hold a meeting with all event volunteers and go over the tasks and schedule. Be clear on what you expect every volunteer to do. Tell volunteers what to wear for the event. Get everyone's contact information (phone number and e-mail) in case you need to communicate any changes or reminders.

Execution

1. Come in early to decorate, set up tables and food, check the lighting and sound systems, and make the author comfortable.

2. Have volunteers collect tickets as well as sell more tickets at the event.

3. Follow your script. Have volunteers control lines for book signings and pictures.

4. Initiate cleanup at the designated end time.

Tip(s)

• Make sure the author will have everything possibly needed (a microphone, water, a comfortable seat, a podium, a pen or marker for autographs, etc.)

Celebrity Cookout

Feature a local or national celebrity at a community cookout. Charge a high fee for general admission to the event, and schedule a time guests can meet one-on-one with the celebrity.

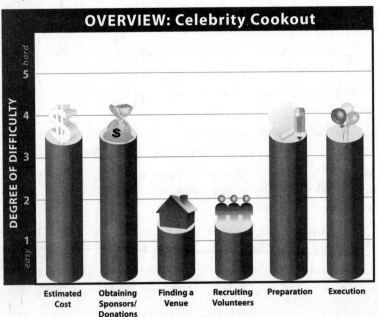

Special Materials/Equipment
- Grilling and serving supplies

Sponsors/Donations
- Find a celebrity who will agree to attend the event, and find additional sponsors who correspond with the celebrity's interests. (i.e. If your celebrity is a famous author, ask a bookstore to help sponsor the event.)

Possible Venue(s)
This is an event that will benefit greatly from being in the outdoors at a location like a large park, forest preserve, or beach where you can have a picnic barbecue. However, for the sake of the celebrity, you might choose a private park/beach or less popular outdoors venue.

Recommended Volunteer
10+ including 5 to 7 committee heads to handle such tasks as venue, food, decorations, entertainment, advertising, ticket sales, and celebrity involvement

Preparation
Prep Time: 8 months to 1 year

1. Start with a central committee of five to seven people who will serve as committee heads for the venue, food, celebrity, decorations, sponsors/donations, advertising, ticket sales, entertainment, setup, and cleanup.

2. Find a celebrity who is willing to be the spotlight of the event, and make a solid contractual agreement to seal the commitment and get written permission for things like pictures, autographs, and time spent with supporters.

3. Decide when to have the event. Before you settle on a date, find out what else is going on in your community, and avoid conflicts.

4. Determine your budget. How much are you looking to raise, and what are you willing to spend to raise that amount?

5. Start seeking sponsors and donations immediately.

6. Search for your perfect venue. If you have to change the date of your event to get the right venue, make sure, again, that you will have no competition from similar events that might be scheduled.

7. If you decide to serve food, plan your menu. Four months before the event, schedule a caterer, recruit people to cook, or ask restaurants or grocery stores to donate food.

8. Select what activities will occur at your event. You may want a live or silent auction, raffle, or band. Consider a silent auction that includes packages of exotic meats and spices, or items related to the celebrity (i.e. the author's books, the singer's CD, the athlete's autographed jersey, etc.)

9. Pick an emcee from your organization.

10. Advertise by sending e-mails and letters, posting fliers, putting a notice on your organization's website, and making an announcement in your newsletter. Send press releases to local media outlets like newspapers and magazines, and contact local TV news and radio stations to request coverage and publicity.

11. Use the event's theme in everything from marketing, to graphic design of tickets and programs, to venue decorations.

12. Have your various committees meet regularly and keep the lines of communication open.

13. Three months out from the event, print tickets and have everyone in your organization sell tickets. Offer an incentive to the individuals who sell the most tickets.

14. If you need any special equipment, such as seating, sound, light, or stage equipment, this is a good time to reserve these items. Do this as you think about how the venue will be set up for the event.

15. Do a walk-through of the venue a month before the event to check if all the venue systems work and ask when you can get in to decorate.

16. Write a script to serve as your minute-by-minute flow of activities for the event. Plan a time to thank your sponsors and distribute information promoting your organization.

17. Hold a meeting with all event volunteers and go over the tasks and schedule. Be clear on what you expect every volunteer to do. Tell volunteers what to wear for the event. Get everyone's contact information (phone number and e-mail) in case you need to communicate any changes or reminders.

Execution

1. Come in early to decorate, set up equipment and food, and check the lighting and sound systems.

2. Have volunteers collect tickets as well as sell more tickets at the event.

3. Follow your script to carry out all planned activities.

4. Initiate cleanup at the designated end time.

Tip(s)

- Check out your community's food safety codes to make sure you comply with the food preparation and service requirements.

Chef Competition

Have chefs compete to create the best dish within a time limit. Provide each chef with a box containing identical ingredients. Allow the public to purchase tickets and judge the results.

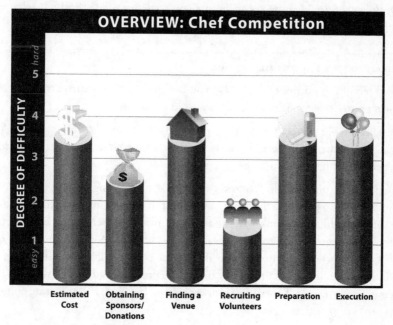

Special Materials/Equipment
- Boxes of ingredients (one per chef)
- Serving dishes
- Cooking utensils and tools
- Eating utensils

Sponsors/Donations
- Upscale restaurants and grocery stores are good sponsors and donors for this event.

Possible Venue(s)
A large upscale restaurant with a kitchen that is large enough to handle multiple working chefs is ideal.

Recommended Volunteer
5+ to handle venue, ingredients, chefs, sponsors/donations, advertising, setup, and cleanup

Preparation
Prep Time: 4 months

1. Start with a committee of three to four people who will serve as committee heads for the venue, talent (chefs), food, hospitality, and marketing.

2. Decide when to have the event. Before you settle on a date, find out what else is going on in your community, and avoid conflicts.

3. Determine your budget. How much are you looking to raise, and what are you willing to spend to raise that amount?

4. Start recruiting a number of chefs so you can cover various courses from appetizers through to desserts. Also, seek sponsors and donations.

5. Search for your perfect venue. If you have to change the date of your event to get the right venue, make sure, again, that you will have no competition from similar events that might be scheduled.

6. Decide the rules for the contest, such as the following: Offer each chef the opportunity to prepare a dish from a given list of ingredients. Set a time frame that the chefs will have to cook within, and a set number of servings. Every supporter who purchases a ticket to your event will be served a portion from each of the chefs. The portions will not be identified by chef but by plate color. The supporters will vote by filling out comment cards. The comment cards will ask the diner to suggest a rating (say, 1 – 10) total for each dish. The chef with the most points will win the competition.

7. Determine a prize for the winning chef.

8. Select what additional activities will occur at your event. You might want a live or silent auction, raffle, or band to entertain guests while you tally the votes.

9. Pick an emcee — either an organization member or a local celebrity. A celebrity can help you market the event.

10. Advertise by sending e-mails and letters, posting fliers, putting a notice on your organization's website, and making an announcement in your newsletter. Send press releases to local media outlets like newspapers and magazines, and contact local TV news and radio stations to request coverage and publicity.

11. Use the event's theme in everything from marketing, to graphic design of tickets and programs, to venue decorations.

12. Have your various committees meet regularly and keep the lines of communication open.

13. Three months out from the event, print tickets and have everyone in your organization sell tickets. Offer an incentive to the individuals who sell the most tickets.

14. If you need any special equipment, such as seating, sound, light, or stage equipment, this is a good time to reserve these items. Do this as you think about how the venue will be set up for the event.

15. Do a walk-through of the venue a month before the event to check if all the venue systems work and ask when you can get in to decorate.

16. Write a script to serve as your minute-by-minute flow of activities for the event. Be sure to plan a time to thank your chefs and sponsors, and distribute information about your organization.

17. Hold a meeting with all event volunteers and go over the tasks and schedule. Be clear on what you expect every volunteer to do. Tell volunteers what to wear for the event. Get everyone's contact information (phone number and e-mail) in case you need to communicate any changes or reminders.

Execution

1. Come in early to decorate, set up equipment and food, and check the lighting and sound systems.

2. Have volunteers collect tickets as well as sell more tickets at the event.

3. Have a go-to person in the kitchen as well as in the dining room. It is vital that these individuals can answer any questions, but also that they stay out of the chef's way.

4. Follow your script to carry out all planned activities.

5. When you ask that your supporters fill out their voting cards, remind them of the rules of the competition. Set a time for the voting cards to be filled out. Let diners know when they have, say, five minutes remaining to submit their votes.

6. Initiate cleanup at the designated end time.

Tip(s)

- Make sure that all the ingredients you supply the chef are as fresh as possible.
- Put voting cards and writing utensils at every diner's place for fast, easy voting.
- Allow your supporters to enjoy their meals before you ask that they fill out their comment cards. Do not rush this part of the event.

Variation(s)

- Promote this event for any aspiring cooks (no experience necessary) who want to try making a dish, and charge the novices an entry fee.

Chocolate Tasting Party

Invite supporters of your organization to a party where they can indulge in a decadent variety of chocolate. Send out fun-size chocolates or personalized candy bars with your invitations to ensure a sweet response. Charge a fee for admission.

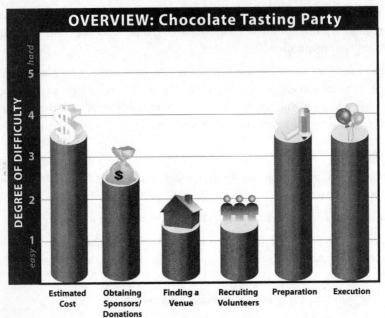

Special Materials/Equipment
- Presentation equipment and materials   • Chocolate
- Chocolate related food items

Sponsors/Donations
- A local chocolatier, chocolate shop, or candy company could be the best sponsor.
- Research your community for local chefs and bakers that do great things with chocolate. Ask these individuals to take part in your event. You can make a strong case for their involvement if you agree to give them a good amount of publicity.
- Consider partnering with a small nonprofit arts organization such as a chamber music group or jazz ensemble to perform at your event.

Possible Venue(s)
A nice upscale hotel with comfortable meeting and/or banquet facilities is ideal.

Recommended Volunteer

10+ including 4 to 5 to organize things such as venue, personnel, chocolate, and ticket sales. Consider having volunteers be servers.

Preparation

Prep Time: 4 to 6 months

1. Identify your venue and date. Before you settle on a date, find out what else is going on in your community, and avoid conflicts.

2. Determine your budget. How much are you looking to raise, and what are you willing to spend to raise that amount?

3. Seek a partnership with a local chocolatier or chocolate shop, if possible. The partnership will bring customers to the shop and will bring you a price break on the chocolate. Ask the merchant if you can sell tickets through their store. Also find chefs and bakers to donate their services.

4. Select what activities will occur at your event. You may want a live or silent auction, raffle, or band.

5. Advertise by sending e-mails and letters, posting fliers, putting a notice on your organization's website, and making an announcement in your newsletter. Send press releases to local media outlets like newspapers and magazines, and contact local TV news and radio stations to request coverage and publicity.

6. Use the event's theme in everything from marketing, to graphic design of tickets and programs, to venue decorations.

7. Three months out from the event, print tickets and have everyone in your organization sell tickets. Offer an incentive to the individuals who sell the most tickets.

8. If you need any special equipment, such as serving dishes and seating, this is a good time to reserve these items. Do this as you think about how the venue will be set up for the event.

9. With the help of your chocolate expert partners, put together a detailed description of each featured chocolate as well as a presentation about the history of chocolate and the different kinds available.

10. Do a walk-through of the venue a month before the event to check if all the venue systems work and ask when you can get in to decorate.

11. Write a script to serve as your minute-by-minute flow of activities for the event. Plan a time to thank your sponsors and distribute information promoting your organization.

12. Hold a meeting with all event volunteers and go over the tasks and schedule. Be clear on what you expect every volunteer to do. Tell volunteers what to wear for the event. Get everyone's contact information (phone number and e-mail) in case you need to communicate any changes or reminders.

Execution

1. Come in early to decorate, set up equipment and food, and check the lighting and sound systems.

2. Have volunteers collect tickets as well as sell more tickets at the event.

3. Follow your script to carry out all planned activities.

4. Initiate cleanup at the designated end time.

Variation(s)

- Throw an Ice Cream Tasting Party.
- Have a Coffee Tasting Party.

Cooking Demonstrations

Ask local chefs to perform a cooking demonstration and charge a fee for the event. If the chefs have their own cookbook, have a book signing to raise additional funds.

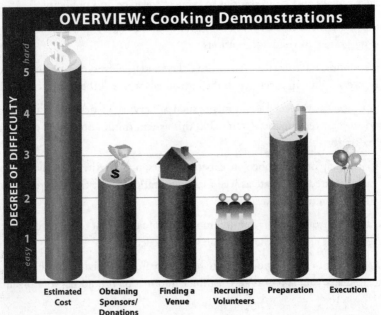

Special Materials/Equipment
- Food preparation and presentation supplies

Sponsors/Donations
- Seek a partnership with a local upscale restaurant with a well-known chef, if possible. The partnership will bring customers to the restaurant and may bring you a price break on the food. Ask the restaurateur if you can sell tickets through his or her establishment.

- Research your community for local chefs and bakers who do great things with food, and ask these individuals to take part in your event. You can make a strong case for their involvement if you agree to give them a good amount of publicity.

- Consider partnering with a small nonprofit arts organization such as a chamber music group or jazz ensemble to perform at your event.

Possible Venue(s)
The venue may be a nice upscale restaurant or a hotel with a comfortable meeting and/or banquet facility, a local school, or a department store during off hours.

Recommended Volunteer
5+ to organize things such as venue, food, ticket sales, sponsors/donations, advertising, setup, and cleanup

Preparation
Prep Time: 4 to 6 months

1. Start with a central committee of five to seven people who will serve as committee heads for the venue, food, decorations, sponsors/donations, advertising, ticket sales, entertainment, setup, and cleanup.

2. Decide when to have the event. Before you settle on a date, find out what else is going on in your community, and avoid conflicts.

3. Determine your budget. How much are you looking to raise, and what are you willing to spend to raise that amount?

4. Start seeking sponsors and donations immediately.

5. Search for your perfect venue. If you have to change the date of your event to get the right venue, make sure, again, that you will have no competition from similar events that might be scheduled.

6. Decide what events you will feature besides the cooking demonstrations. You may want a live or silent auction, raffle, or jazz band. Good items for a raffle or auction are fancy kitchen utensils, electronics (mixers, blenders, processors, etc.), and

gourmet food items.

7. Advertise by sending e-mails and letters, posting fliers, putting a notice on your organization's website, and making an announcement in your newsletter. Send press releases to local media outlets like newspapers and magazines, and contact local TV news and radio stations to request coverage and publicity.

8. Use the event's theme in everything from marketing, to graphic design of tickets and programs, to venue decorations.

9. Have your various committees meet regularly and keep the lines of communication open.

10. Three months out from the event, print tickets and have everyone in your organization sell tickets. Offer an incentive to the individuals who sell the most tickets.

11. If you need any special equipment, such as seating, sound, light, or stage equipment, this is a good time to reserve these items. Do this as you think about how the venue will be set up for the event.

12. Do a walk-through of the venue a month before the event to check if all the venue systems work and ask when you can get in to decorate.

13. Write a script to serve as your minute-by-minute flow of activities for the event. Plan a time to thank your sponsors and distribute information promoting your organization.

14. Hold a meeting with all event volunteers and go over the tasks and schedule. Be clear on what you expect every volunteer to do. Tell volunteers what to wear for the event. Get everyone's contact information (phone number and e-mail) in case you need to communicate any changes or reminders.

Execution

1. Come in early to decorate, set up equipment and food, and check the lighting and sound systems.

2. Have volunteers collect tickets as well as sell more tickets at the event.

3. Follow your script to carry out all planned activities.

4. Initiate cleanup at the designated end time.

Dining with the Stars

Give paying participants the opportunity of a lifetime: to enjoy a meal in the company of a celebrity. The famous person could be a sports star, singer, politician, entertainer, or key leader in the community.

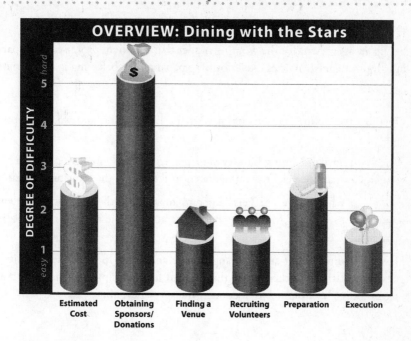

OVERVIEW: Dining with the Stars

Sponsors/Donations
- Ask local restaurant owners to donate dinners. They will be glad to get the free publicity.
- Ask celebrities to participate.

Possible Venue(s)
Popular restaurants in your community work well.

Recommended Volunteer
2 to 4 per dinner including a high-level member of your organization to approach the star and handle accommodations

Preparation
Prep Time: 8 months to 1 year

1. Have a high-level member of your board of directors ask celebrities and restaurants to participate, and make the commitment official by drawing up a contract including a deadline by which the dinner will have taken place.

2. Register your event for auction on an online bidding site like eBay, or choose a time and place for the auction. Set a beginning bid price.

3. Advertise by sending e-mails and letters, posting fliers, putting a notice on your organization's website, and making an announcement in your newsletter. Send press releases to local media outlets like newspapers and magazines, and contact

local TV news and radio stations to request coverage and publicity.

4. Set up an agreement for the winning bidder that has them promise not to partake in compromising activities like informing paparazzi or behaving inappropriately.

Execution

1. Open up the online auction site or start the live auction and watch people bid away.

2. When you have a winning bid, forward the agreement you have prepared to the winner. Contact the celebrity immediately and confirm the location and date.

3. Follow up when the event gets closer to make sure the celebrity and winner remember to attend. Make any necessary accommodations for their arrival, privacy, and comfort.

4. Have a volunteer meet at the arranged time and place to greet the celebrity and guest, escort them to their table, thank them for participating, and wish them a nice evening. Take photos to document the special evening.

Tip(s)

- To make the offer even more attractive, allow the winner to bring a guest.
- Choose a volunteer with public relations experience to insure professionalism in communicating with the celebrity and representing your company.

Variation(s)

- Hold a live auction with local celebrities.
- Auction dinners prepared by celebrity chefs.

Exotic Meat Barbecue

Give participants the chance to chew on something different. Charge for samples of wild animals, including antelope, alligator, buffalo, black bear, crocodile, iguana, ostrich, llama, and wild boar. You can plan this event like a large picnic, but with a beast of a menu.

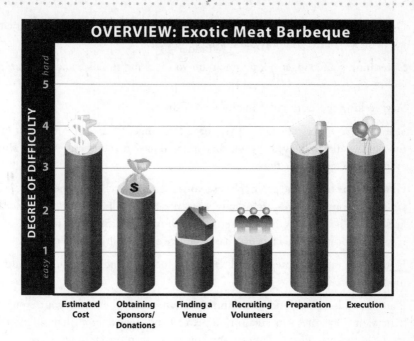

Special Materials/Equipment
- Exotic meat
- Wood and barbecue equipment

Sponsors/Donations
- Ask sporting good businesses to sponsor the event.
- Approach hunting and fishing clubs or other such social clubs and ask them to be sponsors.

Possible Venue(s)
An outdoor location where meat can be barbecued on an open fire, like a large park, is appropriate.

Recommended Volunteer
10+ including 5 to 7 to serve as committee heads for the venue, food, decorations, sponsors/donations, advertising, ticket sales, entertainment, setup, and cleanup

Preparation
Prep Time: 8 months to 1 year

1. Start with a central committee of five to seven people who will serve as committee heads for the venue, food, decorations, sponsors/donations, advertising, ticket sales, entertainment, setup, and cleanup.

2. Decide when to have the event. Before you settle on a date, find out what else is going on in your community, and avoid conflicts.

3. Determine your budget. How much are you looking to raise, and what are you willing to spend to raise that amount?

4. Start seeking sponsors and donations immediately.

5. Search for your perfect venue. If you have to change the date of your event to get the right venue, make sure, again, that you will have no competition from similar events that may be scheduled.

6. Four months before the event, choose your menu and schedule the caterer. Have your food committee research the types of meat you will offer. Begin your search locally and, if necessary, do an internet search for procuring these items. Also, see if you can locate a local chef that has experience in preparing exotic meats.

7. Figure out a means to prepare and serve food that is in line with your community's food safety codes.

8. Plan what additional fundraisers and entertainment will occur at your event. You may want a live or silent auction, raffle, or band. Consider a silent auction that includes packages of exotic meats and spices to use in preparation.

9. Pick an emcee — either an organization member or a local celebrity. A celebrity can help you market the event.

10. Advertise by sending e-mails and letters, posting fliers, putting a notice on your organization's website, and making an announcement in your newsletter. Send press releases to local media outlets like newspapers and magazines, and contact local TV news and radio stations to request coverage and publicity.

11. Use the event's theme in everything from marketing, to graphic design of tickets and programs, to venue decorations.

12. Have your various committees meet regularly and keep the lines of communication open.

13. Three months out from the event, print tickets and have everyone in your organization sell tickets. Offer an incentive to the individuals who sell the most tickets.

14. If you need any special equipment, such as seating, sound, light, or stage equipment, this is a good time to reserve these items. Do this as you think about how the venue will be set up for the event.

15. Do a walk-through of the venue a month before the event to check if all the venue systems work and ask when you can get in to decorate.

16. Write a script to serve as your minute-by-minute flow of activities for the event. Plan a time to thank your sponsors and distribute information promoting your organization.

17. Hold a meeting with all event volunteers and go over the tasks and schedule. Be clear on what you expect every volunteer to do. Tell volunteers what to wear for the event. Get everyone's contact information (phone number and e-mail) in case you need to communicate any changes or reminders.

Execution

1. Come in early to decorate, set up equipment and food, and check the lighting and sound systems.

2. Have volunteers collect tickets as well as sell more tickets at the event.

3. Follow your script to carry out all planned activities.

4. Initiate cleanup at the designated end time.

Martini Mingle

Shake things up with a martini party. Charge a fee for admission to the event, as well as a small cost for drinks. Play cool jazz music in the background to set a hip, relaxed vibe. Add a fun twist by offering interactive martini mixing stations.

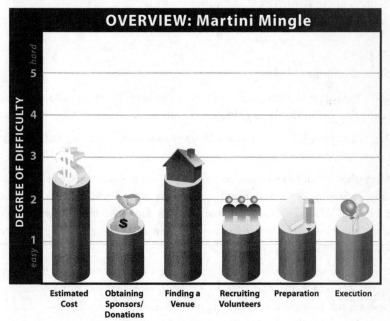

Special Materials/Equipment

- Martini glasses
- Martini recipes and ingredients
- Traditional garnishes (like assorted stuffed olives, cocktail onions and twists of lemon)
- Sound equipment (microphone, speakers)

Sponsors/Donations

- Ask a bar that makes great martinis to host your organization's event for the evening. Generally, you will charge admission to the bar and the bar will make money on the liquor sales. You can make other arrangements with the bar, such as increasing the price of drinks and you getting a percentage of drink sales, but you have to make it attractive to them, as well. If you plan your event for a night that is considered an "off night" for the bar, such as a Monday or Tuesday, and you can guarantee them a full house of your supporters, they should be more than happy to do the event.

Possible Venue(s)

The ideal venue is an upscale bar that is known to make great martinis.

Recommended Volunteer

5+ to book the venue and music, advertise, and set up the event

Preparation

Prep Time: 2 months+

1. Find a bar to sponsor you, and decide when to have the event. Before you settle on a date, find out what else is going on in your community, and avoid conflicts.

2. Determine your budget. How much are you looking to raise, and what are you willing to spend to raise that amount?

3. Select what activities will occur at your event. You may want a live or silent auction, raffle, or jazz band. Consider raffling off some expensive battles of gin, vermouth, and vodka. You can also set up a martini-glass decorating station where guests can design their own personalized glass with glass markers and fun embellishments. You can charge for these or offer them as party favors.

4. Advertise by sending e-mails and letters, posting fliers, putting a notice on your organization's website, and making an announcement in your newsletter. Send press releases to local media outlets like newspapers and magazines, and contact local TV news and radio stations to request coverage and publicity.

5. Use the event's theme in everything from marketing, to graphic design of tickets and programs, to venue decorations.

6. Print tickets and have everyone in your organization sell tickets. Offer an incentive to the individuals who sell the most tickets.

Execution

1. Have volunteers collect tickets as well as sell more tickets at the event.

2. Run the activities and be sure to make an announcement thanking the venue and telling about your organization.

Tip(s)

- Have a volunteer or two on hand to act as designated drivers for guests who might have a little too much to drink.

- Offer a non-alcoholic option. Include mixed fruit juices, iced tea, and seltzer to make sophisticated non-alcoholic martinis.

- Have a few volunteers on hand to act as designated drivers for guests.

Variation(s)

- Serve martinis at a Sex & the City Party, and tell guests to dress up as their favorite character or sporting the latest fashions.

Taste of the Town

This food-sampling event is meant to give supporters a good taste of some of the community's top local restaurants. Community members can pay an entry fee to sample savory specialties and signature dishes prepared by local chefs.

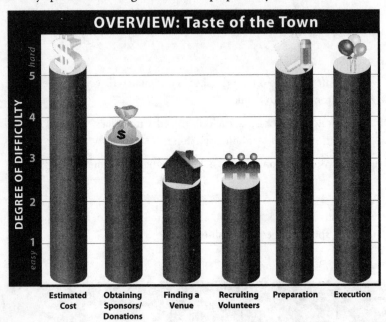

Special Materials/Equipment

- Cooking and serving supplies
- Ingredients

Sponsors/Donations

- See if your local chamber of commerce will sponsor this event, because the fundraiser may generate a large amount of business for local restaurants.
- Ask restaurants to donate the time of their chefs and the ingredients of the prepared dishes. Talk to the restaurants about the free advertising they will receive with their participation. Work to get the participation of restaurants and chefs that are highly regarded. Expensive and trendy restaurants do well at events such as this. Keep in mind that people want to sample new foods, not foods they might have every day.
- Seek your local restaurant association, and/or a media company such as a local newspaper, TV or radio station to help pay for any remaining costs.

Possible Venue(s)

A large hotel with kitchen facilities and space to seat a large number of people is best. Other options include a church, social club, or school with a kitchen and open space for tables and chairs.

Recommended Volunteer

10+ including 5 to 7 to serve as committee heads for the venue, food, decorations, sponsors/donations, advertising, ticket sales, entertainment, setup, and cleanup

Preparation

Prep Time: 8 months to 1 year

1. Start with a central committee of five to seven people who will serve as committee heads for the venue, food, decorations, sponsors/donations, advertising, ticket sales, entertainment, setup, and cleanup.

2. Decide when to have the event. Before you settle on a date, find out what else is going on in your community, and avoid conflicts.

3. Determine your budget. How much are you looking to raise, and what are you willing to spend to raise that amount?

4. Start seeking sponsors and donations immediately. Four months before the event, try to have your restaurants and chefs lined up.

5. Search for your perfect venue. If you have to change the date of your event to get the right venue, make sure, again, that you will have no competition from similar events that may be scheduled.

6. Determine a means to prepare and serve food that is in line with your community's food safety codes.

7. Select what additional activities will occur at your event. You may want a band, raffle, or live or silent auction that includes dinner packages at participating restaurants.

8. If you plan on an outdoor event, make a backup plan in case of bad weather.

9. Pick an emcee — either an organization member or a local celebrity. A celebrity can help you market the event.

10. Advertise by sending e-mails and letters, posting fliers, putting a notice on your organization's website, and making an announcement in your newsletter. Send press releases to local media outlets like newspapers and magazines, and contact local TV news and radio stations to request coverage and publicity.

11. Use the event's theme in everything from marketing, to graphic design of tickets and programs, to venue decorations.

12. Have your various committees meet regularly and keep the lines of communication open.

13. Three months out from the event, print tickets and have everyone in your organization sell tickets. Offer an incentive to the individuals who sell the most tickets.

14. If you need any special equipment, such as seating, sound, light, or stage equipment, this is a good time to reserve these items. Do this as you think about how the venue will be set up for the event.

15. Do a walk-through of the venue a month before the event to check if all the venue systems work and ask when you can get in to decorate.

16. Write a script to serve as your minute-by-minute flow of activities for the event. Plan a time to thank your sponsors and distribute information promoting your organization.

17. Hold a meeting with all event volunteers and go over the tasks and schedule. Be clear on what you expect every volunteer to do. Tell volunteers what to wear for the event. Get everyone's contact information (phone number and e-mail) in case you need to communicate any changes or reminders.

Execution

1. Come in early to decorate, set up equipment and food, and check the lighting and sound systems.

2. Have volunteers collect tickets as well as sell more tickets at the event.

3. Follow your script to carry out all planned activities.

4. Initiate cleanup at the designated end time.

Tip(s)

- Sell tickets at a central ticket booth. This cuts down on your volunteer need and keeps the money in a central location. Also, when people buy tickets directly from the food stations, they only purchase as many tickets as they need. When people purchase tickets at a central desk, they are likely to overbuy.

You must pay extra attention to fundraisers that involve alcoholic beverages. Most states have specific laws to encourage nonprofit organizations to obtain a one day special alcoholic liquor license. You must allocate sufficient time for the application of this license. In addition you will need to comply with all state laws governing the sale and dispensing of alcoholic beverages. The organization will also be required in most cases to carry an insurance rider for the sale of alcoholic beverages, this insurance will protect the organization should someone be over served, or involved in an accident of some kind. Again allow sufficient time to speak with your insurance agent and do not even try to hold the event without the proper licensing and insurance.

Thrilling Theater Dinner

Offer supporters of your organization a night on the town where they can dine with the thrill of a live show happening right around their dinner tables.

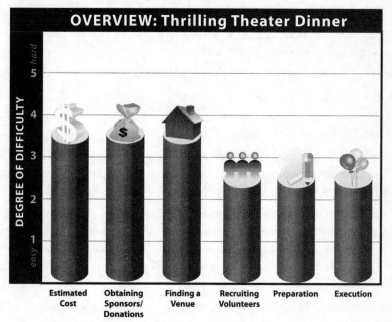

Special Materials/Equipment
- Costumes
- Scripts
- Props

Sponsors/Donations
- Contact a local theater group to provide performers and a script.

Possible Venue(s)
You will need a location that can offer a theatrical atmosphere suitable for a dinner or the capability of handling a caterer as well as plenty of space for a performance area and an audience. An inn or a lodge is ideal, but a restaurant or club works well too.

Recommended Volunteer
10+ including 5 to 7 to serve as committee heads for the venue, food, decorations, sponsors/donations, advertising, ticket sales, entertainment, setup, and cleanup

Preparation
Prep Time: 6 months

1. Start with a central committee of five to seven people who will serve as committee heads for the venue, food, decorations, sponsors/donations, advertising, ticket sales, entertainment, setup, and cleanup.

2. Decide when to have the event. Before you settle on a date, find out what else is going on in your community, and avoid conflicts.

3. Determine your budget. How much are you looking to raise, and what are you willing to spend to raise that amount?

4. Start seeking sponsors and donations immediately.

5. Search for your perfect venue. If you have to change the date of your event to get the right venue, make sure, again, that you will have no competition from similar events that may be scheduled.

6. If you decide to serve food, plan your menu. Four months before the event, schedule a caterer, recruit people to cook, or ask restaurants or grocery stores to donate food. Decide on a flat fee per person for dinner.

7. Allow about three months to advertise by sending e-mails and letters, posting fliers, putting a notice on your organization's website, and making an announcement in your newsletter. Send press releases to local media outlets like newspapers and magazines, and contact local TV news and radio stations to request coverage and publicity.

8. Use the event's theme in everything from marketing, to graphic design of tickets and programs, to venue decorations.

9. Have your various committees meet regularly and keep the lines of communication open.

10. Three months out from the event, print tickets and have everyone in your organization sell tickets. Offer an incentive to the individuals who sell the most tickets.

11. If you need any special equipment, such as seating, sound, light, or stage equipment, this is a good time to reserve these items. Do this as you think about how the venue will be set up for the event.

12. Do a walk-through of the venue with the theater company a month before the event to check if all the venue systems work and ask when you can get in to decorate.

13. Write a script to serve as your minute-by-minute flow of activities for the event. Plan a time to thank your sponsors and distribute information promoting your organization.

14. Hold a meeting with all event volunteers and go over the tasks and schedule. Be clear on what you expect every volunteer to do. Tell volunteers what to wear for the event. Get everyone's contact information (phone number and e-mail) in case you need to communicate any changes or reminders.

Execution

1. Come in early to decorate, set up equipment and food, and check the lighting and sound systems.

2. Have volunteers collect tickets as well as sell more tickets at the event.

5. Follow your script to carry out all planned activities.

6. Initiate cleanup at the designated end time.

Tip(s)

• It may be a fun way to earn a little more money by having your volunteers act as wait staff for the evening

• When you are contracting with the theater company, be sure you clarify who is responsible for paying royalties for the play that is performed.

• Your best bet is to work with a community theater. These groups are often excited by the prospect of a way to earn a little extra money and are well suited to provide the materials you need, like a good script, to make your event a success.

Variation(s)

• Increase your fundraising by coupling this event with a silent auction. Have local businesses donate auction items, and work with the theater group to offer things like singing telegrams for auction.

• Earn a little more money by having your volunteers act as wait staff for the evening. All tips, of course, are considered donations to your cause.

Wine Tasting

Your organization can toast to a successful wine tasting with finger food, live music, dancing, and an auction. Be sure to serve many varieties of vino.

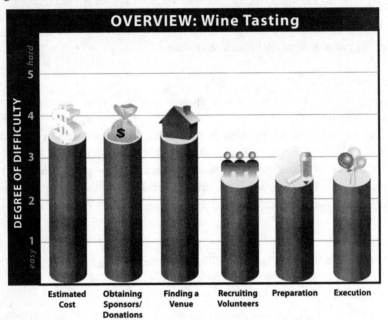

Special Materials/Equipment

- Wine
- Music
- Sound equipment (microphone, speakers)
- Wine glasses
- Finger food

Sponsors/Donations

- Find sponsors to offer items to auction or raffle, like a weekend trip to California wine country, bottles of wine, specialty cheeses, or gourmet cookbooks.
- Seek a partnership with a local wine merchant who can offer you his or her expertise and access to a good variety of wine. The merchant will get customers through you and may be able to offer you a price break on the wine. Ask to sell tickets through their store.
- Consider partnering with a small nonprofit arts organization such as a chamber music group or jazz ensemble to perform at your event.

Possible Venue(s)

A country vineyard or chateau, a garden or other scenic outdoor setting, or an atmospheric inn or lodge is perfect for this event.

Recommended Volunteer

10 to 15 or more including 5 to 7 to serve as committee heads for the venue, food, decorations, sponsors/donations, advertising, ticket sales, entertainment, setup, and cleanup. Consider having volunteers be servers and wine pourers.

Preparation

Prep Time: 4 to 6 months

1. Start with a central committee of five to seven people who will serve as committee heads for the venue, food, decorations, sponsors/donations, advertising, ticket sales, entertainment, setup, and cleanup.

2. Decide when to have the event. Before you settle on a date, find out what else is going on in your community, and avoid conflicts.

3. Determine your budget. How much are you looking to raise, and what are you willing to spend to raise that amount?

4. Start seeking sponsors and donations immediately.

5. Seek out a wine expert or two and form a partnership with a local wine merchant. Plan to have the wine experts give detailed descriptions of each featured wine while volunteers will move from table to table and pour as the wine is described.

6. Search for your perfect venue. If you have to change the date of your event to get the right venue, make sure, again, that you will have no competition from similar events that may be scheduled.

7. Four months before the event, choose your menu of hors d'oeuvres and schedule the caterer, if you decide to serve food. Assign some volunteers to float from table to table as servers and wine pourers.

8. Plan what additional fundraisers and entertainment will occur at your event. You may want a live or silent auction, raffle, or band.

9. If you plan on an outdoor event, work out a rain date or a backup plan.

10. Pick an emcee — either an organization member or a local celebrity. A celebrity can help you market the event.

11. About three months in advance, start to advertise by sending e-mails and letters, posting fliers, putting a notice on your organization's website, and making an announcement in your newsletter. Send press releases to local media outlets like newspapers and magazines, and contact local TV news and radio stations to request coverage and publicity.

12. Use the event's theme in everything from marketing, to graphic design of tickets and programs, to venue decorations.

13. Have your various committees meet regularly and keep the lines of communication open.

14. Three months out from the event, print tickets and have everyone in your organization sell tickets. Offer an incentive to the individuals who sell the most tickets.

15. If you need any special equipment, such as seating, sound, light, or stage equipment, this is a good time to reserve these items. Do this as you think about how the venue will be set up for the event.

16. Do a walk-through of the venue a month before the event to check if all the venue systems work and ask when you can get in to decorate.

17. Write a script to serve as your minute-by-minute flow of activities for the event. Plan a time to thank your sponsors and distribute information promoting your organization.

18. Hold a meeting with all event volunteers and go over the tasks and schedule. Be clear on what you expect every volunteer to do. Tell volunteers what to wear for the event. Get everyone's contact information (phone number and e-mail) in case you need to communicate any changes or reminders.

Execution

1. Come in early to decorate, set up equipment and food, and check the lighting and sound systems.

2. Have volunteers collect tickets as well as sell more tickets at the event.

3. Follow your script to carry out all planned activities.

4. Initiate cleanup at the designated end time.

You must pay extra attention to fundraisers that involve alcoholic beverages. Most states have specific laws to encourage non-profit organizations to obtain a one day special alcoholic liquor license. You must allocate sufficient time for the application of this license. In addition you will need to comply with all state laws governing the sale and dispensing of alcoholic beverages. The organization will also be required in most cases to carry an insurance rider for the sale of alcoholic beverages, this insurance will protect the organization should someone be over served, or involved in an accident of some kind. Again allow sufficient time to speak with your insurance agent and do not even try to hold the event with out the proper licensing and insurance.

Tip(s)

• Have a few volunteers on hand to act as designated drivers for guests who might need a safe lift home.

Chapter 14

Games and Contests

These events appeal to people's competitive spirits, combining contests and games with fundraising. The projects you will find in this chapter include:

- ◎ Amazing Race
- ◎ Cow-Chip Bingo
- ◎ Dart Tournament
- ◎ Quiz Show
- ◎ Scavenger Hunt
- ◎ Scrabble Tournament
- ◎ Snow/Sand Sculptures

Amazing Race

Much like the popular television show, participating teams will have to travel to several checkpoints where they will face challenges before making it to the finish line. The winning team is the team that conquers all of the challenges and arrives at a set location before any other racers. Charge a fee per team to enter the competition. For additional profits, require an individual pledge donation to your organization.

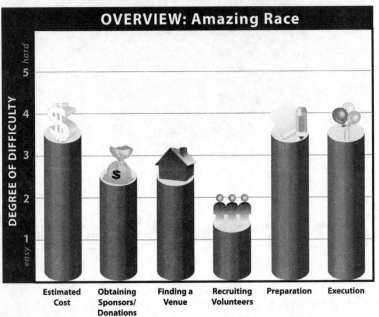

Sponsors/Donations

- Have teams gather sponsor donations as they would for a walk-a-thon or other similar events. (See the example sponsorship sheet in the back of this book).
- Seek donations for prizes for each member of the winning team.

Possible Venue(s)

You may require multiple venues that your teams will travel to in order to participate in a variety of challenges. You need a large venue like a meeting hall or a school gym as a start and finish place.

Recommended Volunteer

5 to 10 or more to handle venue(s), decorations, race rules, challenges, sign ups, judging, food, and prizes. If you travel to a variety of venues, you will need volunteers at each venue.

Preparation

Prep Time: Up to 1 year

1. Start with three to five volunteers to handle venues, race rules, challenges, sign ups, judging, food, and prizes.

2. Decide when to have the event. Before you settle on a date, find out what else is going on in your community, and avoid conflicts.

3. Determine your budget. How much are you looking to raise, and what are you willing to spend to raise that amount?

4. Start seeking sponsors and donations immediately.

5. Search for venues.

6. Determine the scope of your Amazing Race. This decision will be guided, to some extent, by the teams that will be participating. If you have teams of kids, you do not want to have hunt items that will require them to drive across town. Make sure your race and challenges are age-appropriate.

7. Create specific rules of play. Plan to have a volunteer travel with each team of racers to act as a referee.

8. Advertise by sending e-mails and letters, posting fliers, putting a notice on your organization's website, and making an announcement in your newsletter. Send press releases to local media outlets like newspapers and magazines, and contact local TV news and radio stations to request coverage and publicity.

9. Sign teams up and collect entry fees in advance.

10. Do a run-through of the race to work out any glitches in the plan.

11. Offer games, like Twister or board games, and other fundraising activities, like a raffle, that teams can participate in as they arrive back at the venue and wait for other teams to finish the race.

12. Write a script to serve as your minute-by-minute flow of activities for the event. Plan a time to thank your sponsors and distribute information promoting your organization.

13. Hold a meeting with all event volunteers and go over the tasks and schedule. Be clear on what you expect every volunteer to do. Tell volunteers what to wear for the event. Get everyone's contact information (phone number and e-mail) in case you need to communicate any changes or reminders. Spend some time just prior to the event going over the rules with the judges.

Execution

1. At the specified event time, gather the participants to hand out the first clues. Go over the rules of the race with the participants.

2. Start all racers at the same time.

3. As racers arrive at each challenge venue, have two judges monitor each team and mark their performance.

4. Run planned games and other fundraising activities.

5. At the appointed hour, award prizes.

Tip(s)

- Rules of play should be very specific to avoid discrepancies.
- Have a variety of prizes for things like "The Silliest Team" or "The Team That Traveled the Farthest."

Cow-Chip Bingo

Find a well-fed cow and a large area, such as a football field, to divide into one-square-yard portions. Sell $30 tickets that give participants a portion of the field as well as a meal. Release the cow and allow it to roam the field until it eliminates. The owner of this spot wins a prize. Raise additional profits by selling refreshments, holding raffles, and offering prizes.

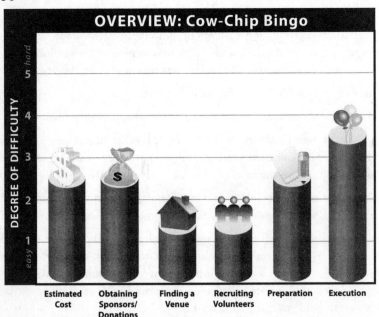

Special Materials/Equipment

- Well-fed cow
- Chalk (to grid the field)
- Fence

Sponsors/Donations
- The best sponsor for this event is a farmer or local dairy who will lend its cow.

Possible Venue(s)
Any cow-friendly and spectator-friendly place with a large field is good.

Recommended Volunteer
3 to 5 to handle the animal, ticket sales, and marking the field

Preparation
Prep Time: 1 month+

1. Put a committee together to handle the tasks of identifying the cow, the field, ticket sales, and any additional activities that may go along with your field day.

2. Decide when to have the event. Before you settle on a date, find out what else is going on in your community, and avoid conflicts.

3. Determine your budget. How much are you looking to raise, and what are you willing to spend to raise that amount?

4. Start seeking sponsors and donations immediately.

5. Search for your perfect venue. If you have to change the date of your event to get the right venue, make sure, again, that you will have no competition from similar events that may be scheduled.

6. Select what activities will occur at your event. You may want a live or silent auction, raffle, or band. Arrange for refreshments as well.

7. Advertise by sending e-mails and letters, posting fliers, putting a notice on your organization's website, and making an announcement in your newsletter. Send press releases to local media outlets like newspapers and magazines, and contact local TV news and radio stations to request coverage and publicity.

8. Use the event's theme in marketing and graphic design of tickets.

9. Print tickets and have everyone in your organization sell tickets. Offer an incentive to the individuals who sell the most tickets.

10. Plan a time to thank your sponsors and distribute information promoting your organization.

11. Hold a meeting with all event volunteers and go over the tasks and schedule. Be clear on what you expect every volunteer to do. Tell volunteers what to wear for the event. Get everyone's contact information (phone number and e-mail) in case you need to communicate any changes or reminders.

Execution

1. Arrive early to set up.

2. Have volunteers collect tickets as well as sell more tickets at the event.

3. Carry out all planned activities.

4. Initiate cleanup at the designated end time.

Tip(s)

- Be sure to make clear rules to determine the outcome of the bingo event.
- This is a good fundraising event for schools.
- This is an event that does well combined with another event, such as a field day party or picnic.

Dart Tournament

For an entry fee, participants can compete in games of darts. Have local bars, pubs, or clubs organize teams for the event.

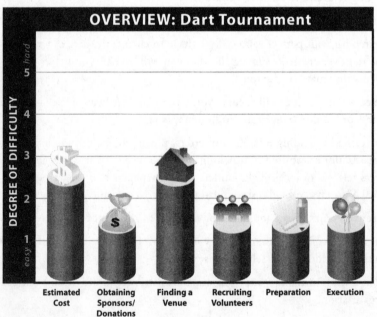

Special Materials/Equipment

- Dart boards
- Darts

Sponsors/Donations

- Ask a venue to host your organization for an evening. Generally, you will charge an admission to the bar and a fee or sponsorship of the gamers. The bar will take the alcohol sales. You can make other arrangements with the bar, but you have to make it attractive to them, as well. If you plan your event for a night that is considered an off night for the bar, such as a Monday or Tuesday, and you can guarantee them a full house of your supporters, they should be more than happy to do the event for the sales at the bar.
- In addition to charging an entry fee at the door, have gamers collect pledges and ask for sponsorships. (See the sample pledge forms in the back of this book.)
- Try to get a local beer distributor to sponsor the event.

Possible Venue(s)

A bar, club, hotel, restaurant, school, church, or any venue equipped for a darts tournament works, especially one that is already set up with dart boards.

Recommended Volunteer

1 if you plan it at an outfitted bar. If you choose to do it at a location not set up such an event, you will need a small committee of 3 to 5 to handle venue, hospitality, marketing, and games.

Preparation

Prep Time: 2 months+

1. Decide when to have the event. Before you settle on a date, find out what else is going on in your community, and avoid conflicts.

2. Determine your budget. How much are you looking to raise, and what are you willing to spend to raise that amount?

3. Start seeking sponsors and donations immediately.

4. Search for your perfect venue. If you have to change the date of your event to get the right venue, make sure, again, that you will have no competition from similar events that may be scheduled.

5. Select what additional activities will occur at your event. You may want a live or silent auction, raffle, or band.

6. Plan for an attractive prize for the tournament winner(s). Consider having several different classes of competition.

7. About a month before your event, advertise by sending e-mails and letters, posting fliers, putting a notice on your organization's website, and making an announcement in your newsletter. Send press releases to local media outlets like newspapers and magazines, and contact local TV news and radio stations to request coverage and publicity. Put an ad in the sports section of your local newspaper, and be sure to flier bars, especially ones with darts.

8. Use the event's theme in everything from marketing, to graphic design of tickets and programs, to venue decorations.

9. Print tickets and have everyone in your organization sell them. Offer an incentive to the individuals who sell the most tickets.

10. Plan a time to thank your sponsors and distribute information about your organization.

11. Hold a meeting with all event volunteers and go over the tasks and schedule. Be clear on what you expect every volunteer to do. Tell volunteers what to wear for the event. Get everyone's contact information (phone number and e-mail) in case you need to communicate any changes or reminders.

12. Make sure that all involved in the tournament are clear on the rules of play. Have printed copies available, and read them aloud just prior to play.

Execution

1. Come in early to set up.

2. Have volunteers collect tickets as well as sell more tickets at the event.

3. Carry out the tournament and other designated activities, award prizes, and give your organization's pitch.

4. Initiate cleanup at the designated end time.

Variation(s)

- Host a Foosball Tournament.
- Try an Air Hockey Tournament.
- Have a Pinball Tournament.

Quiz Show

Smarties will flock to this fun competition to prove their knowledge in a friendly setting.

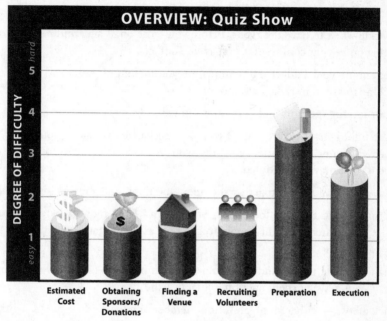

Special Materials/Equipment

- List of quiz questions and answers
- Lighting
- Sound equipment (microphone, speakers)
- Stage
- Table and chairs

Sponsors/Donations

- Find local businesses to donate their services and items to serve as door prizes for the event.
- An ideal sponsor for such an event is a media sponsor, like a local radio station that could get the word out about the event and provide an emcee.

Possible Venue(s)

A location with a stage, adequate stage lighting, and an in-house sound system is best. Consider a local community theater, a banquet hall, or a large meeting room at a hotel.

Recommended Volunteer

5+ for the venue, sponsors/donations, advertising, ticket sales, host, and quiz questions

Preparation

Prep Time: 3 months to 1 year

1. Start with a central committee of five people who will serve as committee heads for the venue, sponsors/donations, advertising, ticket sales, quiz questions, rules, and setup.

2. Decide when to have the event. Before you settle on a date, find out what else is going on in your community, and avoid conflicts.

3. Determine your budget. How much are you looking to raise, and what are you willing to spend to raise that amount?

4. Start seeking sponsors and donations immediately.

5. Search for your perfect venue. If you have to change the date of your event to get the right venue, make sure, again, that you will have no competition from similar events that may be scheduled.

6. Have a committee put together the rules, questions, and answers for the quiz.

7. If you decide to serve food, plan your menu. Four months before the event, schedule a caterer, recruit people to cook, or ask restaurants or grocery stores to donate food.

8. Plan what additional fundraisers and entertainment will occur at your event. You may want a live or silent auction, raffle, or band.

9. Pick a host — either an organization member or a local celebrity. A celebrity can help you market the event.

10. Advertise by sending e-mails and letters, posting fliers, putting a notice on your organization's website, and making an announcement in your newsletter. Send press releases to local media outlets like newspapers and magazines, and contact local TV news and radio stations to request coverage and publicity.

11. Use the event's theme in everything from marketing, to graphic design of tickets and programs, to venue decorations.

12. Have your various committees meet regularly and keep the lines of communication open.

13. Three months out from the event, print tickets and have everyone in your organization sell tickets. Offer an incentive to the individuals who sell the most tickets.

14. If you need any special equipment, such as seating, sound, light, or stage equipment, this is a good time to reserve these items. Do this as you think about how the venue will be set up for the event.

15. Do a walk-through of the venue a month before the event to check if all the venue systems work and ask when you can you get in to decorate.

16. Write a script to serve as your minute-by-minute flow of activities for the event. Plan a time to thank your sponsors and distribute information promoting your organization.

17. Hold a meeting with all event volunteers and go over the tasks and schedule. Be clear on what you expect every volunteer to do. Tell volunteers what to wear for the event. Get everyone's contact information (phone number and e-mail) in case you need to communicate any changes or reminders.

Execution

1. Come in early to decorate, set up equipment and food, and check the lighting and sound systems.

2. Have volunteers collect tickets as well as sell more tickets at the event.

3. Follow your script to carry out all planned activities.

4. Initiate cleanup at the designated end time.

Tip(s)

• Make sure the rules are clear in order to avoid discrepancies.
• Double-check the answers to your quiz questions to ensure validity.

Scavenger Hunt

Send participating groups on an unforgettable adventure race across town with a list of items and a limited amount of time; charge a sign-up fee to make money for your organization. Everyone can regroup at the end and wait for you to announce the winners. This is a great fundraising event for a church, school, or civic organization.

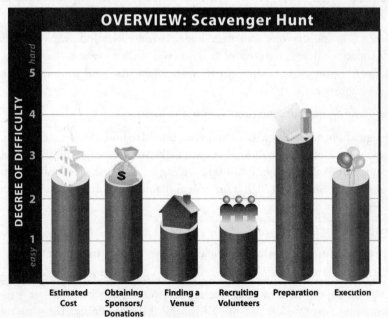

Sponsors/Donations

- Seek food donors if you plan to serve food at the post-hunt gathering.
- Have teams gather sponsor donations as they would for a walk-a-thon or other similar event. (See the example sponsorship sheet in the back of this book.)
- Seek donations for prizes for the winners. Remember to secure multiple prizes to accommodate all members of the winning team.

Possible Venue(s)

A meeting hall, a school gym, or any place where a large crowd can gather works well.

Recommended Volunteer

10+ including 5 to 7 committee heads to handle the venue, prizes, scavenger hunt rules and lists, setup, participation, food, advertising, and judging

Preparation

Prep Time: 1 to 3 months

1. Start with a central committee of five to seven people who will serve as committee heads for the venue, prizes, scavenger hunt rules and lists, setup, participation, food, advertising, and judging.

2. Decide when to have the event. Before you settle on a date, find out what else is going on in your community, and avoid conflicts.

3. Determine your budget. How much are you looking to raise, and what are you willing to spend to raise that amount?

4. Plan the scope of your scavenger hunt, bearing in mind who will likely be participating. If you have teams of kids, you do not want to have hunt items that will require them to drive across town. Make sure your scavenger hunt list is age-appropriate.

5. Start seeking sponsors and donations immediately.

6. Design a hunt and create a list of items teams need to find with detailed instructions about what is and is not allowed. As you make your scavenger hunt list, give each item a point value. Assign items that are easy to find low point values and items that are difficult to find high point values. Point values make the teams consider different strategies of play.

7. Search for venues.

8. Choose an entrance fee that participating teams will pay to register.

9. Create specific rules of play. Indicate that each team must return to the designated venue by a specified time, and that anyone who returns late will lose points for each minute they are late or will be disqualified from winning. The winning team

is the team that returns by the specified time and has the most items on the list. If there is a tie, the winning team is the one that has the most items and returned to the specified venue in the least amount of time.

10. Assign some volunteers to be judges. Be sure that your team of judges understands the rules of the competition. Spend some time just prior to the event going over the rules with the judges.

11. Plan on games that can be played and snacks that can be served as teams arrive back at the venue and wait for other teams to arrive.

12. Advertise by sending e-mails and letters, posting fliers, putting a notice on your organization's website, and making an announcement in your newsletter. Send press releases to local media outlets like newspapers and magazines, and contact local TV news and radio stations to request coverage and publicity.

13. Have your various committees meet regularly and keep the lines of communication open.

14. Do a run-through of the scavenger hunt within the week before the event to make sure all items are still attainable.

15. Plan a time to thank your sponsors and distribute information promoting your organization.

16. Hold a meeting with all event volunteers and go over the tasks and schedule. Be clear on what you expect every volunteer to do. Tell volunteers what to wear for the event. Get everyone's contact information (phone number and e-mail) in case you need to communicate any changes or reminders.

Execution

1. Gather the participants to hand out the scavenger hunt lists, and go over the rules.

2. Start your timer and begin the race.

3. As hunters return to the venue, two judges should mark each team's return time, go over their findings, and determine their scores.

4. Have volunteers run game stations and serve food as teams wait for everyone to arrive.

5. At the appointed hour, announce the winners and award prizes.

Tip(s)

- Make rules of play clear and specific to avoid discrepancies.
- Have a variety of prizes for things like "The Silliest Team," "The Team That Traveled the Farthest," or "The Youngest/Oldest Team." It is always fun to have many winners.

Scrabble Tournament

Participants can have a blast playing with words at a fundraising scrabble tournament. Teams of four, six, or eight will be provided a scrabble board and letters. Start each group with the same word, and give them 20 minutes to fill the board up with their own words. A judge will be present at every table, and players who need extra help can donate money to glance at a dictionary. Charge an entry fee for each player in the tournament. Sell concessions or hold a raffle to make extra profits.

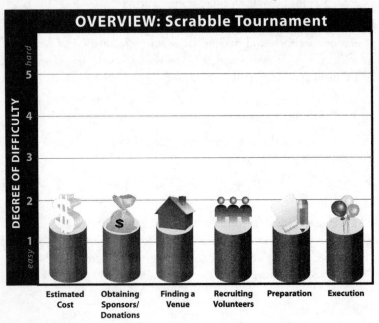

Special Materials/Equipment

- Scrabble games
- Tables and chairs

Sponsors/Donations

- A toy store, game store, or large department store that sells games might be a good sponsor for this event. Ideally, you can get your games donated.
- Find a venue to host the event. For a place like a pub, generally, you will collect an admission fee and a sponsorship fee for gamers, and the pub will take the alcohol sales. If you plan your event for a night that is considered and "off night" for the facility, such as a Monday or Tuesday, and you can guarantee them a full house of your supporters, they will likely be glad to do the event for the sales at the bar.
- You can also have gamers collect pledges. (See the sample pledge forms in the back of this book.)

Possible Venue(s)

Consider holding this event at a hotel, restaurant, school, church, pub, or other venue that can accommodate your players.

Recommended Volunteer

5+ to handle the venue, sponsors/donations, advertising, ticket sales, and to moderate games

Preparation

Prep Time: 2 months

1. Start with two to four people who will serve as committee heads for the venue, sponsors/donations, advertising, ticket sales, and games.

2. Decide when to have the event. Before you settle on a date, find out what else is going on in your community, and avoid conflicts.

3. Determine your budget. How much are you looking to raise, and what are you willing to spend to raise that amount?

4. Start seeking sponsors and donations immediately.

5. Book your venue.

6. Choose your menu and schedule the caterer, if you decide to serve food.

7. Select what additional activities will occur at your event. You may want a live or silent auction or a raffle.

8. Plan for an attractive prize for the tournament winner(s). Consider having several different classes of competition.

9. One month prior to your event, advertise by sending e-mails and letters, posting fliers, putting a notice on your organization's website, and making an announcement in your newsletter. Send press releases to local media outlets like newspapers and magazines, and contact local TV news and radio stations to request coverage and publicity.

10. Use the event's theme in everything from marketing, to graphic design of tickets and programs, to venue decorations.

11. Have your various committees meet regularly and keep the lines of communication open.

12. Three months out from the event, print tickets and have everyone in your organization sell tickets. Offer an incentive to the individuals who sell the most tickets.

13. If you need any special equipment, such as seating, sound, light, or stage equipment, this is a good time to reserve these items. Do this as you think about how the venue will be set up for the event.

14. Do a walk-through of the venue a month before the event to check if all the venue systems work and ask when you can get in to decorate.

15. Write a script to serve as your minute-by-minute flow of activities for the event. Plan a time to thank your sponsors and distribute information promoting your organization.

16. Hold a meeting with all event volunteers and go over the tasks and schedule. Be clear on what you expect every volunteer to do. Tell volunteers what to wear for the event. Get everyone's contact information (phone number and e-mail) in case you need to communicate any changes or reminders. Make sure that all involved in the tournament are clear on the rules of play. Have them in print form and plan to read them aloud to participants just prior to play. Appoint volunteer judges to monitor the games and settle disputes.

Execution

1. Come in early to set up.

2. Have volunteers collect tickets as well as sell more tickets at the event.

3. Follow your script to carry out all planned activities.

4. Initiate cleanup at the designated end time.

Variation(s)

- Hold a Monopoly Tournament.
- Have an Uno Tournament.
- Host a Boggle Tournament.

Snow/Sand Sculptures

Fancy snow or sand sculptures always catch the eyes of passersby. Find an expert sculptor who can create something attention-grabbing in a highly-trafficked public place. People will be eager to meet the individual and learn a few tips on his or her skill. Allow teams or individuals to participate, and set an entrance fee.

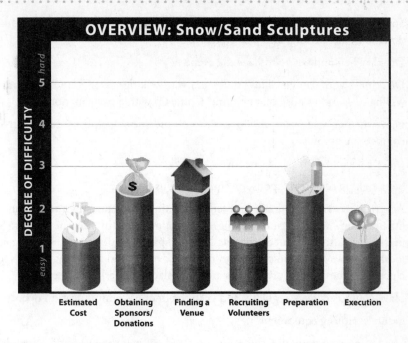

OVERVIEW: Snow/Sand Sculptures

DEGREE OF DIFFICULTY — 5 hard, easy

Estimated Cost · Obtaining Sponsors/Donations · Finding a Venue · Recruiting Volunteers · Preparation · Execution

Special Materials/Equipment

- Sand or snow
- Shovels and other sculpting tools

Sponsors/Donations

- Participants can seek sponsors for their work in the same manner that they might for a walk-a-thon or other similar events. (See the example sponsorship sheet in the back of this book.)
- Your organization can seek sculptors to offer their time and services for a sculpting workshop.

Possible Venue(s)

The beach is great for sand sculptures, and a large parking lot works well for snow sculptures. A park is a fine place for smaller sculptures.

Recommended Volunteer

5+ to serve as committee heads for the venue, sponsors/donations, advertising, and participation

Preparation

Prep Time: 3 to 4 months

1. Start with a committee of three to five volunteers to handle the venue, sponsors/donations, advertising, and participation.

2. Decide when and where to have the event.

3. Determine your budget. How much are you looking to raise, and what are you willing to spend to raise that amount? Come up with a participation fee.

4. Plan whether you want to do a simple sand/snow-sculpting exhibition or a competitive event.

5. Make a backup plan in case bad weather strikes.

6. Start seeking sculptors, sponsors, and donations immediately.

7. Advertise by sending e-mails and letters, posting fliers, putting a notice on your organization's website, and making an announcement in your newsletter. Send press releases to local media outlets like newspapers and magazines, and contact local TV news and radio stations to request coverage and publicity. Schools, civic clubs, churches, and youth centers are good places to market your event.

8. Have volunteers meet regularly and keep the lines of communication open.

9. Secure sculpting equipment.

10. Hold a meeting with all event volunteers and go over the tasks and schedule. Be clear on what you expect every volunteer to do. Tell volunteers what to wear for the event. Get everyone's contact information (phone number and e-mail) in case you need to communicate any changes or reminders.

Execution

1. Arrive early to set up.

2. Sign participants up and watch them sculpt away.

3. Have a few volunteer judges determine winners, if you choose.

4. Initiate cleanup at the designated end time.

Tip(s)

- If you are in a snowy climate and are considering doing large-scale snow sculptures, talk to the local authorities about bringing snow cleared from city streets to your location for the event. By providing this much extra snow, you can promote the possibility of building giant sculptures.

Variation(s)

- Turn the event into a summer/winter carnival by adding games and other activities you can charge people to participate in.
- Hold a silent auction or raffle at your event to increase your ability to raise funds. A good auction/raffle item for a snow-sculpting event is a vacation to a warm and sunny climate.

Chapter 15

Holidays and Special Occasions

Holidays and special events call for celebrations, and what better combination than a celebration for a cause? The projects you will find in this chapter include:

- ๏ Birthday Banquet
- ๏ Bloody Halloween Banquet
- ๏ "Hats Off to Mom" Tea Party
- ๏ Holiday Carnival
- ๏ Oscar Party
- ๏ Pumpkin Fest
- ๏ White Wonderland Gift Exchange

- ๏ Black and Orange Ball
- ๏ Christmas Tree Sale
- ๏ Holiday Card Mailings
- ๏ Mardi Gras Party
- ๏ Parent Appreciation Banquet
- ๏ "Soup"er Bowl Sale

Birthday Banquet

Your organization can offer to throw a birthday bash for a regular supporter or donor. Set the theme for the event around the person's favorite hobby, movie, or other interest. Charge a fee to cover general admission and dinner expenses. Food and drinks can also focus on the theme chosen by the birthday honoree.

Special Materials/Equipment

- Banquet tables
- Chairs
- Sound equipment (microphone, speakers)
- Specialty lighting

Sponsors/Donations

- The best donation that you might possibly get is that of a venue.

Possible Venue(s)

If you are having this as a school fundraiser, consider having the event in the school gymnasium. If the event is for your church, and you can the event in the social hall in your building. If you want to go all out for this event, consider having it at an upscale hotel in your community or any venue with a fancy banquet room.

Recommended Volunteer

10+ including 5 to 7 to serve as committee heads for the venue, food, decorations, sponsors/donations, advertising, ticket sales, entertainment, setup, and cleanup

Preparation
Prep Time: 6 months to1 year

1. Start with a central committee of five to seven people who will serve as committee heads for the venue, food, decorations, sponsors/donations, advertising, ticket sales, entertainment, and setup and cleanup.

2. Decide when to have the event. Before you settle on a date, find out what else is going on in your community, and avoid conflicts.

3. Determine your budget. How much are you looking to raise, and what are you willing to spend to raise that amount?

4. Search for your perfect venue. If you have to change the date of your event to get the right venue, make sure, again, that you will have no competition from similar events that may be scheduled.

5. If you decide to serve food, plan your menu. Four months before the event, schedule a caterer, recruit people to cook, or ask restaurants or grocery stores to donate food.

6. Select what activities will occur at your event. You may want a live or silent auction, raffle, or band. Because your basic purpose (beyond raising money) is to recognize a birthday, decide how you will recognize and appreciate the honoree(s) in attendance. You may have a gift presentation ceremony of some kind.

7. Pick an emcee — either an organization member or a local celebrity. A celebrity can help you market the event.

8. Advertise by sending e-mails and letters, posting fliers, putting a notice on your organization's website, and making an announcement in your newsletter. Send press releases to local media outlets like newspapers and magazines, and contact local TV news and radio stations to request coverage and publicity.

9. Use the event's theme in everything from marketing, to graphic design of tickets and programs, to venue decorations.

10. Have your various committees meet regularly and keep the lines of communication open.

11. Three months out from the event, print tickets and have everyone in your organization sell tickets. Offer an incentive to the individuals who sell the most tickets.

12. If you need any special equipment such as sound, lights, staging, or seating, this is a good time to reserve these items. Do this as you think about how the venue will be set up for the event.

13. Do a walk-through of the venue a month before the event to check if all the venue systems work and ask when you can get in to decorate.

14. Write a script to serve as your minute-by-minute flow of activities for the event. Plan a time to thank your sponsors and distribute information promoting your organization.

15. Hold a meeting with all event volunteers and go over the tasks and schedule. Be clear on what you expect every volunteer to do. Tell volunteers what to wear for the event. Get everyone's contact information (phone number and e-mail) in case you need to communicate any changes or reminders.

Execution

1. Come in early to decorate, set up equipment and food, and check the lighting and sound systems.

2. Have volunteers collect tickets as well as sell more tickets at the event.

3. Follow your script to carry out all planned activities.

4. Initiate cleanup at the designated end time.

Variation(s)

- Celebrate the anniversary of a company, a big accomplishment, or a couple at an Anniversary Banquet.
- Gather people and their fury friends for a Pets Birthday Banquet.

Black and Orange Ball

Celebrate Halloween with an elegant evening at which guests can dance in their finest black and orange attire. Charge an admission fee. Buy or create black and orange invitations, decorations, and party favors.

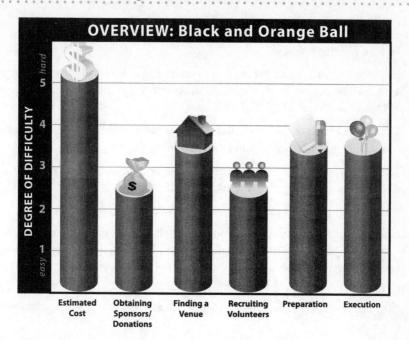

Special Materials/Equipment

- Black and orange decorations
- Sound system
- Dance floor
- Music

Sponsors/Donations

- Consider asking a major supporter to sponsor the entire event, or at least to cover the cost of the venue.
- You can also seek sponsors for tables. A sponsor might purchase a table that seat 10 for dinner. The sponsor might then give the tickets to employees, friends, or family.
- If you have a silent auction or raffle, you can also have sponsors donate big-ticket items to auction or raffle such as trips, large electronics, or jewelry.

Possible Venue(s)

Nice hotels are great places for such balls because they can usually handle the catering and provide an in-house sound system, lighting, and large ballrooms that accommodate many people. Unusual locations, like large old houses or inns, are also fitting.

Recommended Volunteer

10 to 15 or more including 5 to 7 to handle the venue, food, decorations, sponsors/donations, advertising, ticket sales, entertainment, setup, and cleanup

Preparation

Prep Time: 6 months to1 year

1. Start with a central committee of five to seven people who will serve as committee heads for the venue, food, decorations, sponsors/donations, advertising, ticket sales, entertainment, setup, and cleanup.

2. Decide when to have the event. Before you settle on a date, find out what else is going on in your community, and avoid conflicts.

3. Determine your budget. How much are you looking to raise, and what are you willing to spend to raise that amount?

4. Start seeking sponsors and donations immediately.

5. Search for your perfect venue. If you have to change the date of your event to get the right venue, make sure, again, that you will have no competition from similar events that may be scheduled.

6. If you decide to serve food, plan your menu. Four months before the event, schedule a caterer, recruit people to cook, or ask restaurants or grocery stores to donate food.

7. Select what activities will occur at your event. You may want a live or silent auction, raffle, or band.

8. Pick an emcee — either an organization member or a local celebrity. A celebrity can help you market the event.

9. Advertise by sending e-mails and letters, posting fliers, putting a notice on your organization's website, and making an announcement in your newsletter. Send press releases to local media outlets like newspapers and magazines, and contact local TV news and radio stations to request coverage and publicity.

10. Use the event's theme in everything from marketing, to graphic design of tickets and programs, to venue decorations.

11. Have your various committees meet regularly and keep the lines of communication open.

12. Three months out from the event, print tickets and have everyone in your organization sell tickets. Offer an incentive to the individuals who sell the most tickets.

13. If you need any special equipment such as sound, lights, staging, or seating, this is a good time to reserve these items. Do this as you think about how the venue will be set up for the event.

14. Do a walk-through of the venue a month before the event to check if all the venue systems work and ask when you can get in to decorate.

15. Write a script to serve as your minute-by-minute flow of activities for the event. Plan a time to thank your sponsors and distribute information promoting your organization.

16. Hold a meeting with all event volunteers and go over the tasks and schedule. Be clear on what you expect every volunteer to do. Tell volunteers what to wear for the event. Get everyone's contact information (phone number and e-mail) in case you need to communicate any changes or reminders.

Execution

1. Come in early to decorate, set up equipment and food, and check the lighting and sound systems.

2. Have volunteers collect tickets as well as sell more tickets at the event.

3. Follow your script to carry out all planned activities.

4. Initiate cleanup at the designated end time.

Bloody Halloween Banquet

This bloody gathering will be sure to intrigue Halloween enthusiasts willing to support your cause. Put up Halloween decorations covered in fake blood, and serve blood-red drinks. Charge an admission fee.

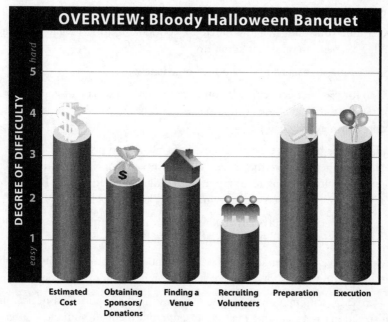

Special Materials/Equipment

• Bloody-looking Halloween decorations

Sponsors/Donations

- Local theaters and performing arts organizations are great places to seek donations of costumes and props for this event.
- Theatrical prop companies are also good places to locate supplies for the event.

Possible Venue(s)

Large old churches, community buildings, or schools might be suitable.

Recommended Volunteer

10 to 15+ including 5 to 7 to serve as committee heads for the venue, food, decorations, sponsors/donations, advertising, ticket sales, entertainment, setup, and cleanup

Preparation

Prep Time: 6 months to 1 year

1. Start with a central committee of five to seven people who will serve as committee heads for the venue, food, decorations, sponsors/donations, advertising, ticket sales, entertainment, setup, and cleanup.

2. Decide when to have the event. Before you settle on a date, find out what else is going on in your community, and avoid conflicts.

3. Determine your budget. How much are you looking to raise, and what are you willing to spend to raise that amount?

4. Start seeking sponsors and donations immediately.

5. Search for your perfect venue. If you have to change the date of your event to get the right venue, make sure, again, that you will have no competition from similar events that may be scheduled.

6. Four months before the event, choose your menu and be creative in connecting it with the theme. Have the caterer work with your ideas, if you decide to use a caterer. Consider serving a variety of unidentifiable meats, beets, Bloody Marys, cranberry juice, strawberry ice-cream, and red Jell-O molds.

7. Select what activities will occur at your event. You may want a live or silent auction, or raffle. Consider having a live band or DJ and dancing.

8. Pick an emcee — either an organization member or a local celebrity — and have him or her dress up as Dracula. A celebrity can help you market the event.

9. Advertise by sending e-mails and letters, posting fliers, putting a notice on your organization's website, and making an announcement in your newsletter. Send press releases to local media outlets like newspapers and magazines, and contact local TV news and radio stations to request coverage and publicity.

10. Use the event's theme in everything from marketing, to graphic design of tickets and programs, to venue decorations.

11. Have your various committees meet regularly and keep the lines of communication open.

12. Three months out from the event, print tickets and have everyone in your organization sell tickets. Offer an incentive to the individuals who sell the most tickets.

13. If you need any special equipment such as sound, lights, staging, or seating, this is a good time to reserve these items. Do this as you think about how the venue will be set up for the event.

14. Do a walk-through of the venue a month before the event to check if all the venue systems work and ask when you can get in to decorate.

15. Write a script to serve as your minute-by-minute flow of activities for the event. Plan a time to thank your sponsors and distribute information promoting your organization.

16. Hold a meeting with all event volunteers and go over the tasks and schedule. Be clear on what you expect every volunteer to do. Tell volunteers what to wear for the event. Get everyone's contact information (phone number and e-mail) in case you need to communicate any changes or reminders.

Execution

1. Come in early to decorate, set up equipment and food, and check the lighting and sound systems.

2. Have volunteers collect tickets as well as sell more tickets at the event.

3. Follow your script to carry out all planned activities.

4. Initiate cleanup at the designated end time.

Tip(s)

- Hold a costume contest at the banquet, and encourage people to dress up as vampires, bloody butchers, bloody brides, bloody mimes, etc. Give prizes for the best and bloodiest costumes.
- Play a horror/slasher movie to further set the mood. "Dracula" and "Halloween" are classic choices, and "Texas Chainsaw Massacre" and "Saw" will amp up the gore. "The Addams Family" is a more child-friendly choice.

Christmas Tree Sale

Set up a colorfully lit, festive lot and offer a variety of healthy trees and wreaths for sale. Profit from these big purchases and the tips that come from cutting the trees and loading them into customers' vehicles. Play Christmas music to get everyone in the holiday spirit, and sell Christmas cookies and hot chocolate for extra profit.

Special Materials/Equipment

- Tent
- Tree stands
- Christmas lights
- Chainsaw (to cut bases of trees)
- Netting, rope, razor etc. (to package trees)
- Giant sign (to make it easy to read from the road)

- Christmas trees
- Outdoor lighting
- Christmas music

Sponsors/Donations

- Try to find tree farmers who are willing to donate trees or sell them at a reduced price to support your cause.
- Ask stores that sell tree stands if they will donate stands or sell them at a reduced price.

Possible Venue(s)

A supermarket parking lot, your organization's lot, or a space bordering a main road is great to catch drivers who are on the hunt for a tree.

Recommended Volunteer

15 to 20+ to unload trees, set them up in stands, water them, set up the tent and decorations, handle sales, and load trees into vehicles. You will need several strong people to handle the labor.

Preparation

Prep Time: 6 months

1. In late summer or early fall, start planning by forming a central committee of five to seven people to be in charge of the venue, decorations, sponsors/donations, advertising, trees, pricing/sales, setup, labor, and cleanup.

2. Determine your budget. How much are you looking to raise, and what are you willing to spend to raise that amount?

3. Start seeking sponsors and donations immediately.

4. Contact local tree farmers immediately. For assistance, try the Department of Agriculture and Forestry. Get price quotes from about four tree farmers, and choose the one that fits your budget best. Nicer trees will sell for more money than crooked or less healthy ones. To make a nice profit, consider charging about twice as much as you paid for them.

5. Find a venue, and clear your location with your city planning or zoning office.

6. Decide when you will open your lot for sales (November or December), and what your hours will be. Create a schedule to make sure there are at least three volunteers there at all times.

7. Plan any other fundraisers you would like to have on the site, such as selling hot chocolate, cookies, or even handmade ornaments.

8. Starting in November, advertise by sending e-mails and letters, posting fliers, putting a notice on your organization's website, and making an announcement in your newsletter. Send press releases to local media outlets like newspapers and magazines, and contact local TV news and radio stations to request coverage and publicity.

9. Have your various committees meet regularly and keep the lines of communication open.

10. Secure any special materials and equipment you will need. Do a walk-through of the venue a month before the event. Locate your lot's electrical sources for lighting and the chainsaw. You may need extension cords.

11. Prepare ways to accept a variety of payments, like credit cards, checks and cash.

12. Hold a meeting with all event volunteers and go over the tasks and schedule. Be clear on what you expect every volunteer to do. Tell volunteers what to wear for the event. Get everyone's contact information (phone number and e-mail) in case you need to communicate any changes or reminders.

Execution

1. Come in early to decorate, set up trees, equipment and food, and check the lighting and sound systems.

2. Have volunteers sell trees and carry out all planned activities.

3. Initiate cleanup at the designated end time.

Tip(s)
- Put lights on your sign to ensure that your lot is visible to shoppers at night.
- Advertise free hot chocolate to get more people in.
- Sell hand-made ornaments for additional profit.

Variation(s)
- Offer a service picking up old Christmas trees for a set fee or donation. Advertise with fliers at tree lots, shopping centers, and neighborhoods throughout December and early January.

"Hats Off to Mom" Tea Party

Mothers and daughters will enjoy a delightful and dainty afternoon wearing hats and gloves, eating finger sandwiches, and sipping tea from fancy tea sets. Put a box of fun craft supplies on each table, and have guests make their own hats to model at the end. Set up a photo booth, and sell mother-daughter photos to guests.

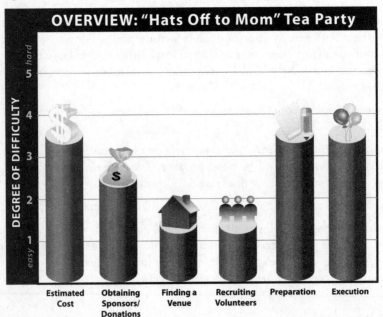

Special Materials/Equipment

- Basic straw hats
- Banquet tables and chairs
- Hat decorations (scarves, ribbons, feathers, fake flowers, tissue paper, streamers)
- Tea and tea sets
- Sound system (microphone, speakers)

Sponsors/Donations

- If there is a hat shop in your community, this could be your best sponsor.
- Find a venue to lend their facility for free.
- Contact local craft stores for donations of decorations.
- Consider partnering with a small nonprofit arts organization, such as a chamber music group or jazz ensemble to perform at your event.

Possible Venue(s)

A nice upscale hotel with comfortable meeting and/or banquet facilities is ideal. Also, an upscale restaurant or country club could be nice.

Recommended Volunteer

10 to 15+ to organize the overall event, and take part in the decorations committee, food and beverage committee, the entertainment committee, and the marketing and ticket committee

Preparation

Prep Time: 4 months to 6 months

1. Start with a central committee of five to seven people who will serve as committee heads for the venue, food, decorations, sponsors/donations, advertising, ticket sales, entertainment, setup and cleanup.

2. Decide when to have the event. This is an event that can happen over a brunch, lunch, or in the mid-afternoon. Before you settle on a date, find out what else is going on in your community, and avoid conflicts.

3. Determine your budget. How much are you looking to raise, and what are you willing to spend to raise that amount?

4. Start seeking sponsors and donations immediately.

5. Search for your perfect venue. If you have to change the date of your event to get the right venue, make sure, again, that you will have no competition from similar events that may be scheduled.

6. If you decide to serve food, plan your menu. Four months before the event, schedule a caterer, recruit people to cook, or ask restaurants or grocery stores to donate food.

7. Select what activities will occur at your event. You may want a live or silent auction, raffle, or jazz band in addition to decorating hats, taking photos, and serving tea.

8. Pick an emcee — either an organization member or a local celebrity. A celebrity can help you market the event.

9. Advertise by sending e-mails and letters, posting fliers, putting a notice on your organization's website, and making an announcement in your newsletter. Send press releases to local media outlets like newspapers and magazines, and contact local TV news and radio stations to request coverage and publicity.

10. Use the event's theme in everything from marketing, to graphic design of tickets and programs, to venue decorations.

11. Have your various committees meet regularly and keep the lines of communication open.

12. Three months out from the event, print tickets and have everyone in your organization sell tickets. Offer an incentive to the individuals who sell the most tickets.

13. If you need any special equipment, such as seating, sound, light, or stage equipment, this is a good time to reserve these items. Do this as you think about how the venue will be set up for the event.

14. Do a walk-through of the venue a month before the event to check if all the venue systems work and ask when you can get in to decorate.

15. Write a script to serve as your minute-by-minute flow of activities for the event. Plan a time to thank your sponsors and distribute information promoting your organization.

16. Hold a meeting with all event volunteers and go over the tasks and schedule. Be clear on what you expect every volunteer to do. Tell volunteers what to wear for the event. Get everyone's contact information (phone number and e-mail) in case you need to communicate any changes or reminders.

Execution

1. Come in early to decorate, set up equipment and food, and check the lighting and sound systems.

2. Have volunteers collect tickets as well as sell more tickets at the event.

3. Follow your script to carry out all planned activities.

4. Initiate cleanup at the designated end time.

Tip(s)

- Schedule this event around Mother's Day.

Variation(s)

- Have a Mother-Daughter Spa Day.

- Have a father-son event, like a sailing, golfing, or fishing tournament.

Holiday Card Mailings

While everyone is in the spirit of giving, wish them happy holidays and make it easy for them to give your organization a gift in return. Enclose a donation card and no-postage-necessary envelopes. Send them early so you are one of the first to ask for donations.

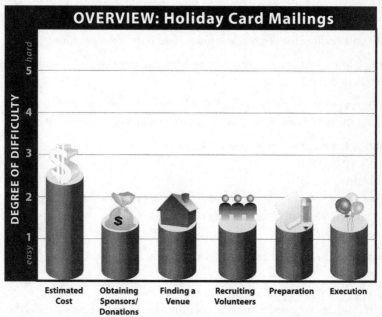

OVERVIEW: Holiday Card Mailings

DEGREE OF DIFFICULTY (easy → hard), scale 1 to 5

- Estimated Cost
- Obtaining Sponsors/Donations
- Finding a Venue
- Recruiting Volunteers
- Preparation
- Execution

Special Materials/Equipment
- Card paper
- No-postage-necessary return envelops
- Address labels (unless you plan to print the information directly on the envelop)
- Envelopes

Sponsors/Donations
- A local hobby or craft store is the ideal sponsor for such an event.

Possible Venue(s)
You can make these in a spacious, empty room (i.e. the break room or conference room) at your organization's office where it is OK if you make a bit of a mess.

Recommended Volunteer
5 to 10 to assemble and mail the cards

Preparation
Prep Time: 2 months

1. Decide how you would like to produce your cards, and who will produce them.

2. Choose when and where you will meet.

3. Determine and gather the materials you will need to have on hand. You can choose to have very labor intensive hand-made cards, with every card being an individual "masterpiece," or you can have cards that are designed by the artist on a computer and mass produced with a printer.

4. Obtain a mailing list of previous donors and potential new donor.

5. Print address labels and return address labels, or print this information directly on the envelope.

6. Print simple donation cards that include boxes the donors can check based on the amount they would like to donate as well as donor information lines.

7. Obtain the no-purchase-necessary return envelopes.

Execution

1. Throw a card making party at which you make the cards, address the envelops, and stuff the envelops with the greeting card, donation card, and no-postage-necessary return envelop.

2. Drop them in the mail and wait for the donations to come in.

Tip(s)

- To maximize efficiency, form assembly lines in which one person puts the address labels on the envelope, one stuffs the envelope, and one seals it.
- You can do this event for any kind of holiday or event that people send cards on, but the big payday will come as you approach Christmas.

Variation(s)

- Instead of sending the traditional, store-bought cards, you can make yours stand out by making them. You could have an event or two leading up to the mailing where families, groups, etc. are invited to craft cards with the aid of instructors. Ask volunteers to bring their own scissors, glue, and other craft supplies, if needed, to make the process quicker and easier.

Holiday Carnival

Celebrate the holidays with festive decorations and music as well as themed food and games. The possibilities are endless.

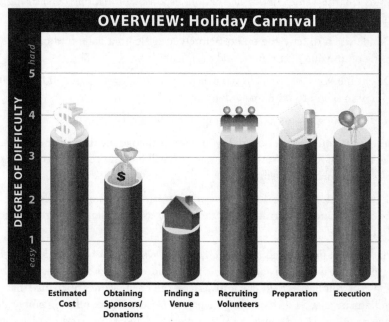

Special Materials/Equipment
- Holiday decorations
- Holiday game/activity equipment
- Holiday food
- Sound system (microphone, speakers)

Sponsors/Donations
- Find people to donate food, games, and crafts that will be used to generate holiday spirit and revenue.

Possible Venue(s)
Whether your organization is a church, school, or community center, the best possible venue for a holiday festival is your organization's home.

Recommended Volunteer
15 to 20+ to handle the venue, food, decorations, sponsors/donations, advertising, ticket sales, entertainment, setup, and cleanup, as well as to man the games

Preparation

Prep Time: 6 months to 1 year

1. Start with a central committee of five to seven people who will serve as committee heads for the venue, food, decorations, sponsors/donations, advertising, ticket sales, entertainment, setup, and cleanup.

2. Decide when to have the event. Before you settle on a date, find out what else is going on in your community, and avoid conflicts.

3. Determine your budget. How much are you looking to raise, and what are you willing to spend to raise that amount?

4. Start seeking sponsors and donations immediately.

5. Search for your perfect venue. If you have to change the date of your event to get the right venue, make sure, again, that you will have no competition from similar events that may be scheduled.

6. If you decide to serve food, plan your menu. Four months before the event, schedule a caterer, recruit people to cook, or ask restaurants or grocery stores to donate food.

7. Plan your games and activities. Perhaps you will have a band, a dunking booth, carnival rides, and inflatable rentals that children would enjoy, such as a bounce house. If you have a field day festival, you can create games of chance that people will donate, say, $1 a chance to take part in. Also consider offering pony rides and face painting. Decide early on if you plan on having any kind of silent auction, raffle, or any other event that may require donated prizes.

8. About three months in advance, advertise by sending e-mails and letters, posting fliers, putting a notice on your organization's website, and making an announcement in your newsletter. Send press releases to local media outlets like newspapers and magazines, and contact local TV news and radio stations to request coverage and publicity.

9. Use the event's theme in everything from marketing, to graphic design of tickets and programs, to venue decorations.

10. Have your various committees meet regularly and keep the lines of communication open.

11. Three months out from the event, print tickets and have everyone in your organization sell tickets. Offer an incentive to the individuals who sell the most tickets.

12. If you need any special equipment, such as seating, sound, light, or stage equipment, this is a good time to reserve these items. Do this as you think about how the venue will be set up for the event.

13. Do a walk-through of the venue a month before the event to check if all the venue systems work and ask when you can get in to decorate.

14. Write a script to serve as your minute-by-minute flow of activities for the event. Plan a time to thank your sponsors and distribute information promoting your organization.

15. Hold a meeting with all event volunteers and go over the tasks and schedule. Be clear on what you expect every volunteer to do. Tell volunteers what to wear for the event. Get everyone's contact information (phone number and e-mail) in case you need to communicate any changes or reminders.

Execution

1. Decorate, set up equipment and food, and check the lighting and sound systems before the event.

2. Have volunteers collect tickets as well as sell more tickets at the event.

3. Follow your script to carry out all planned activities.

4. Initiate cleanup at the designated end time.

Tip(s)

• Weekend afternoons work best for this event.

Variation(s)

• Cater the theme to the time of year. For example, celebrate the changing colors of leaves and crisp fall air by holding a fall fiesta. Feature a buffet-style dinner and auction fall food favorites, like honey ham, turkey, or pumpkin pie. Offer activities such as pumpkin carving, pumpkin painting, and scarecrow making, and offer prizes in different categories (most creative, silliest, etc.). If you hold the event in the park, consider equipment and materials for field activities such as a hayride, corn maze, or game of gourd toss.

Mardi Gras Party

This celebration will offer participants a chance to eat, drink, and be merry while dressed in outrageous costumes and beaded necklaces. Be sure to serve delectable New Orleans-style food and feature a live band for the event. With this theme, you can incorporate many different fundraisers, such as raffles, wine tasting, gourmet food, and auctions.

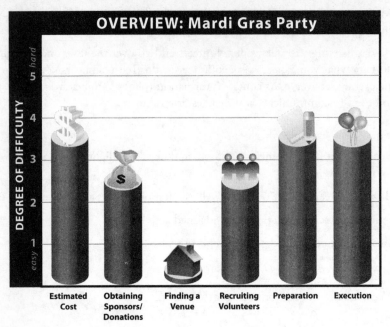

Special Materials/Equipment

- Mardi Gras decorations
- Beads
- Masks
- Party favors

Sponsors/Donations

- Ask New Orleans-style restaurants to donate food.
- Request donations of crafts supplies for decorations from craft stores.

Possible Venue(s)

A fun venue for a holiday festival is your organization's home, whether it is a church, school, or community center.

Recommended Volunteer

10 to 15+ including 5 to 7 to serve as committee heads for the venue, food, decorations, sponsors/donations, advertising, ticket sales, entertainment, setup, and cleanup

Preparation

Prep Time: 6 months to 1 year

1. Start with a central committee of five to seven people who will serve as committee heads for the venue, food, decorations, sponsors/donations, advertising, ticket sales, entertainment, setup, and cleanup.

2. Decide when to have the event. Before you settle on a date, find out what else is going on in your community, and avoid conflicts.

3. Determine your budget. How much are you looking to raise, and what are you willing to spend to raise that amount?

4. Start seeking sponsors and donations immediately.

5. Prepare your venue.

6. Plan what additional fundraisers and entertainment will occur at your event. You may want a live or silent auction, raffle, or band. Try to book your band at least 6 months in advance.

7. Four months before the event, choose your New Orleans-style menu and schedule the caterer, if you decide to serve food.

8. Pick an emcee — either an organization member or a local celebrity. A celebrity can help you market the event.

9. Advertise by sending e-mails and letters, posting fliers, putting a notice on your organization's website, and making an announcement in your newsletter. Send press releases to local media outlets like newspapers and magazines, and contact local TV news and radio stations to request coverage and publicity.

10. Use the event's theme in everything from marketing, to graphic design of tickets and programs, to venue decorations.

11. Have your various committees meet regularly and keep the lines of communication open.

12. Three months out from the event, print tickets and have everyone in your organization sell tickets. Offer an incentive to the individuals who sell the most tickets.

13. If you need any special equipment, such as seating, sound, light, or stage equipment, this is a good time to reserve these items. Do this as you think about how the venue will be set up for the event.

14. Do a walk-through of the venue a month before the event to check if all the venue systems work and ask when you can get in to decorate.

15. Write a script to serve as your minute-by-minute flow of activities for the event. Plan a time to thank your sponsors and distribute information promoting your organization.

16. Hold a meeting with all event volunteers and go over the tasks and schedule. Be clear on what you expect every volunteer to do. Tell volunteers what to wear for the event. Get everyone's contact information (phone number and e-mail) in case you need to communicate any changes or reminders.

Execution

1. Come in early to decorate, set up equipment and food, and check the lighting and sound systems.

2. Have volunteers collect tickets as well as sell more tickets at the event.

3. Follow your script to carry out all planned activities.

4. Initiate cleanup at the designated end time.

Variation(s)

- Throw a St. Patrick's Day Party.
- Host an Independence Day Festival.
- Hold a Valentine's Day Party.

Oscar Party

Encourage participants to dress in elegant attire fit for a star and walk the red carpet as they arrive at your Oscar-inspired banquet. Charge a fee for admission to the event and provide a catered dinner with gourmet food. Present an award for the best dressed male and female at the event.

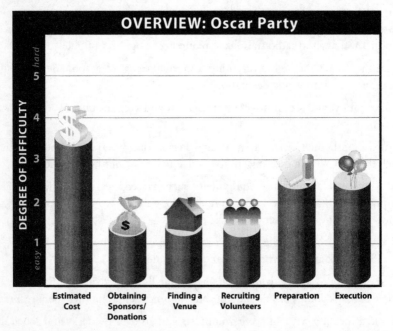

Special Materials/Equipment

- Banquet tables
- Specialty lighting
- Sound equipment (microphone, speakers)
- Chairs
- Red carpet

Sponsors/Donations

- The best donation that you might possibly get is that of a venue.

- Try to find someone to sponsor the entire event or see if you can get sponsors for each banquet table.

Possible Venue(s)

Consider having it at an upscale hotel in your community or any venue with a fancy banquet room.

Recommended Volunteer

10 to 15+ including 5 to 7 to serve as committee heads for the venue, food, decorations, sponsors/donations, advertising, ticket sales, entertainment, setup, and cleanup

Preparation

Prep Time: 6 months to1 year

1. Start with a central committee of five to seven people who will serve as committee heads for the venue, food, decorations, sponsors/donations, advertising, ticket sales, entertainment, setup, and cleanup.

2. Decide when to have the event. Before you settle on a date, find out what else is going on in your community, and avoid conflicts.

3. Determine your budget. How much are you looking to raise, and what are you willing to spend to raise that amount?

4. Search for your perfect venue. If you have to change the date of your event to get the right venue, make sure, again, that you will have no competition from similar events that may be scheduled.

5. If you decide to serve food, plan your menu. Four months before the event, schedule a caterer, recruit people to cook, or ask restaurants or grocery stores to donate food.

6. Select what activities will occur at your event. You may want a live or silent auction, raffle, or band. Plan to ask that attendees dress in the style of the Academy Awards. Determine what awards you will hand out and how you will handle that. What will your awards be? Remember that the "Oscar" is a copyrighted name and award.

7. Pick an emcee — either an organization member or a local celebrity. A celebrity can help you market the event.

8. Advertise by sending e-mails and letters, posting fliers, putting a notice on your organization's website, and making an announcement in your newsletter. Send press releases to local media outlets like newspapers and magazines, and contact local TV news and radio stations to request coverage and publicity.

9. Use the event's theme in everything from marketing, to graphic design of tickets and programs, to venue decorations.

10. Have your various committees meet regularly and keep the lines of communication open.

11. Three months out from the event, print tickets and have everyone in your organization sell tickets. Offer an incentive to the individuals who sell the most tickets.

12. If you need any special equipment such as sound, lights, staging, or seating, this is a good time to reserve these items. Do this as you think about how the venue will be set up for the event.

13. Do a walk-through of the venue a month before the event to check if all the venue systems work and ask when you can get in to decorate.

14. Write a script to serve as your minute-by-minute flow of activities for the event. Plan a time to thank your sponsors and distribute information promoting your organization.

15. Hold a meeting with all event volunteers and go over the tasks and schedule. Be clear on what you expect every volunteer to do. Tell volunteers what to wear for the event. Get everyone's contact information (phone number and e-mail) in case you need to communicate any changes or reminders.

Execution

1. Come in early to decorate, set up equipment and food, and check the lighting and sound systems.

2. Have volunteers collect tickets as well as sell more tickets at the event.

3. Follow your script to carry out all planned activities.

4. Initiate cleanup at the designated end time.

Tip(s)

- Hold this event on the night of the Oscars for a fun, classy viewing party.
- Remember that you cannot use the words "Oscar" or "Academy Award" in your marketing unless you obtain permission to do so.

Parent Appreciation Banquet

Teens will have the opportunity to express their love and gratitude for their parents in this fundraising event. Gather several students from local schools to send out invitations to their parents and charge a fee for attendance. The teens will act as the servers at the banquet. Play interactive games with all the guests involved.

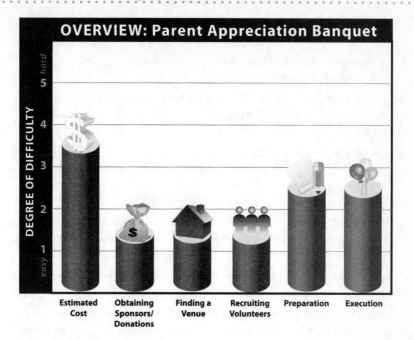

Special Materials/Equipment
- Banquet tables
- Sound equipment (microphone, speakers)
- Specialty lighting
- Chairs

Sponsors/Donations
- The best donation that you might possibly get is that of a venue.

Possible Venue(s)
If you are doing this fundraiser for your school Parent-Teacher Organization, consider having the event in the gymnasium of the school. If the event is for your church and you have a social hall in your building, have the event there. If you want to go all out, consider having it at an upscale hotel in your community or any venue with a fancy banquet room.

Recommended Volunteer
10+ including 5 to 7 to serve as committee heads for the venue, food, decorations, sponsors/donations, advertising, ticket sales, entertainment, setup, and cleanup.

Preparation
Prep Time: 6 months to 1 year

1. Start with a central committee of five to seven people who will serve as committee heads for the venue, food, decorations, sponsors/donations, advertising, ticket sales, entertainment, setup, and cleanup.

2. Decide when to have the event. Before you settle on a date, find out what else is going on in your community, and avoid conflicts.

3. Determine your budget. How much are you looking to raise, and what are you willing to spend to raise that amount?

4. Search for your perfect venue. If you have to change the date of your event to get the right venue, make sure, again, that you will have no competition from similar events that may be scheduled.

5. If you decide to serve food, plan your menu. Four months before the event, schedule a caterer, recruit people to cook, or ask restaurants or grocery stores to donate food.

6. Select what activities will occur at your event. You may want a live or silent auction, raffle, or band. Because your basic purpose for this event (beyond raising money) is parent appreciation, decide how you will recognize and appreciate the parents in attendance. You may have an award ceremony of some kind.

7. Pick an emcee — either an organization member or a local celebrity. A celebrity can help you market the event.

8. Advertise by sending e-mails and letters, posting fliers, putting a notice on your organization's website, and making an announcement in your newsletter. Send press releases to local media outlets like newspapers and magazines, and contact local TV news and radio stations to request coverage and publicity.

9. Use the event's theme in everything from marketing, to graphic design of tickets and programs, to venue decorations.

10. Have your various committees meet regularly and keep the lines of communication open.

11. Three months out from the event, print tickets and have everyone in your organization sell tickets. Offer an incentive to the individuals who sell the most tickets.

12. If you need any special equipment such as sound, lights, staging, or seating, this is a good time to reserve these items. Do this as you think about how the venue will be set up for the event.

13. Do a walk-through of the venue a month before the event to check if all the venue systems work and ask when you can get in to decorate.

14. Write a script to serve as your minute-by-minute flow of activities for the event. Plan a time to thank your sponsors and distribute information promoting your organization.

15. Hold a meeting with all event volunteers and go over the tasks and schedule. Be clear on what you expect every volunteer to do. Tell volunteers what to wear for the event. Get everyone's contact information (phone number and e-mail) in case you need to communicate any changes or reminders.

Execution

1. Come in early to decorate, set up equipment and food, and check the lighting and sound systems.

2. Have volunteers collect tickets as well as sell more tickets at the event.

3. Follow your script to carry out all planned activities.

4. Initiate cleanup at the designated end time.

Tip(s)

- Have a special presentation from a guest speaker.
- Have kids make cards, crafts, or placemats to put at their parents' seat or to give to them at a designated time.

Variation(s)

- Have a Kid Appreciation Banquet.
- Put on a Spouse Appreciation Banquet.
- Hold a Teacher Appreciation Banquet.

Pumpkin Fest

Have a pumpkin-filled festival featuring a pumpkin pie bake-off, pumpkin juice, pumpkin carving and painting stations, and pumpkin games for people of all ages. Charge a fee for admission.

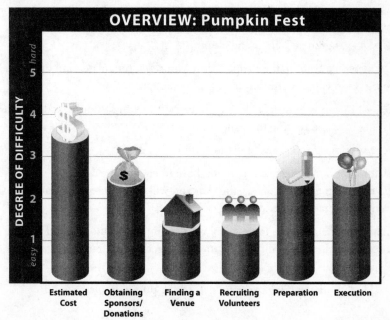

Special Materials/Equipment

- Pumpkins
- Brushes
- Serving utensils (for the pies)
- Pumpkin game supplies
- Paint
- Carving knives
- Pumpkin juice

Sponsors/Donations

- Ask pumpkin patches and grocery stores to donate or give you a price break on pumpkins and carving supplies.
- Ask a craft store to donate paint.

Possible Venue(s)

If you are doing an outdoor festival, secure a park pavilion. You can also consider holding the event in your organization's parking lot, especially if your organization is a church or school with heavy foot traffic.

Recommended Volunteer

10 to 15+ including 5 to 7 to serve as committee heads for the venue, food, decorations, sponsors/donations, advertising, ticket sales, entertainment, setup, and cleanup.

Preparation

Prep Time: 10 months to 1 year

1. Start with a central committee of five to seven people who will serve as committee heads for the venue, food, decorations, sponsors/donations, advertising, ticket sales, entertainment, setup, and cleanup.

2. Decide when to have the event. Before you settle on a date, find out what else is going on in your community, and avoid conflicts.

3. Determine your budget. How much are you looking to raise, and what are you willing to spend to raise that amount?

4. Start seeking sponsors and donations immediately.

5. Search for your perfect venue. If you have to change the date of your event to get the right venue, make sure, again, that you will have no competition from similar events that may be scheduled.

6. If you decide to serve food, plan your menu. Four months before the event, schedule a caterer, recruit people to cook, or ask restaurants or grocery stores to donate food.

7. Decide the rules and select the judges for the pumpkin pie bake-off.

8. Select what activities will occur at your event beyond the pie bake-off and the carving and painting stations. For pumpkin games, consider Pin the Stem on the Pumpkin, Pumpkin Passing (like hot potato), Pumpkin Golf (hit a golf ball into a hollowed pumpkin), or a Mini-Pumpkin Hunt (hide miniature pumpkins in a designated area and give a prize to the person who finds the most in the time limit). You may also want a live or silent auction, raffle, or band.

9. Pick an emcee — either an organization member or a local celebrity. A celebrity can help you market the event.

10. Advertise by sending e-mails and letters, posting fliers, putting a notice on your organization's website, and making an announcement in your newsletter. Send press releases to local media outlets like newspapers and magazines, and contact local TV news and radio stations to request coverage and publicity.

11. Use the event's theme in everything from marketing, to graphic design of tickets and programs, to venue decorations.

12. Have your various committees meet regularly and keep the lines of communication open.

13. Three months out from the event, print tickets and have everyone in your organization sell tickets. Offer an incentive to the individuals who sell the most tickets.

14. If you need any special equipment, such as seating, sound, light, or stage equipment, this is a good time to reserve these items. Do this as you think about how the venue will be set up for the event.

15. Do a walk-through of the venue a month before the event to check if all the venue systems work and ask when you can get in to decorate.

16. Write a script to serve as your minute-by-minute flow of activities for the event. Plan a time to thank your sponsors and distribute information promoting your organization.

17. Hold a meeting with all event volunteers and go over the tasks and schedule. Be clear on what you expect every volunteer to do. Tell volunteers what to wear for the event. Get everyone's contact information (phone number and e-mail) in case you need to communicate any changes or reminders.

Execution

1. Come in early to decorate, set up equipment and food, and check the lighting and sound systems.

2. Have volunteers collect tickets as well as sell more tickets at the event.

3. Follow your script to carry out all planned activities.

4. Initiate cleanup at the designated end time.

"Soup"er Bowl Sale

Sell hand-painted soup bowls for Super Bowl Sunday. Have artistic volunteers paint soup bowls with the Super Bowl logo, competing teams' colors, or general football theme. Have the bowls fired in a kiln, and sell them with a recipe for or a dried package of starter contents for a delicious chili, stew, or other soup that could be made for Super Bowl Sunday. This is a great project for an art school or an organization with ties to artists.

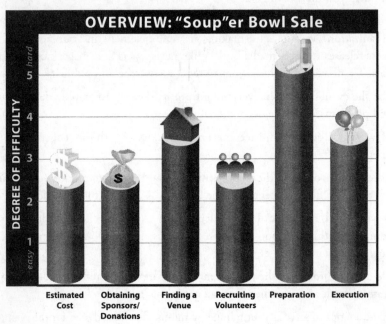

OVERVIEW: "Soup"er Bowl Sale

DEGREE OF DIFFICULTY (easy 1 to hard 5)

Estimated Cost | Obtaining Sponsors/Donations | Finding a Venue | Recruiting Volunteers | Preparation | Execution

Special Materials/Equipment
- Bowls
- Kiln
- Paint and brushes

Sponsors/Donations
- Ask local art, craft, or ceramic pottery store for donations of bowls and paints.
- Partner with a ceramics studio or an art school for help painting, and seek permission to use its kiln.
- See if a soup company will donate the dried soup mixes and recipes to put with the bowls.

Possible Venue(s)

A church social hall, school cafeteria, or any place with room for large tables to work at is fine for painting. Find a ceramic pottery studio that has a kiln you can use to fire the bowls. Sell bowls through your website and by setting up tables outside of sports bars and at your organization's facility the month leading up to the Super Bowl.

Recommended Volunteer

15+ to organize the specific logistics of and take part in the painting, firing, and sales

Preparation

Prep Time: 3 months+

1. Start with a central committee of five to seven people who will serve as committee heads for the venues, sponsors/donations, advertising, painting, firing, packaging, sales, and delivery.

2. Decide when to paint, package, fire, and sell the bowls to have them delivered before the Super Bowl. Keep in mind that after you have painted the bowls and allowed them to dry, you need to allow at least a week to fire them in a kiln, glaze them, and re-fire them. Plan on being able to deliver your orders one to two weeks prior to the big game.

3. Determine your budget. How much are you looking to raise, and what are you willing spend to raise that amount?

4. Decide early on whether you will offer recipes with your bowls or soup. Soup, stew, or chili can be offered in the form of dried mix. Frontier Soups offers dried soup mixes that can be ordered online.

5. Start seeking artists, sponsors, and donations immediately.

6. Search for the right venues for painting, firing, packaging, and selling the bowls.

7. Make a brochure with pictures and descriptions of what you will be selling, and have your members take pre-orders. If you have your brochure ready three months before your event, you can give volunteers a month to six weeks to sell bowls. This will then give you plenty of lead-time to put your orders together.

8. Advertise by sending e-mails and letters, posting fliers, putting a notice on your organization's website, and making an announcement in your newsletter. Send press releases to local media outlets like newspapers and magazines, and contact local TV news and radio stations to request coverage and publicity.

9. Use the event's theme in everything from marketing, to graphic design of tickets and programs, to venue decorations.

10. Have your various committees meet regularly and keep the lines of communication open.

11. Hold a meeting with all event volunteers and go over the sales tasks and schedule.

Execution

1. Sell bowls through your website.

2. Set up tables outside of sports bars and at your organization's facility the month leading up to the Super Bowl to sell bowls.

Tip(s)

- Advertise them as great bowls for serving other snacks like chips, dip, salsa, guacamole, candy, or popcorn at your Super Bowl party.
- Make sure the materials used will make a final product that is safe to eat out of.

Variation(s)

- Sell tickets for a soup lunch where you get to take home the hand-painted bowl you ate out of.
- Buy pre-made bowls that are in team colors, and sell them with soup-mix or recipes.
- Sell painted holiday cookie jars filled with cookies or cookie-making ingredients inside.

White Wonderland Gift Exchange

Let it snow with gifts and donations. During the holidays, catch guests in the spirit of giving by asking them to bring snow-white gifts wrapped in white paper and ribbon to a gift exchange. Set up a donation table, and encourage guests to bring a gift to trade and a gift to donate, or to make monetary donations to your organization.

OVERVIEW: White Wonderland Gift Exchange

Special Materials/Equipment

- Festive, white decorations
- Chairs
- Sound equipment (microphone, speakers)
- Banquet tables
- Specialty lighting

Sponsors/Donations

- Ask local supermarkets and restaurants to donate food or cater the event.

Possible Venue(s)

If you plan for a large event, consider doing your party at a nice hotel with banquet facilities. For a smaller party, consider doing it at someone's home.

Recommended Volunteer

10+ handle the venue, food, decorations, sponsors/donations, advertising, ticket sales, entertainment, setup, and cleanup

Preparation

Prep Time: 10 months to 1 year

1. Start with a central committee of 10 people to handle the venue, food, decorations, sponsors/donations, advertising, ticket sales, entertainment, setup, and cleanup.

2. Decide when to have the event. Before you settle on a date, find out what else is going on in your community, and avoid conflicts.

3. Determine your budget. How much are you looking to raise, and what are you willing to spend to raise that amount?

4. Start seeking sponsors and donations immediately.

5. Search for your perfect venue. If you have to change the date of your event to get the right venue, make sure, again, that you will have no competition from similar events that may be scheduled.

6. If you decide to serve food, plan your menu. Four months before the event, schedule a caterer, recruit people to cook, or ask restaurants or grocery stores to donate food.

7. Select what activities will occur at your event. You may want a live or silent auction, raffle, or band.

8. Pick an emcee — either an organization member or a local celebrity. A celebrity can help you market the event.

9. Advertise by sending e-mails and letters, posting fliers, putting a notice on your organization's website, and making an announcement in your newsletter. Send press releases to local media outlets like newspapers and magazines, and contact local TV news and radio stations to request coverage and publicity.

10. Use the event's theme in everything from marketing, to graphic design of tickets and programs, to venue decorations.

11. Have your various committees meet regularly and keep the lines of communication open.

12. Three months out from the event, print tickets and have everyone in your organization sell tickets. Offer an incentive to the individuals who sell the most tickets.

13. If you need any special equipment such as sound, lights, staging, or seating, this is a good time to reserve these items. Do this as you think about how the venue will be set up for the event.

14. Do a walk-through of the venue a month before the event to check if all the venue systems work and ask when you can get in to decorate.

15. Write a script to serve as your minute-by-minute flow of activities for the event. Plan a time to thank your sponsors and distribute information promoting your organization.

16. Hold a meeting with all event volunteers and go over the tasks and schedule. Be clear on what you expect every volunteer to do. Tell volunteers what to wear for the event. Get everyone's contact information (phone number and e-mail) in case you need to communicate any changes or reminders.

Execution

1. Come in early to decorate, set up equipment and food, and check the lighting and sound systems.

2. Have volunteers collect tickets as well as sell more tickets at the event.

3. Follow your script to carry out all planned activities.

4. Initiate cleanup at the designated end time.

Tip(s)

- Paper snowflakes are inexpensive, easy-to-make winter decorations.

Variation(s)

- Rent a snow machine. While parents do a gift exchange and socialize, they can pay for their kids to play in the snow and enter a snowman-building contest. The winner will get a prize.

Chapter 16

Shows

The following events combine good times with good causes, requiring more preparation to create large-scale shows. The projects you will find in this chapter include:

- Antique Show
- Car Show
- Concert in the Park
- Home and Garden Show
- Host a Radio Show
- Male Beauty Pageant
- Superstar Idol Singing Show
- Tickets Sales for Touring Shows

- Art Show
- Comedy Club Night
- Fashion Show
- Horse Show
- Karaoke Celebration
- Movie Premier
- Talent Show
- Truck Show

Antique Show

Contact numerous antique dealers in your area and charge each for their own space in the show. Come up with an admission fee, and provide food and beverages at the event. Make program books and distribute them to participants.

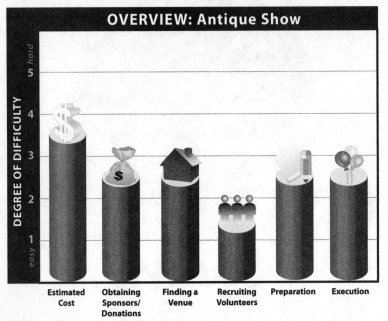

OVERVIEW: Antique Show

Special Materials/Equipment
- Booths or tables (to showcase antiques)

Sponsors/Donations
- Seek a corporate or business sponsor, like a high-end antique dealer, to cover the venue cost and/or the cost of display materials.

Possible Venue(s)
Nice hotels with large banquet rooms are ideal because they offer plenty of space and can usually provide catering. If you are going to be showing high-end antiques, be sure that you offer the collectors and dealers a secure venue.

Recommended Volunteer
10 including 5 to 7 committee heads for the venue, food, decorations, sponsors/donations, advertising, ticket sales, entertainment, antiques, security, setup, and cleanup

Preparation

Prep Time: 8 months to 1 year

1. Start with a central committee of five to seven people who will serve as committee heads for the venue, food, sponsors/donations, advertising, ticket sales, entertainment, antiques, security, setup, and cleanup.

2. Decide when to have the event. Before you settle on a date, find out what else is going on in your community, and avoid conflicts.

3. Determine your budget. How much are you looking to raise, and what are you willing to spend to raise that amount?

4. Start seeking sponsors and donations immediately.

5. Search for your perfect venue. If you have to change the date of your event to get the right venue, make sure, again, that you will have no competition from similar events that may be scheduled.

6. Consider your options and decide how you will raise funds. Beside selling admission tickets, you can sell booths to dealers and collectors. You can also consider taking a percentage of each sale the dealer makes at the event. Before you consider this option, you need to know that the antiques should be appraised before it is priced for sale at your fundraiser. An independent third party professional appraiser should do the appraisal.

7. If you decide to serve food, plan your menu. Four months before the event, schedule a caterer, recruit people to cook, or ask restaurants or grocery stores to donate food.

8. Select what activities will occur at your event. You may want a live or silent auction, raffle, or band.

9. Pick an emcee — either an organization member or a local celebrity. A celebrity can help you market the event.

10. As you settle on the dealers and collectors, plan to put a catalogue together. The catalogue will help to market your event and it will guide your supporters through your event. You should be prepared to print your catalogue three months prior to your event. The catalogue can pay for itself if you sell ad space in it.

11. Three months prior to the event, advertise by sending e-mails and letters, posting fliers, putting a notice on your organization's website, and making an announcement in your newsletter. Send press releases to local media outlets like newspapers and magazines, and contact local TV news and radio stations to request coverage and publicity.

12. Use the event's theme in everything from marketing, to graphic design of tickets and programs, to venue decorations.

13. Have your various committees meet regularly and keep the lines of communication open.

14. Three months out from the event, print tickets and have everyone in your organization sell tickets. Offer an incentive to the individuals who sell the most tickets. When you decide your ticketing structure, you might want to consider a "private showing" period prior to the announced event time. These tickets will be priced a little higher and offer the purchaser early admittance to view the antiques and speak with the dealers and collectors.

15. If you need any special equipment, such as seating, sound, light, or stage equipment, this is a good time to reserve these items. Do this as you think about how the venue will be set up for the event.

16. Do a walk-through of the venue a month before the event to check if all the venue systems work and ask when you can get in to decorate. Map out where each dealer will be stationed. It also helps if the dealers and collectors can attend this walk-through to address any last minute needs.

17. Write a script to serve as your minute-by-minute flow of activities for the event. Plan a time to thank your sponsors and distribute information promoting your organization.

18. Hold a meeting with all event volunteers and go over the tasks and schedule. Be clear on what you expect every volunteer to do. Tell volunteers what to wear for the event. Get everyone's contact information (phone number and e-mail) in case you need to communicate any changes or reminders.

Execution

1. Come in early to set up equipment and food, and check the lighting and sound systems.

2. Have volunteers collect tickets as well as sell more tickets at the event.

3. Follow your script to carry out all planned activities.

4. Initiate cleanup at the designated end time.

Tip(s)

• Attract dealers and collectors by offering to pass along any mailing lists you generate from this event.

• Meet with the dealers and collectors individually to work out any marketing hooks that will help you to advertise your event and their items.

• Consider offering the antique show along with dinner and/or cocktails. Consider having a wide selection of antiques for show and for sale. Offer a little something for everyone to increase the appeal of the show and increase the likelihood that the dealers will find new customers.

Art Show

Everyone can appreciate quality art and feel good about supporting local artists. Sell tickets for an art gala at which the public can meet with the artists as well as bid for artwork during an auction.

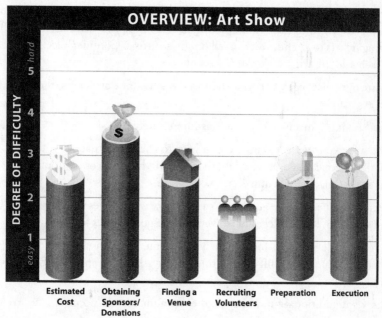

Special Materials/Equipment
- Supplies for displaying the art

Sponsors/Donations
- Find a corporate or business sponsor to cover the venue cost and/or the cost of display materials. Art supply stores are good places to go.
- Find a caterer or people to cook and/or donate food.

Possible Venue(s)
Hotels that offer larger banquet rooms and allow catering are ideal.

Recommended Volunteer
10 to 15 starting with a committee of 5 to 7 individuals who will consider venue, sponsors/donations, art/sales, advertising, setup, and cleanup

Preparation
Prep Time: 4 to 8 months

1. Start with a central committee of five to seven people who will serve as committee heads for the venue, sponsors/donations, advertising, ticket sales, entertainment, setup, and cleanup.

2. Decide when to have the event. Before you settle on a date, find out what else is going on in your community, and avoid conflicts.

3. Determine your budget. How much are you looking to raise, and what are you willing to spend to raise that amount? Decide how you will raise funds. Besides selling tickets to attend, you can sell booths to artists. Consider taking a percentage of each sale the artist makes at the event.

4. Figure out what type of art you want to showcase (fine art, crafts, themed art, kids art, etc.).

5. Start seeking sponsors and donations immediately.

6. Search for your perfect venue. If you have to change the date of your event to get the right venue, make sure, again, that you will have no competition from similar events that may be scheduled.

7. Decide whether you are going to jury the show with judges who give prizes for the best art. If so, local colleges or universities are good places to find judges.

8. If you decide to serve food, plan your menu. Four months before the event, schedule a caterer, recruit people to cook, or ask restaurants or grocery stores to donate food.

9. Plan what additional fundraisers and entertainment will occur at your event. You may want a live or silent auction, raffle, or band.

10. Arrange with the artists who will be featured in your show, and have the art appraised by an independent third party professional appraiser to determine sale prices.

11. Advertise by sending e-mails and letters, posting fliers, putting a notice on your organization's website, and making an announcement in your newsletter. Send press releases to local media outlets like newspapers and magazines, and contact local TV news and radio stations to request coverage and publicity.

12. Use the event's theme in everything from marketing, to graphic design of tickets and programs, to venue decorations.

13. Have your various committees meet regularly and keep the lines of communication open.

14. Three months out from the event, print tickets and have everyone in your organization sell tickets. Offer an incentive to the individuals who sell the most tickets.

15. If you need any special equipment, such as supplies and lighting equipment for the art's display, this is a good time to reserve these items. Do this as you think about how the venue will be set up for the event.

16. Work out a schedule of events and map out a specific plan of where each artist's work will be shown. Go over these plans with your volunteers and artists during a walk-through, and indicate who will be stationed where for the show. Tell volunteers what to wear for the event. Get everyone's contact information (phone number and e-mail) in case you need to communicate any changes or reminders.

17. If you have security in place, go over planned security measures.

18. Write a script to serve as your minute-by-minute flow of activities for the event. Plan a time to thank your sponsors and distribute information promoting your organization.

19. Hold a meeting with all event volunteers and go over the tasks and schedule. Be clear on what you expect every volunteer to do.

Execution

1. Come in early to decorate, set up equipment and food, and check the lighting.

2. Make sure artists arrive early to install their work.

3. Have volunteers collect tickets as well as sell more tickets at the event.

4. Follow your script to carry out all planned activities.

5. Initiate cleanup at the designated end time.

Tip(s)

- To add to the funds you raise, have artists pay a fee for their booths.
- To ensure this is a win-win event for your organization and the artists, make sure you offer to pass along any mailing list you generate from this event to the artists. Also, meet with the artists individually to work out any marketing hooks that will help you to advertise your event and help them promote their works.
- If you are showing high-end art, ensure the safety of artists' work by choosing a secure venue, possibly with security guards.
- Consider having a wide selection of art and pricing structures so there is something for everyone; this will increase the appeal of the show and increase the likelihood that the art will sell.
- Have invitations and tickets designed by an artist and printed on high-quality paper. Make the invitations extra artsy by printing them on CDs, wine glasses, or paper bags.

Variation(s)

- Have a private showing period prior to the event's advertised start time. Sell these tickets separate for a higher price for early admittance to view the art and speak with the artists.
- Introduce your art show fundraiser by hosting a paid preview with dinner.

Car Show

Rev up funds with a classic car show. Have local car dealers exhibit cars, and charge an admission fee for spectators.

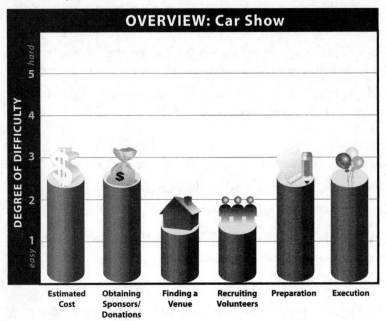

Special Materials/Equipment
- Classic cars

Sponsors/Donations
- The best sponsors you can have for such an event are the classic cars clubs. You can find a car club in your area on Hubcapcafe's website at **www.hubcapcafe.com**.
- New car dealers can be valuable sponsors for such events.

Possible Venue(s)
If your organization has a large parking lot, that is probably the best venue. If you do not have a parking lot, or if you have a small parking lot, consider a city park, a mall parking lot, a new car dealership's parking lot.

Recommended Volunteer
10 including 5+ to take charge of the venue, exhibitors, sponsors/donations, advertising, entry fee, entertainment, setup, cleanup, and other events like the raffle or auction

Preparation

Prep Time: 6 months+

1. Start with a central committee of five to seven people who will serve as committee heads for the venue, food, decorations, sponsors/donations, advertising, ticket sales, entertainment, and setup and cleanup.

2. Find car clubs and new car dealers who will agree to participate.

3. Search for your perfect venue.

4. Decide when to have the event. Before you settle on a date, find out what else is going on in your community, and avoid conflicts. Because this is an outdoor event, you will want to plan on a time of year when people enjoy being outside. You will also want to plan for a time when you have a minimal chance of being rained out. You will, however, have to plan for this possibility.

5. Determine your budget. How much are you looking to raise, and what are you willing to spend to raise that amount?

6. If you decide to serve food, plan your menu. Four months before the event, schedule a caterer, recruit people to cook, or ask restaurants or grocery stores to donate food.

7. Select what activities will occur at your event. You may want a live or silent auction, raffle, or band.

8. Pick an emcee — either an organization member or a local celebrity. A celebrity can help you market the event.

9. Advertise by sending e-mails and letters, posting fliers, putting a notice on your organization's website, and making an announcement in your newsletter. Send press releases to local media outlets like newspapers and magazines, and contact local TV news and radio stations to request coverage and publicity.

10. Use the event's theme in everything from marketing, to graphic design of tickets and programs, to venue decorations.

11. Have your various committees meet regularly and keep the lines of communication open.

12. Three months out from the event, print tickets and have everyone in your organization sell tickets. Offer an incentive to the individuals who sell the most tickets.

13. If you need any special equipment such as sound, lights, staging, or seating, this is a good time to reserve these items. Do this as you think about how the venue will be set up for the event.

14. Do a walk-through of the venue a month before the event to check if all the venue systems work and ask when you can get in to decorate.

15. Write a script to serve as your minute-by-minute flow of activities for the event. Plan a time to thank your sponsors and distribute information promoting your organization.

16. Hold a meeting with all event volunteers and go over the tasks and schedule. Be clear on what you expect every volunteer to do. Tell volunteers what to wear for the event. Get everyone's contact information (phone number and e-mail) in case you need to communicate any changes or reminders.

Execution

1. Come in early to decorate, set up equipment and food, and check the lighting and sound systems.

2. Have volunteers collect tickets as well as sell more tickets at the event.

3. Follow your script to carry out all planned activities.

4. Initiate cleanup at the designated end time.

Variation(s)

- Have a Motorcycle Show.
- A great indoor event is a Classic (Antique) Toy Show.

Comedy Club Night

Have a laugh-out-load evening and smile about your profits. Sell tickets for an evening at a comedy club.

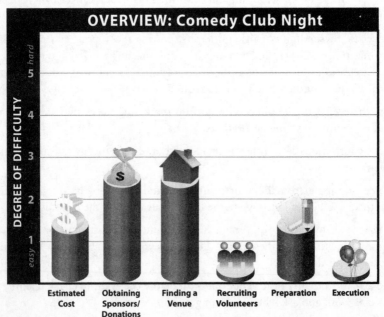

OVERVIEW: Comedy Club Night

DEGREE OF DIFFICULTY: easy 1 — 5 hard

Estimated Cost | Obtaining Sponsors/Donations | Finding a Venue | Recruiting Volunteers | Preparation | Execution

Sponsors/Donations

- Ask a local comedy club to host this event for an evening and have the proceeds donated to your organization. The comedy club will schedule the comedians.

Possible Venue(s)

Besides holding this event at a comedy club, consider having it at a bar, restaurant, school, church, or any venue with a stage.

Recommended Volunteer

3 to 5 to handle the venue, sponsors/donations, advertising, and ticket sales

Preparation

Prep Time: 2 months

1. Find a venue to sponsor you and pick a date. If you book at a venue other than a comedy club, you will have to find the comedians.

2. Advertise by sending e-mails and letters, posting fliers, putting a notice on your organization's website, and making an announcement in your newsletter. Send press releases to local media outlets like newspapers and magazines, and contact local TV news and radio stations to request coverage and publicity.

3. Print tickets and sell as many tickets in advance as you can.

4. Have someone prepare a pitch for your organization that he or she will deliver during the event.

Execution

1. Collect and sell tickets at the door.

2. Have someone make your organization's pitch, and pass a hat or basket for additional donations.

3. Join guests for a hilarious evening.

Tip(s)

- Remember to publicly thank the club during the event.

- Generally, you will take the sales of the admission to the club and the club will take the sales at the bar. You can make other arrangements with the club, but you have to make it attractive to them. If you plan your event for a night that is considered an "off night" for the club, such as a Monday or Tuesday, and you can guarantee them a full house of your supporters, they likely will be more than happy to do the event for the sales at the bar.

Variation(s)

- Hold a Jazz Club Fundraiser.
- Put on a Rock Club Fundraiser.
- Try a Folk Club Fundraiser.

Concert in the Park

Holding a concert in the park can be a huge fundraising success. Local talents will be eager to showcase their skills, and they will likely play for free to gain recognition in the community. This event is ideal for children and teen volunteers.

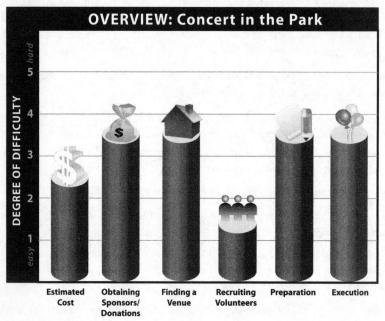

Special Materials/Equipment

- Stage
- Sound equipment (microphone, speakers)
- Seating

Sponsors/Donations

- Contact local businesses to act as event sponsors. Set sponsorship levels and offer potential sponsors advertising rights, select seating, and other perks to make sponsorship attractive.
- Try to find well-known musicians who support your cause to perform.

Possible Venue(s)

A park with a band shell, outdoor amphitheater, or hill to serve as a natural amphitheater work well.

Recommended Volunteer

10 to 15+ including 5 to 7 to serve as committee heads for the venue, food, decorations, sponsors/donations, advertising, ticket sales, entertainment, setup, and cleanup

Preparation

Prep Time: 6 months to 1 year

1. Start with a central committee of five to seven people who will serve as committee heads for the venue, food, decorations, sponsors/donations, advertising, ticket sales, entertainment, setup, and cleanup.

2. Decide when to have the event. Before you settle on a date, find out what else is going on in your community, and avoid conflicts.

3. Determine your budget. How much are you looking to raise, and what are you willing to spend to raise that amount?

4. Start seeking sponsors and donations immediately.

5. Search for your perfect venue. If you have to change the date of your event to get the right venue, make sure, again, that you will have no competition from similar events that may be scheduled.

6. If you decide to serve food, plan your menu. Four months before the event, schedule a caterer, recruit people to cook, or ask restaurants or grocery stores to donate food.

7. Plan what additional fundraisers and entertainment will occur at your event. You may want a live or silent auction or a raffle.

8. Make a backup plan, and set an alternative date in case it rains. Decide what steps will be taken if rain come in the middle of the concert (refunds, relocating, etc.).

9. Pick an emcee — either an organization member or a local celebrity. A celebrity can help you market the event.

10. About three months prior to the event, advertise by sending e-mails and letters, posting fliers, putting a notice on your organization's website, and making an announcement in your newsletter. Send press releases to local media outlets like newspapers and magazines, and contact local TV news and radio stations to request coverage and publicity.

11. Use the event's theme in everything from marketing, to graphic design of tickets and programs, to venue decorations.

12. Have your various committees meet regularly and keep the lines of communication open.

13. Three months out from the event, print tickets and have everyone in your organization sell tickets. Offer an incentive to the individuals who sell the most tickets.

14. If you need any special equipment, such as seating, sound, light, or stage equipment, this is a good time to reserve these items. Do this as you think about how the venue will be set up for the event.

15. Do a walk-through of the venue a month before the event to locate outlets and check if all the venue systems work and ask when you can start setting up.

16. Write a script to serve as your minute-by-minute flow of activities for the event. Plan a time to thank your sponsors and distribute information promoting your organization.

17. Hold a meeting with all event volunteers and go over the tasks and schedule. Be clear on what you expect every volunteer to do. Tell volunteers what to wear for the event. Get everyone's contact information (phone number and e-mail) in case you need to communicate any changes or reminders.

Execution

1. Arrive early to decorate, set up equipment and food, and check the lighting and sound systems.

2. Have volunteers collect tickets as well as sell more tickets at the event.

3. Follow your script to carry out all planned activities.

4. Initiate cleanup at the designated end time.

Tip(s)

• To save the money and hassle of renting and setting up chairs, advertise, "Bring a blanket and sit on the lawn under the stars." If you choose to have the concert near a hill, people can sit toward the top of the hill with a good view of the performers at the bottom of the hill.

Fashion Show

Have models or confident volunteers strut their stuff while excited audience members gain insight into the latest styles and newest trends. A fashion show is a great way to gain immense profits for your organization.

Special Materials/Equipment
- Stage
- Sound equipment (microphone, speakers)
- Catwalk

Sponsors/Donations
- Ask a few larger stores at a mall or some smaller boutiques to show their seasonal fashions for a sponsorship fee of $30 to $50 per item shown, or ask for a sponsorship donation of $500 to $1,000.

Possible Venue(s)
A country club restaurant or a local hotel is an excellent choice if you are serving a meal at your event. If you are just serving hors d'oeuvres and beverages, consider a local community theater, which will provide you with a stage, sound equipment, and lighting.

Recommended Volunteer
15 to 20 including 7 to 10 to serve as committee heads for the venue, food, decorations, emcee, sponsors/donations, advertising, ticket sales, models, stage setup, and cleanup.

Preparation

Prep Time: 4 months

1. Start with a central committee of five to seven people who will serve as committee heads for the venue, models, food, decorations, sponsors/donations, advertising, ticket sales, entertainment, setup, and cleanup.

2. Decide when to have the event. Before you settle on a date, find out what else is going on in your community, and avoid conflicts.

3. Determine your budget. How much are you looking to raise, and what are you willing to spend to raise that amount?

4. Start seeking sponsors and donations immediately.

5. Search for your perfect venue. If you have to change the date of your event to get the right venue, make sure, again, that you will have no competition from similar events that may be scheduled.

6. If you decide to serve food, plan your menu. Four months before the event, schedule a caterer, recruit people to cook, or ask restaurants or grocery stores to donate food.

7. Select what activities will occur at your event. You may want a live or silent auction, raffle, or band.

8. Pick an emcee — either an organization member or a local celebrity. A celebrity can help you market the event.

9. Three months prior to the event, advertise by sending e-mails and letters, posting fliers, putting a notice on your organization's website, and making an announcement in your newsletter. Send press releases to local media outlets like newspapers and magazines, and contact local TV news and radio stations to request coverage and publicity.

10. Use the event's theme in everything from marketing, to graphic design of tickets and programs, to venue decorations.

11. Have your various committees meet regularly and keep the lines of communication open.

12. Three months out from the event, print tickets and have everyone in your organization sell tickets. Offer an incentive to the individuals who sell the most tickets.

13. If you need any special equipment, such as seating, sound, light, or stage equipment, this is a good time to reserve these items. Do this as you think about how the venue will be set up for the event.

14. Do a walk-through of the venue a month before the event to check if all the venue systems work and ask when you can get in to decorate. Test out the runway for safety for the models and visibility for the audience.

15. Plan a place for models to change and fashions to be stored during the event.

16. Write a script to serve as your minute-by-minute flow of activities for the event. Plan a time to thank your sponsors and distribute information promoting your organization.

17. Hold a meeting with all event volunteers and go over the tasks and schedule. Be clear on what you expect every volunteer to do. Tell volunteers what to wear for the event. Get everyone's contact information (phone number and e-mail) in case you need to communicate any changes or reminders.

Execution

1. Come in early to decorate, set up equipment and food, and check the lighting and sound systems. Have models arrive early to get ready and line up.

2. Have volunteers collect tickets as well as sell more tickets at the event.

3. Follow your script to carry out all planned activities.

4. Initiate cleanup at the designated end time.

Tip(s)

- To generate more profit, have volunteer photographers document each look that is showcased, and create a photo book with descriptions of each outfit and sponsors. Include information about your organization. Contact attendees about a week after the event to thank them and ask if they would like to buy a photo book for a memento and fashion guide or gift.

Variation(s)

- Plan an outdoor fashion event such as a garden party.
- Choose to have the items that are modeled designed by students.
- Have experimental fashions that might be considered works of art.
- Feature hairstyles.
- Do a fashion show for children.

Home and Garden Show

Attendees will be excited to beautify their yards by making purchases for their new paradises. At a large meeting center, feature a variety of garden items available for purchase by selling booth space to gardening vendors, nurseries, gazebo suppliers, and others who sell products relating to outdoor home living.

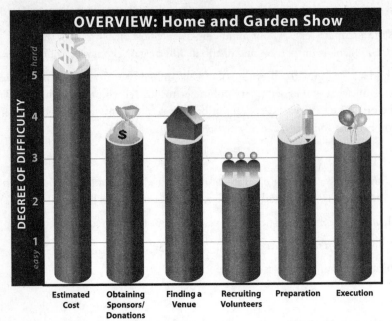

Special Materials/Equipment

- Booths, lighting, and sound equipment (if not provided by the venue)

Sponsors/Donations

- Large local nurseries are ideal sponsors for such events, as are hardware, home, and garden retailers.
- Seek early partnerships with local merchants who will attract people to your event by providing on site expertise in home and gardening matters.
- Consider partnering with a bluegrass band to perform at your event.

Possible Venue(s)

Book a large meeting center, such as a convention center, that is capable of having indoor and outdoor display space.

Recommended Volunteer

10 to 15+ including 5 to 7 to serve as committee heads for the venue, vendor relations, food, decorations, sponsors/donations, advertising, ticket sales, entertainment, setup, and cleanup

Preparation

1. Start with a central committee of five to seven people who will serve as committee heads for the venue, food, decorations, sponsors/donations, advertising, ticket sales, entertainment, setup, and cleanup.

2. Decide when to have the event. Before you settle on a date, find out what else is going on in your community, and avoid conflicts.

3. Determine your budget. How much are you looking to raise, and what are you willing to spend to raise that amount?

4. Search for your perfect venue. If you have to change the date of your event to get the right venue, make sure, again, that you will have no competition from similar events that may be scheduled.

5. If you decide to serve food, plan your menu. Four months before the event, schedule a caterer, recruit people to cook, or ask restaurants or grocery stores to donate food.

6. Select what activities will occur at your event. You may want a live or silent auction, raffle, or band.

7. Pick a host — either an organization member or a local celebrity. A celebrity can help you market the event.

8. Advertise by sending e-mails and letters, posting fliers, putting a notice on your organization's website, and making an announcement in your newsletter. Send press releases to local media outlets like newspapers and magazines, and contact local TV news and radio stations to request coverage and publicity.

9. Use the event's theme in everything from marketing, to graphic design of tickets and programs, to venue decorations.

10. Have your various committees meet regularly and keep the lines of communication open.

11. Three months out from the event, print tickets and have everyone in your organization sell tickets. Offer an incentive to the individuals who sell the most tickets.

12. If you need any special equipment such as sound, lights, staging, or seating, this is a good time to reserve these items. Do this as you think about how the venue will be set up for the event.

13. Do a walk-through of the venue a month before the event to check if all the venue systems work and ask when you can get in to decorate.

14. Write a script to serve as your minute-by-minute flow of activities for the event. Plan a time to thank your sponsors and distribute information promoting your organization.

15. Hold a meeting with all event volunteers and go over the tasks and schedule. Be clear on what you expect every volunteer to do. Tell volunteers what to wear for the event. Get everyone's contact information (phone number and e-mail) in case you need to communicate any changes or reminders.

16. If you plan on an outdoor event and the weather is bad, be sure that you have worked out a rain date or a back-up plan of some sort.

Execution

1. Come in early to decorate, set up equipment and food, and check the lighting and sound systems.

2. Have volunteers collect tickets as well as sell more tickets at the event.

3. Follow your script to carry out all planned activities.

4. Initiate cleanup at the designated end time.

Horse Show

Charge participants to compete in a horse show. Provide cash prizes for first, second, and third place. Charge an admission fee for the audience, and sell concessions and chances at winning door prizes.

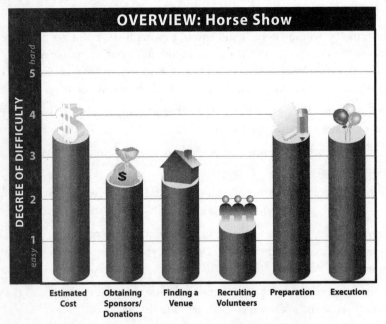

Sponsors/Donations

- A stable, barn, or riding school may be an excellent venue sponsor.
- Companies that make and/or sell riding equipment may also be good sponsors and prize donors.

Possible Venue(s)

An upscale stable or riding school is a great venue for a horse show.

Recommended Volunteer

10 to 15 including 5 to 7 to handle the grounds operations, setup, cleanup, concessions, advertising, ticket sales, identifying and judging contestants, and awarding prizes

Preparation

Prep Time: 1 year

1. Start with a central committee of five to seven people who will handle the grounds operations (map the area and location of planned events), setup, cleanup, food, advertising, ticket sales, identifying and judging contestants, and awarding prizes.

2. Decide when to have the event. Before you settle on a date, find out what else is going on in your community, and avoid conflicts.

3. Determine your budget. How much are you looking to raise, and what are you willing to spend to raise that amount?

4. Choose exactly what kind of horse show you will have, as there are many different styles of horse and rider shows.

5. Start seeking sponsors and donations immediately.

6. Search for your perfect venue and book it a year in advance. If you have to change the date of your event to get the right venue, make sure, again, that you will have no competition from similar events that may be scheduled.

7. Make a decision early on as to what you will do if the weather is bad.

8. Six to eight months before the event, choose your menu and schedule the caterer, if you decide to serve food. Consider a picnic or barbecue. Charge per plate. Plan how you will handle transactions related to food. Having a central ticket location is a good idea. Supporters will purchase tickets at a central booth and then exchange tickets for food.

9. Select what activities will occur at your event. You may want a live or silent auction, raffle, or band.

10. Pick a commentator — either an organization member or a local celebrity. A celebrity can help you market the event.

11. Three months prior to the event, advertise by sending e-mails and letters, posting fliers, putting a notice on your organization's website, and making an announcement in your newsletter. Send press releases to local media outlets like newspapers and magazines, and contact local TV news and radio stations to request coverage and publicity.

12. Use the event's theme in everything from marketing, to graphic design of tickets and programs, to venue decorations.

13. Have your various committees meet regularly and keep the lines of communication open.

14. Three months out from the event, print tickets and have everyone in your organization sell tickets. Offer an incentive to the individuals who sell the most tickets.

15. If you need any special equipment, such as seating, sound, or stage equipment, this is a good time to reserve these items. Do this as you think about how the venue will be set up for the event.

16. Do a walk-through of the venue a month before the event to check if all the venue systems work and ask when you can get in to decorate.

17. Write a script to serve as your minute-by-minute flow of activities for the event. Plan a time to thank your sponsors and distribute information promoting your organization.

18. Hold a meeting with all event volunteers and go over the tasks and schedule. Be clear on what you expect every volunteer to do. Tell volunteers what to wear for the event. Get everyone's contact information (phone number and e-mail) in case you need to communicate any changes or reminders.

Execution

1. Come in early to set up equipment and food, and check the sound system.

2. Have volunteers collect tickets as well as sell more tickets at the event.

3. Follow your script to carry out all planned activities.

4. Initiate cleanup at the designated end time.

Host a Radio Show

Go live on the air and host a talk show promoting your cause. Feature guests who are knowledgeable about your cause or who have some kind of first-hand experience. This is a good fundraiser because people can call in and/or send donations and you can have conversations with listeners interested in your organization.

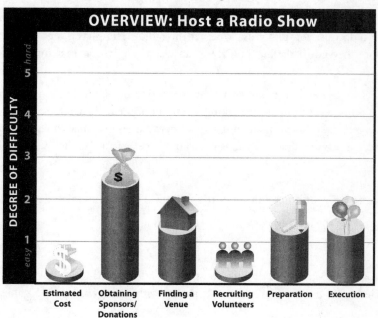

Sponsors/Donations

- The best sponsor you can have for such an event is a popular radio station.

Possible Venue(s)

Ideally, you want a radio station that speaks to your supporters and audience.

Recommended Volunteer

2+ to make arrangements and speak on the air

Preparation

Prep Time: 1 month+

1. Find a radio station to sponsor you, and agree on a date.

2. Prepare your message before your event in much the same way that you might prepare a grant. Tell your organization's story. Explain your mission, vision, and the community need you are addressing.

3. Help your cause by gathering some of your supporters to bring with you to the radio station. Have several people lined up to offer testimonials describing why it is important that people support your cause.

4. Be sure that you have a clear way for people to give to your organization. If you have online fundraising capabilities, be prepared to explain how people can support you in that way.

5. Be prepared to allow people to call in and talk to you about your organization. If you do this, you might ask whether the radio station has a way to screen calls before they go to the air. Prepare to answer any question that may come your way.

6. Advertise by sending e-mails and letters, posting fliers, putting a notice on your organization's website, and making an announcement in your newsletter. Send press releases to local media outlets like newspapers and magazines, and contact local TV news and radio stations to request coverage and publicity.

Execution

1. Arrive with your notes and supporters who will give testimonials.

2. Go live on the air, and convince listeners to donate.

Tip(s)

*   Prepare your statement of need so as not to ask for a handout but, rather, as an invitation to people to work in partnership with you toward your organizational goals.

Karaoke Celebration

Profits from this entertaining evening will be music to your ears as old and new performers alike pay to be in the spotlight for a few songs. Supply contestants with funny, original costumes and props. Participants pay an entry fee and are provided with a song list and pledge sheet before the event takes place. Friends can support karaoke contestants by pledging an amount of their choice. Audience members can also pay to stop performers from singing.

Special Materials/Equipment
- Karaoke machine

Sponsors/Donations
- Contact a local karaoke club and ask if it will donate its club to your organization for an evening. Generally, you will take the sales of the admission to the club and the club will take the sales at the bar. You can make other arrangements with the club, but you have to make it attractive to them, as well. If you plan your event for a night that is considered and "off night" for the club, such as a Monday or Tuesday, and you can guarantee them a full house of your supporters, they likely will be more than happy to do the event for the sales at the bar.
- Ask organization members to lend costumes and props for performers to borrow.

Possible Venue(s)
Ideally, hold this event at a location that is already set up and operating as a karaoke club, because it will have all the equipment you need. Other options are a bar, hotel, restaurant, school, church, or any venue with a stage.

Recommended Volunteer
1 if it is at a karaoke venue. Otherwise, you will need a small committee of 3 to 5 to handle the venue, advertising, sponsors/donations, and DJ or sound equipment and music

Preparation

Prep Time: 2 months+

1. Have one volunteer take charge of this event and make it a priority to book a karaoke venue.

2. Decide when to have the event. Before you settle on a date, find out what else is going on in your community, and avoid conflicts.

3. Determine your budget. How much are you looking to raise, and what are you willing to spend to raise that amount?

4. Start seeking sponsors and donations immediately.

5. Pick an emcee — either an organization member or a local celebrity. A celebrity can help you market the event.

6. Advertise by sending e-mails and letters, posting fliers, putting a notice on your organization's website, and making an announcement in your newsletter. Send press releases to local media outlets like newspapers and magazines, and contact local TV news and radio stations to request coverage and publicity.

7. Use the event's theme in everything from marketing, to graphic design of tickets and programs, to venue decorations.

8. A couple months before the event, print tickets and have everyone in your organization sell tickets. Offer an incentive to the individuals who sell the most tickets.

9. If you need any special equipment, such as seating, sound, light, or stage equipment, this is a good time to reserve these items. Do this as you think about how the venue will be set up for the event.

10. Write a script to serve as your minute-by-minute flow of activities for the event. Plan a time to thank your sponsors and distribute information promoting your organization.

11. Hold a meeting with all event volunteers and go over the tasks and schedule. Be clear on what you expect every volunteer to do. Tell volunteers what to wear for the event. Get everyone's contact information (phone number and e-mail) in case you need to communicate any changes or reminders.

12. Do a walk-through of the venue the day of the event to check if all the venue systems work.

Execution

1. Come in early to decorate and check the lighting and sound systems.

2. Have volunteers collect tickets as well as sell more tickets at the event.

3. Follow your script to carry out all planned activities.

4. Initiate cleanup at the designated end time.

Tip(s)

- Remember to publicly thank the club during the event.

- If you choose to hold your event at a location other than a karaoke club, you can either rent a karaoke machine or hire a DJ to come in and MC the event. The easiest thing to do is to hire a DJ. This may add to your costs, but it will make the event a little easier for you to put together. When you interview DJs to do this type of event, as how big their song selection is. Also ask for references from other event such as this they have done. Check out their references. Ask other organizations that have done similar events for suggestions on DJs.

Male Beauty Pageant

Gather a group of brave males willing to dress up as ladies to help your cause. Hold a pageant where men will compete for best talent, answer questions, and be judged on their dresses. Crown the winner, and provide a sash and bouquet of flowers. Charge an admission fee.

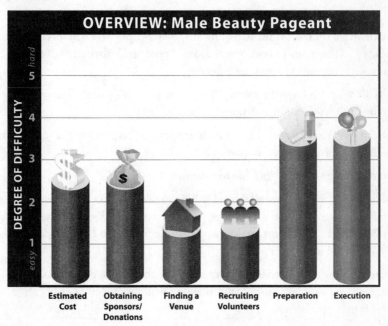

Special Materials/Equipment

- Stage
- Sound system (microphone, speakers)
- Music
- Catwalk
- Specialty lighting
- Fancy dresses (for the men to borrow)

Sponsors/Donations

- Find brave men willing to donate their time as a contestant.
- Ask women to lend their fancy dresses to the men for the evening. Meet at least a month in advance to have the participant try on the dress to make sure it fits well enough to wear.
- Have each participant seek a sponsor.
- You also can sell sponsorships of tables if you chose to serve lunch or dinner.

Possible Venue(s)

Social halls, churches, schools, and hotels are possible venues.

Recommended Volunteer

10 to 15 including 5 to 7 to serve as committee heads for the venue, contestants, food, decorations, sponsors/donations, advertising, ticket sales, entertainment, setup, and cleanup

Preparation

Prep Time: 6 months to 1 year

1. Start with a central committee of five to seven people who will serve as committee heads for the venue, food, decorations, sponsors/donations, advertising, ticket sales, entertainment, setup, and cleanup.

2. Decide when to have the event. Before you settle on a date, find out what else is going on in your community, and avoid conflicts.

3. Determine your budget. How much are you looking to raise, and what are you willing to spend to raise that amount?

4. Start seeking sponsors and donations immediately.

5. Identify a dozen or so men who are willing to take part in your pageant. Be creative in your approach to this. Perhaps you can convince local athletes, firefighters, police officers, and construction workers to compete to be your pageant Queen. Pit one trade against another.

6. Search for your perfect venue. If you have to change the date of your event to get the right venue, make sure, again, that you will have no competition from similar events that may be scheduled.

7. If you decide to serve food, plan your menu. Four months before the event, schedule a caterer, recruit people to cook, or ask restaurants or grocery stores to donate food.

8. Select what additional activities will occur at your event. You may want a live or silent auction, raffle, or band.

9. Pick an emcee — either an organization member or a local celebrity. A celebrity can help you market the event.

10. Advertise by sending e-mails and letters, posting fliers, putting a notice on your organization's website, and making an announcement in your newsletter. Send press releases to local media outlets like newspapers and magazines, and contact local TV news and radio stations to request coverage and publicity.

11. Use the event's theme in everything from marketing, to graphic design of tickets and programs, to venue decorations.

12. Have your various committees meet regularly and keep the lines of communication open.

13. Three months out from the event, print tickets and have everyone in your organization sell tickets. Offer an incentive to the individuals who sell the most tickets.

14. Have participants get their talents and costumes approved by your organization to ensure there will be no inappropriate surprises.

15. If you need any special equipment, such as seating, sound, light, or stage equipment, this is a good time to reserve these items. Do this as you think about how the venue will be set up for the event.

16. Do a walk-through of the venue a month before the event to check if all the venue systems work and ask when you can get in to decorate.

17. Write a script to serve as your minute-by-minute flow of activities for the event. Plan a time to thank your sponsors and distribute information promoting your organization.

18. Hold a meeting with all event volunteers and go over the tasks and schedule. Be clear on what you expect every volunteer to do. Tell volunteers what to wear for the event. Get everyone's contact information (phone number and e-mail) in case you need to communicate any changes or reminders.

19. Have a dress rehearsal with all volunteers, participants, and the emcee to smooth out any bumps in the show beforehand.

Execution

1. Come in early to decorate, set up equipment and food, and check the lighting and sound systems.

2. Have volunteers collect tickets as well as sell more tickets at the event.

3. Follow your script to carry out all planned activities.

4. Initiate cleanup at the designated end time.

Movie Premier

Reserve seats in a large theater for the premier of a highly-anticipated movie, and sell tickets. This can be a big money-maker, depending on the popularity of the movie being premiered.

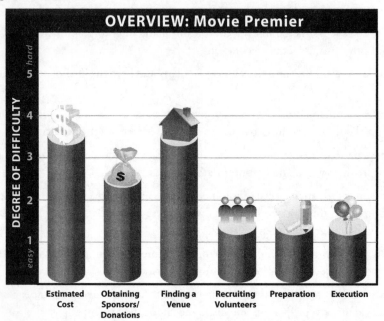

OVERVIEW: Movie Premier

DEGREE OF DIFFICULTY (easy 1 — hard 5)

Estimated Cost | Obtaining Sponsors/ Donations | Finding a Venue | Recruiting Volunteers | Preparation | Execution

Sponsors/Donations

- A local business may sponsor your entire event by purchasing your tickets up-front. You will then sell all the tickets at a straight profit.
- If you can get the theater owner to donate the entire theater, all the better.

Possible Venue(s)

A large local movie theater works well.

Recommended Volunteer

1 to find a venue and as many as possible to sell tickets

Preparation

1. Choose a movie that will likely appeal to your supporters or be popular enough to attract a large public crowd.

2. Make an arrangement with a theater owner to hold choice seats for you as soon as possible. Try to get the theater to allow you to sell your unsold tickets back to the theater owner before a set time. Ask if you can sell concessions or receive a portion

of their concession sales for the evening.

3. Advertise by sending e-mails and letters, posting fliers, putting a notice on your organization's website, and making an announcement in your newsletter. Send press releases to local media outlets like newspapers and magazines, and contact local TV news and radio stations to request coverage and publicity.

4. Allow yourself as much time as possible to sell your tickets.

Execution
1. Arrive early to set up.
2. Collect tickets and sell more tickets at the event.

Tip(s)
- Poll potential supporters to see what kinds of movies they prefer seeing so you can choose the movie that might attract the most people.

Superstar Idol Singing Show

Do your own take on the popular American Idol singing show. Hold auditions, choose contestants, and find three judges who can imitate the personalities of the ones on the show and provide entertaining feedback. Sell tickets for admission. Then let audience members vote on ballots, and announce the winner and runners-up with a special ceremony.

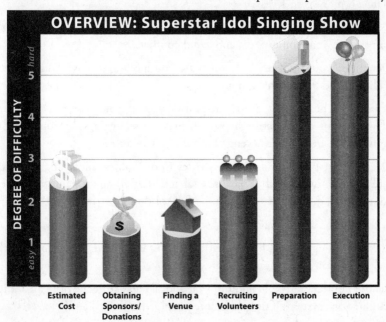

Special Materials/Equipment

- Sound equipment (microphone, speakers)
- Stage
- Music
- Seating

Sponsors/Donations

- Find someone to donate a prize for the winner, like a travel agent who can donate a trip to Los Angeles to see American Idol.
- Ask local grocery stores and restaurants to donate baked goods and snacks that you can sell at the event.

Possible Venue(s)

Your organizational home is a good venue for this kind of event. This event would be great in a school with an auditorium, gym, and/or cafeteria. If you do not have such a venue available to you, a local community theater makes for a nice alternative.

Recommended Volunteer

10 to 15+ including 5 to 7 to serve as committee heads for the venue, food, decorations, sponsors/donations, advertising, ticket sales, entertainment, setup, and cleanup

Preparation

Prep Time: 6 months to 1 year

1. Decide when to have the event. Before you settle on a date, find out what else is going on in your community, and avoid conflicts.

2. Determine your budget. How much are you looking to raise, and what are you willing spend to raise that amount?

3. Search for your perfect venue to sponsor you. If you have to change the date of your event to get the right venue, make sure, again, that you will have no competition from similar events that may be scheduled.

4. Decide what kind of ancillary activities (food, raffles, silent auction, etc.) you will have. You will need to have several activities going on while votes are being counted and during any pauses in the flow of the entertainment.

5. Seek sponsors and donations.

6. Pick three judges and a host — either organization members or local celebrities. Celebrities can help you market the event.

7. Recruit contestants. Hold auditions (at a local karaoke venue or in an auditorium with a sound system) if there are more people interested than there will be time to perform.

8. About three months before the event, advertise by sending e-mails and letters, posting fliers, putting a notice on your organization's website, and making an announcement in your newsletter. Send press releases to local media outlets like newspapers and magazines, and contact local TV news and radio stations to request coverage and publicity.

9. Use the event's theme in everything from marketing, to graphic design of tickets and programs, to venue decorations.

10. Three months out from the event, print tickets and have everyone in your organization sell tickets. Offer an incentive to the individuals who sell the most tickets. Provide a song list and pledge sheet to participants before the event takes place.

11. If you need any special equipment such as sound, lights, staging, or seating, this is a good time to reserve these items. Do this as you think about how the venue will be set up for the event.

12. Determine how the singers will be accompanied. That is, you will need to determine if you will have a live band or musician playing with them, if they will need to provide their own musical accompaniment, or if you will rent a karaoke machine or use a lyric-less CD for the evening.

13. Do a walk-through of the venue a month before the event to check if all the venue systems work and ask when you can get in to decorate.

14. Plan a time to thank your sponsors and distribute information promoting your organization.

Execution

1. Come in early to decorate, set up equipment, and check the lighting and sound systems.

2. Have volunteers collect tickets as well as sell more tickets at the event.

3. Follow your script to carry out all planned activities.

4. Initiate cleanup at the designated end time.

Tip(s)

- Make sure that you are cleared to perform any music that will be used during this event.

Variation(s)

- Do your own take on any popular competitive reality TV show for an evening of fun (i.e. So You Think You Can Dance, Top Chef, America's Next Top Model, The Bachelor).

Talent Show

For an entry fee, participants can witness the talents of members in the community. Advertise for local talent early to get a wide variety of talents. Advertise for everything from musicians to "stupid human tricks." This variety of performances makes the event fun and memorable. Arrange for an array of quick concessions during intermission, like soda, hot dogs, candy, and popcorn.

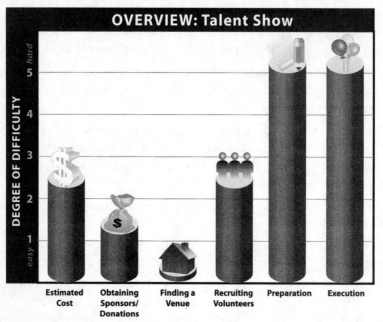

Special Materials/Equipment
- Stage
- Sound equipment (microphone, speakers)
- Seating

Sponsors/Donations
- Find someone to donate a prize for the winner.
- Ask local grocery stores and restaurants to donate baked goods and snacks that you can sell at the event.

Possible Venue(s)
Your organizational home is a good venue for this kind of event. This event would be great in a school with an auditorium, gym, and/or cafeteria. If you do not have such a venue available to you, a local community theater makes for a nice alternative.

Recommended Volunteer

10 to 15 including 5 to 7 to serve as committee heads to handle the venue, decorations, sponsors/donations, auditions/contestants, advertising, ticket sales, setup, and cleanup.

Preparation

Prep Time: 8 months to 1 year

1. Decide when to have the event. Before you settle on a date, find out what else is going on in your community, and avoid conflicts.

2. Determine your budget. How much are you looking to raise, and what are you willing to spend to raise that amount?

3. Search for your perfect venue to sponsor you. If you have to change the date of your event to get the right venue, make sure, again, that you will have no competition from similar events that may be scheduled.

4. Decide what kind of ancillary activities (food, raffles, silent auction, etc.) you will have. You may want to have several activities going on during intermission.

5. Seek sponsors and donations.

6. Recruit contestants. Hold auditions (at a local karaoke venue or in an auditorium with a sound system) if there are more people interested than there will be time to perform.

7. Pick a handful of judges and a host — either organization members or local celebrities. Celebrities can help you market the event.

8. Advertise by sending e-mails and letters, posting fliers, putting a notice on your organization's website, and making an announcement in your newsletter. Send press releases to local media outlets like newspapers and magazines, and contact local TV news and radio stations to request coverage and publicity.

9. Use the event's theme in everything from marketing, to graphic design of tickets and programs, to venue decorations.

10. Three months out from the event, print tickets and have everyone in your organization sell tickets. Offer an incentive to the individuals who sell the most tickets. Provide a song list and pledge sheet to participants before the event takes place.

11. If you need any special equipment such as sound, lights, staging, or seating, this is a good time to reserve these items. Do this as you think about how the venue will be set up for the event.

12. Have a dress rehearsal with the contestants, emcee, and staging and lighting volunteers to make sure everyone is prepared for the show.

13. Do a walk-through of the venue a month before the event to check if all the venue systems work and ask when you can get in to decorate.

14. Plan a time to thank your sponsors and distribute information promoting your organization.

Execution

1. Come in early to decorate, set up equipment, and check the lighting and sound systems.

2. Have volunteers collect tickets as well as sell more tickets at the event.

3. Follow your script to carry out all planned activities.

4. Initiate cleanup at the designated end time.

Tickets Sales for Touring Shows

Traveling shows such as plays or circuses offer great fundraising opportunities. Locate a touring company that is scheduled to stop in your area and purchase tickets for its events. Sell tickets at a higher price, and the difference in amounts will go toward your cause.

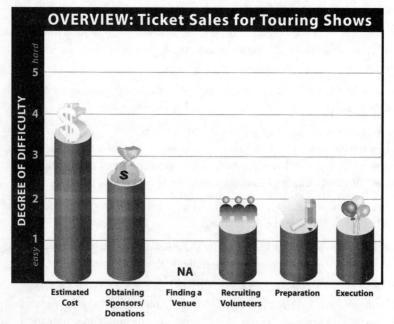

OVERVIEW: Ticket Sales for Touring Shows

DEGREE OF DIFFICULTY — 5 hard ... 1 easy

Estimated Cost | Obtaining Sponsors/Donations | Finding a Venue (NA) | Recruiting Volunteers | Preparation | Execution

Sponsors/Donations

• A local business may sponsor your entire event by purchasing your tickets up-front. You can then sell the tickets for a full profit.

Recommended Volunteer

1+ to find a company and set up ticket sales, and as many people as possible to sell tickets

Preparation

1. Find out what events will be visiting your community and what events will likely appeal to your supporters.

2. Arrange with the producing entity to hold choice seats for you, and to let you sell your unsold tickets back to the producer before a set time.

3. Allow yourself as much time as possible to sell your tickets.

Execution

Sell as many tickets as you can.

Tip(s)

• Poll your supporters to see what kinds of events they prefer seeing before you reserve the tickets.

Variation(s)

• Sell a holiday travel package. Arrange with a travel agent, and sell the travel packages for an amount higher than the travel agent sells them to you. You can arrange a London theater tour, an African safari, Alaskan cruise, etc.

Truck Show

Ask community and organization members who own large vehicles like trucks, tractors, or earthmovers to park them at your venue. Kids will jump at the chance to see these large trucks and have a chance to hop in the driver's seat. Charge an admission fee, sell photographs, and have the owners available to answer questions.

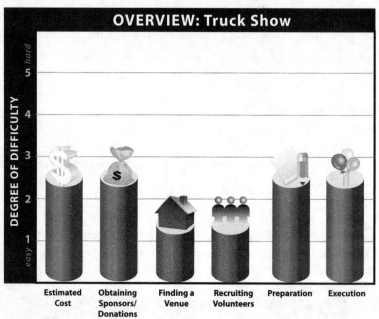

OVERVIEW: Truck Show

DEGREE OF DIFFICULTY (easy 1 – 5 hard)

- Estimated Cost
- Obtaining Sponsors/Donations
- Finding a Venue
- Recruiting Volunteers
- Preparation
- Execution

Special Materials/Equipment
- Large vehicles

Sponsors/Donations
- The best sponsors you can have for such an event are local trucking companies, construction companies, and fire houses.

Possible Venue(s)
This event will call for a large, outdoor venue in an area with high traffic to attract people passing by, like your organization's parking lot (if it is large enough) or the parking lot of a large vehicle dealer, city park, or mall.

Recommended Volunteer
10 including 5 to serve as committee heads to handle the venue, exhibitors, advertising, ticket sales, and additional events

Preparation

Prep Time: 6 months+

1. Start with a central committee of five to seven people who will serve as committee heads for the venue, exhibitors, advertising, ticket sales, entertainment, setup, and cleanup.

2. Decide when to have the event. Before you settle on a date, find out what else is going on in your community, and avoid conflicts.

3. Determine your budget. How much are you looking to raise, and what are you willing to spend to raise that amount?

4. Start seeking sponsors and donations immediately. Find and ask old and new truck owners and dealers to participate in your event.

5. Search for your perfect venue. If you have to change the date of your event to get the right venue, make sure, again, that you will have no competition from similar events that may be scheduled.

6. Make a back up plan in case of rain.

7. If you decide to serve food, plan your menu. Four months before the event, schedule a caterer, recruit people to cook, or ask restaurants or grocery stores to donate food.

8. Select what activities will occur at your event. You may want a live or silent auction, a raffle, games or a band.

9. Pick an emcee — either an organization member or a local celebrity. A celebrity can help you market the event.

10. Advertise by sending e-mails and letters, posting fliers, putting a notice on your organization's website, and making an announcement in your newsletter. Send press releases to local media outlets like newspapers and magazines, and contact local TV news and radio stations to request coverage and publicity.

11. Use the event's theme in everything from marketing, to graphic design of tickets and programs, to venue decorations.

12. Have your various committees meet regularly and keep the lines of communication open.

13. Three months out from the event, print tickets and have everyone in your organization sell tickets. Offer an incentive to the individuals who sell the most tickets.

14. If you need any special equipment, such as seating, sound, light, or stage equipment, this is a good time to reserve these items. Do this as you think about how the venue will be set up for the event.

15. Do a walk-through of the venue a month before the event to check if all the venue systems work and ask when you can get in to decorate.

16. Write a script to serve as your minute-by-minute flow of activities for the event. Plan a time to thank your sponsors and distribute information promoting your organization.

17. Hold a meeting with all event volunteers and go over the tasks and schedule. Be clear on what you expect every volunteer to do. Tell volunteers what to wear for the event. Get everyone's contact information (phone number and e-mail) in case you need to communicate any changes or reminders.

Execution

1. Come in early to decorate, set up equipment and food, and check the lighting and sound systems.

2. Have volunteers collect tickets as well as sell more tickets at the event.

3. Follow your script to carry out all planned activities.

4. Initiate cleanup at the designated end time.

Tip(s)

• Plan on a time of year when people enjoy being outside and there is a minimal chance of being rained out.

Chapter 17

Sports

These events will bring supporters together for a good time while supporting a good cause and being active. The projects you will find in this chapter include:

- Boat Race
- Fishing Tournament
- Golf Tournament
- Hot-Air Balloon Race
- Mudfest
- Rock Climbing
- Sky Diving
- Soccer Tournament
- Water Sports Challenge

Boat Race

Locate a venue to host a boating race, and charge an entry fee for viewing and participating in the event. Provide prizes for race winners, and offer concessions to spectators.

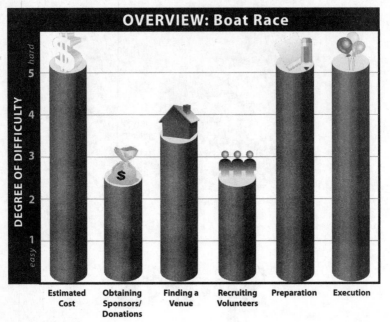

OVERVIEW: Boat Race

Special Materials/Equipment
- Buoys (to mark the racecourse)

Sponsors/Donations
- A local marina is a good choice for a sponsor in areas that are near larger bodies of water.
- Local outdoors clubs, sporting goods, and boating stores are also good sponsor possibilities.
- Have racers collect sponsorships in the same manner that they would in an event such as a walk-a-thon (see sample form and rules in Appendices).

Possible Venue(s)
Your venue can range from a small farm pond to the Pacific Ocean and everything in between.

Recommended Volunteer
10+ to run the event including 5 to serve as committee heads to handle venue, race, sponsors, marketing, and hospitality. You will need a number of people on these committees that have boating experience.

Preparation

Prep Time: 6 months to 1 year

1. Start with a central committee of five to seven people who will serve as committee heads for the venue, food, sponsors/donations, advertising, ticket sales, entertainment, setup, and cleanup.

2. Decide when to have the event. Before you settle on a date, find out what else is going on in your community, and avoid conflicts.

3. Determine your budget. How much are you looking to raise, and what are you willing to spend to raise that amount?

4. Start seeking sponsors and donations immediately.

5. Search for your perfect venue. If you have to change the date of your event to get the right venue, make sure, again, that you will have no competition from similar events that may be scheduled.

6. Four months before the event, choose your menu (barbecue food is popular at outdoor events), and schedule the caterer, if you decide to serve food.

7. Select what additional activities and entertainment will occur at your event. You may want a live or silent auction, raffle, or DJ.

8. Determine the rules of your contest, and publicize them from the very beginning.

9. Make a backup plan in case of bad weather.

10. Three months before the event, start advertising by sending e-mails and letters, posting fliers, putting a notice on your organization's website, and making an announcement in your newsletter. Send press releases to local media outlets like newspapers and magazines, and contact local TV news and radio stations to request coverage and publicity.

11. Use the event's theme in everything from marketing, to graphic design of tickets and programs, to venue decorations.

12. Have your various committees meet regularly and keep the lines of communication open.

13. Three months out from the event, print tickets and have everyone in your organization sell tickets. Offer an incentive to the individuals who sell the most tickets.

14. If you need any special equipment, such as seating, sound, light, or stage equipment, this is a good time to reserve these items. Do this as you think about how the venue will be set up for the event.

15. Do a walk-through of the venue a month before the event to check if all the venue systems work and ask when you can get in to decorate.

16. Write a script to serve as your minute-by-minute flow of activities for the event. Plan a time to thank your sponsors and distribute information promoting your organization.

17. Hold a meeting with all event volunteers and go over the tasks and schedule. Be clear on what you expect every volunteer to do. Tell volunteers what to wear for the event. Get everyone's contact information (phone number and e-mail) in case you need to communicate any changes or reminders.

Execution

1. Come in early to decorate, set up equipment and food, and check the lighting and sound systems.

2. Have volunteers collect tickets as well as sell more tickets at the event.

3. Follow your script to carry out all planned activities.

4. Initiate cleanup at the designated end time.

Fishing Tournament

Participants will have a "reel" good time competing in a fishing tournament while you catch some profits. Gather corporate sponsors, and provide prizes for the event.

Special Materials/Equipment
• Fishing gear (poles, lures, bait, etc.)

Sponsors/Donations

- Sporting goods stores are excellent sponsors for such events. Local sporting social clubs are also possible sponsors and may be able to help with equipment.

Possible Venue(s)

A city park with a lake or river is a good venue. If you are in a location situated on a larger body of water, consider a pier, dock, or boat.

Recommended Volunteer

10 including 5 committee heads to handle the venue, sponsors/donations, advertising, fees, prizes, setup, and cleanup. You will then need a number of people on hand at the event to help those with little fishing experience.

Preparation

Prep Time: 4 to 6 months

1. Start with a central committee of five to seven people who will serve as committee heads for the venue, food, decorations, sponsors/donations, advertising, ticket sales, entertainment, setup, and cleanup.

2. Decide when to have the event. Before you settle on a date, find out what else is going on in your community, and avoid conflicts.

3. Determine your budget. How much are you looking to raise, and what are you willing to spend to raise that amount?

4. Search for your perfect venue. If you have to change the date of your event to get the right venue, make sure, again, that you will have no competition from similar events that may be scheduled.

5. If you decide to serve food, plan your menu. Four months before the event, schedule a caterer, recruit people to cook, or ask restaurants or grocery stores to donate food.

6. Select what activities will occur at your event to raise more money. You may want a shore lunch, live or silent auction, or raffle. You can start by charging a fee for those who fish in your tournament. Alternatively, you can have those who plan to fish collect sponsorships in the same manner that they would in an event such as a walk-a-thon (see sample form and rules in Appendices).

7. Be sure to plan a rain date or a back-up plan in case the weather is bad.

8. Pick an emcee — either an organization member or a local celebrity. A celebrity can help you market the event.

9. Advertise by sending e-mails and letters, posting fliers, putting a notice on your organization's website, and making an announcement in your newsletter. Send press releases to local media outlets like newspapers and magazines, and contact local TV news and radio stations to request coverage and publicity.

10. Use the event's theme in everything from marketing, to graphic design of tickets and programs, to venue decorations.

11. Have your various committees meet regularly and keep the lines of communication open.

12. Three months out from the event, print tickets and have everyone in your organization sell tickets. Offer an incentive to the individuals who sell the most tickets.

13. If you need any special equipment such as sound, lights, staging, or seating, this is a good time to reserve these items. Do this as you think about how the venue will be set up for the event.

14. Do a walk-through of the venue a month before the event to check if all the venue systems work and ask when you can get in to decorate.

15. Write a script to serve as your minute-by-minute flow of activities for the event. Plan a time to thank your sponsors and distribute information promoting your organization.

16. Hold a meeting with all event volunteers and go over the tasks and schedule. Be clear on what you expect every volunteer to do. Tell volunteers what to wear for the event. Get everyone's contact information (phone number and e-mail) in case you need to communicate any changes or reminders.

Execution

1. Come in early to decorate, set up equipment and food, and check the lighting and sound systems.

2. Have volunteers collect tickets as well as sell more tickets at the event.

3. Follow your script to carry out all planned activities.

4. Initiate cleanup at the designated end time.

Tip(s)

- This event can be held any time of year if you are in a location where ice fishing is popular.
- Make additional profits by selling T-shirts or having a vendor fair.

Golf Tournament

Give participants the opportunity to tee-off for a good cause.

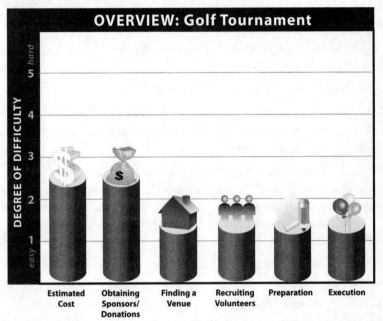

Sponsors/Donations

- Try to find a company, business, or individual who can sponsor the entire event by covering greens fees for the tournament. That way, whatever the golfers give goes straight to your organization.
- Also consider finding people and businesses to sponsor a hole or a golfer's game. Each golfer can sign up sponsors who will pay a per-hole sponsorship pledge to the golfer. Pledges of $100 each for 18 holes will quickly add up.
- Attempt to get golf clubs, bags, and assorted golf related items donated to be bid on throughout the day in a silent auction.

Possible Venue(s)

A public golf course or a country club will provide what you need.

Recommended Volunteer

5 to 10 to handle the venue, food, sponsors/donations, advertising, and ticket sales, including a volunteer pro golfer if possible

Preparation

Prep Time: 8 to 10 months

1. Start with a central committee of five to ten people to handle the venue, food, decorations, sponsors/donations, advertising, ticket sales, entertainment, setup, and cleanup.

2. Decide when to have the event. Before you settle on a date, find out what else is going on in your community, and avoid conflicts.

3. Determine your budget. How much are you looking to raise, and what are you willing to spend to raise that amount?

4. Start seeking sponsors and donations immediately.

5. Search for your perfect venue. If you have to change the date of your event to get the right venue, make sure, again, that you will have no competition from similar events that may be scheduled.

6. If you decide to serve food, plan your menu. Four months before the event, schedule a caterer, recruit people to cook, or ask restaurants or grocery stores to donate food. Decide if you would like to have a before-golf breakfast or an after-golf dinner. Consider having a beverage cart to drive the course and sell snacks and beverages.

7. Plan what additional fundraisers will occur at your event. You may want a live or silent auction or a raffle.

8. About three months prior to your event, advertise by sending e-mails and letters, posting fliers, putting a notice on your organization's website, and making an announcement in your newsletter. Send press releases to local media outlets like newspapers and magazines, and contact local TV news and radio stations to request coverage and publicity.

9. Use the event's theme in everything from marketing, to graphic design of tickets and programs, to venue decorations.

10. Have your various committees meet regularly and keep the lines of communication open.

11. Three months out from the event, print tickets and have everyone in your organization sell tickets. Offer an incentive to the individuals who sell the most tickets.

12. If you need any special equipment, such as seating, sound, light, or stage equipment, this is a good time to reserve these items. Do this as you think about how the venue will be set up for the event.

13. Do a walk-through of the venue a month before the event.

14. Write a script to serve as your minute-by-minute flow of activities for the event. Plan a time to thank your sponsors and distribute information promoting your organization.

15. Hold a meeting with all event volunteers and go over the tasks and schedule. Be clear on what you expect every volunteer to do. Tell volunteers what to wear for

the event. Get everyone's contact information (phone number and e-mail) in case you need to communicate any changes or reminders.

Execution

1. Arrive early to set up.

2. Have volunteers collect tickets as well as sell more tickets at the event.

3. Follow your script to carry out all planned activities.

4. Initiate cleanup at the designated end time.

Tip(s)

- Find a good course with many amenities. The nicer the course, the better turnout you will have.
- Get a volunteer golf pro to attend as a way to advertise and attract more golfers.

Variation(s)

- Have a miniature golf tournament to attract family participation.

Hot-Air Balloon Race

Find a large, open field and gather several professional hot-air balloonists. Choose a day with favorable winds and comfortable temperatures. Possible areas for this event include a construction site of a shopping mall, large parks, farm fields, or lawns of estates. Charge a fee for watching the race, or take bets on balloons, and obtain sponsorship on each balloon. Make additional profits by holding raffles, selling food, or selling pictures of participants inside the balloon baskets.

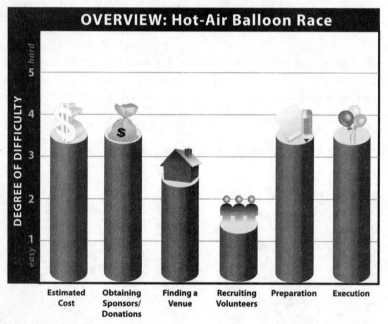

OVERVIEW: Hot-Air Balloon Race

DEGREE OF DIFFICULTY (easy 1 to hard 5): Estimated Cost, Obtaining Sponsors/Donations, Finding a Venue, Recruiting Volunteers, Preparation, Execution

Special Materials/Equipment
- Hot-air balloons

Sponsors/Donations
- Corporate sponsors who already sponsor your organization are likely to agree to serve as individual balloon sponsors and/or event sponsors.

Possible Venue(s)
You need a large open area, such as a park, school field, or mall parking lot.

Recommended Volunteer
10 to 15+ to find balloons and a venue as well as to sign up participants and manage the race

Preparation

Prep Time: Up to 1 year

1. Form committees to take care of setup, food, entertainment, advertising, and ticket sales. Have someone who understands the technical aspects of balloon racing head up a committee that will handle the grounds operations and identifying balloon racers. This individual will be in charge of mapping the area and placing the variety of events you will have.

2. Decide when to have the event. Before you settle on a date, find out what else is going on in your community, and avoid conflicts.

3. Determine your budget. How much are you looking to raise, and what are you willing to spend to raise that amount?

4. Start seeking sponsors and donations immediately.

5. Search for your perfect venue. If you have to change the date of your event to get the right venue, make sure, again, that you will have no competition from similar events that may be scheduled.

6. Eight to ten months in advance, book balloonists and plan events. Select what activities will occur at your event. You may want games, a live or silent auction, a raffle, or a band.

7. If you decide to serve food, plan your menu. Four months before the event, schedule a caterer, recruit people to cook, or ask restaurants or grocery stores to donate food.

8. At an outdoor event such as this is, nice weather is a must. Ideal locations for such events are booked early. Make the decision early on what you will do if the balloons cannot fly due to bad weather.

9. Pick an emcee — either an organization member or a local celebrity. A celebrity can help you market the event.

10. About three months before the event, advertise by sending e-mails and letters, posting fliers, putting a notice on your organization's website, and making an announcement in your newsletter. Send press releases to local media outlets like newspapers and magazines, and contact local TV news and radio stations to request coverage and publicity.

11. Use the event's theme in everything from marketing, to graphic design of tickets and programs, to venue decorations.

12. Have your various committees meet regularly and keep the lines of communication open.

13. Three months out from the event, print tickets and have everyone in your organization sell tickets. Offer an incentive to the individuals who sell the most tickets. At the event, plan on having a central ticket location where supporters can purchase tickets and then exchange them for food and games at different booths.

14. If you need any special equipment, such as seating, sound, light, or stage equipment, this is a good time to reserve these items. Do this as you think about how the venue will be set up for the event.

15. Do a walk-through of the venue a month before the event to check if all the venue systems work and ask when you can get in to decorate.

16. Write a script to serve as your minute-by-minute flow of activities for the event. Plan a time to thank your sponsors and distribute information promoting your organization.

17. Hold a meeting with all event volunteers and go over the tasks and schedule. Be clear on what you expect every volunteer to do. Tell volunteers what to wear for the event. Get everyone's contact information (phone number and e-mail) in case you need to communicate any changes or reminders.

Execution

1. Come in early to decorate, set up equipment and food, and check the lighting and sound systems.

2. Have volunteers collect tickets as well as sell more tickets at the event.

3. Follow your script to carry out all planned activities.

4. Initiate cleanup at the designated end time.

Mudfest

People will gladly pay for a chance to play in the mud, or to watch the messy action from the sidelines — especially in a college atmosphere. Create a mud pit by having a pit dug and filled with clay and water. Hold a week-long competition in which teams can pay to play mud games including mud tug, mud volleyball, mud polo, and mud Frisbee. Award trophies to the winning teams. Have T-shirt decorating contests, spirit points, and money wars. Hold a mud dance at the end of the games, complete with a DJ and an outdoor photo backdrop, and charge an admission fee.

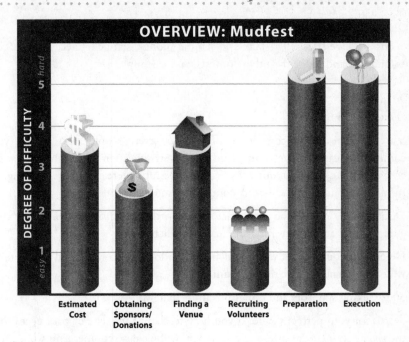

Special Materials/Equipment

- Hose or outdoor shower
- Water polo ball and two goals
- Tug-of-war rope
- Volleyball and volleyball net
- Frisbee
- Cones (to mark the "field")
- Mud pit (hire a backhoe to dig a pit, and have clay imported; add water)
- Whistles (for referees)
- Empty water or milk jugs (for the money wars)

Sponsors/Donations

- This type of event is ideal for local beverage distributor sponsorships.
- Seek local sports stores to donate old sports equipment for the mud games.
- Try to find a DJ who would offer free services for the dance.
- Ask a T-shirt company to donate or give discounted custom-made shirts, and offer sponsors advertising space on the back of the shirt.

Possible Venue(s)

An ideal venue might be a large, grassy field in a convenient location for spectators and that you have permission to dig up. Make sure showers and hoses can be stationed nearby so contestants can wash off. A local county fair grounds, where you might find arena seating around an open dirt floor normally used for rodeo shows, might work too.

Recommended Volunteer

15 to 20+ to advertise, sell tickets and handle money, setup, referee, keep track of points, and run and judge the other contests, and cleanup

Preparation

Prep Time: 6 to 8 months

1. Start with a central committee of five to seven people who will serve as committee heads for the venue/mud pit, advertising, sign-ups/money collection, entertainment, sponsors/donations, setup, cleanup, refereeing, score-keeping, and running and judging the T-shirt contest and money wars.

2. Decide when to have the event. Before you settle on a date, find out what else is going on in your community, and avoid conflicts.

3. Determine your budget. How much are you looking to raise, and what are you willing to spend to raise that amount?

4. Start seeking sponsors and donations immediately.

5. Search for your perfect venue. If you have to change the date of your event to get the right venue, make sure, again, that you will have no competition from similar events that may be scheduled.

6. Four months before the event, schedule a contractor to dig you a pit about the size of a shallow swimming pool only a few feet deep and fill it with clay and water.

7. Select what mud games will occur at your event (mud tug, mud volleyball, mud polo, and mud Frisbee), and print up a schedule of the game times. Leave room to fill in the names of the teams that will be playing.

8. Plan additional activities that will occur at your event, like a T-shirt design contest and a money war between teams. (Money wars is a competition between teams to see who can collect the most money using a special system — paper bills count as positive money in your money jug and coins count as negative money, so place bills in your jug and coins in competitors' jugs). Decide how you will award spirit points. Make preparations for a mud dance for the end of the week of mud games, book a DJ, and invite the public to the dance for an admission fee.

9. Find referees and judges. Compile a book of rules to be shared with participants for all games and contests. Give a copy to each team captain.

10. Order trophies, plaques, or certificates to award to the winning teams in each event, and to an overall winner.

11. Advertise by sending e-mails and letters, posting fliers, putting a notice on your organization's website, and making an announcement in your newsletter. Send press releases to local media outlets like newspapers and magazines, and contact local TV news and radio stations to request coverage and publicity.

12. Use the event's theme in everything from marketing, to graphic design of tickets and programs, to venue decorations.

13. Have your various committees meet regularly and keep the lines of communication open.

14. Three months out from the event, start signing up teams and hype up the competition.

15. If you need any special equipment, such as seating, sound, light, or stage equipment, this is a good time to reserve these items. Do this as you think about how the venue will be set up for the event.

16. Do a walk-through of the venue a month before the event to check if all the venue systems work and ask when you can you get in to decorate.

17. Write a script to serve as your minute-by-minute flow of activities for the event. Plan a time to thank your sponsors and distribute information promoting your organization.

18. Hold a meeting with all event volunteers and go over the tasks and schedule. Be clear on what you expect every volunteer to do. Tell volunteers what to wear for the event. Get everyone's contact information (phone number and e-mail) in case you need to communicate any changes or reminders.

Execution

1. Have everything set up before teams arrive to sign in.

2. Have volunteers sign teams in, collect submissions of T-shirt designs (or take a picture of the printed T-shirts), and show them the money jar that will be theirs to fill for the week for money wars.

3. Post a giant schedule up in an obvious place near the mud pit.

4. Charge spectators an entry fee, and let the games begin.

5. Start games on time, and follow your script to carry out all planned activities.

6. Initiate cleanup at the designated end time.

Tip(s)

- Because the mud may be slippery and sports activities involve a certain amount of risk, have all participants sign liability waivers.

Variation(s)

- Have a Snowfest, and set up the same games in the snow (snow volleyball, snow tug, snow polo, and snow Frisbee) and of course, the traditional snowman-building contest. If it is in a place that does not get snow, import a heap of snow.

Rock Climbing

Promote excitement and adventure by letting participants climb to the top of a rock wall for a fee.

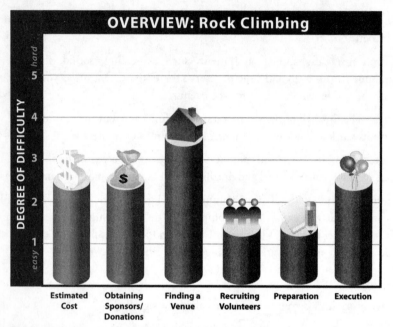

OVERVIEW: Rock Climbing

DEGREE OF DIFFICULTY (5 hard — easy)

Estimated Cost | Obtaining Sponsors/Donations | Finding a Venue | Recruiting Volunteers | Preparation | Execution

Special Materials/Equipment

- Rock wall and climbing equipment
- Loudspeaker
- Music/sound equipment

Sponsors/Donations

- Ask a rock climbing rental company to lend their climbing wall, equipment, and services for free or at a discount.
- Ask local food stores to donate snacks and beverages to sell to spectators.

Possible Venue(s)

Consider a gym, basketball court, or field.

Recommended Volunteer

5+ to handle the venue, sponsors/donations, advertising, ticket sales, and setup

Preparation

Prep Time: 3 to 4 months

1. Find a rock climbing rental company to donate a wall, equipment, and services. Arrange a central location that has a good sight line of the event to draw more participants in while others are rock climbing, and to gather spectators.

2. Make sure your organization and the venue have the necessary insurance to cover the event.

3. Make an arrangement with a local food vendor to sell hot dogs, ice cream, and fun refreshments to spectators and participants.

4. Choose a date.

5. Advertise by sending e-mails and letters, posting fliers, putting a notice on your organization's website, and making an announcement in your newsletter. Send press releases to local media outlets like newspapers and magazines, and contact local TV news and radio stations to request coverage and publicity.

6. Have every member of your organization pre-sell opportunities to rock climb.

Execution

1. Set up your equipment and refreshments, put out a sign to advertise to passersby, and start selling.

2. As people sign up to rock climb, have them write a message they would like read about themselves or to friends who are watching, and have them write how they might support your organization.

3. Use a loudspeaker to read each rock climber's message. Make sure they are appropriate for the setting before reading them.

4. Have music that plays as the climbs are made.

Tip(s)

- Holding this event in a highly populated downtown area during the early evening of a weekday is best to ensure you have a large audience. Friday evening at 5 p.m. is ideal.
- Though people will pay to rock climb, they can also get other donors to sponsor their activity. This is a good way to add additional donations.

Sky Diving

Fundraising does not get much more thrilling than jumping out of a plane for a cause. Create a personal campaign on **www.skydive4free.com**. Once you collect $500 in donations, take a free jump for your organization. Encourage other friends and supporters of your cause to follow suit.

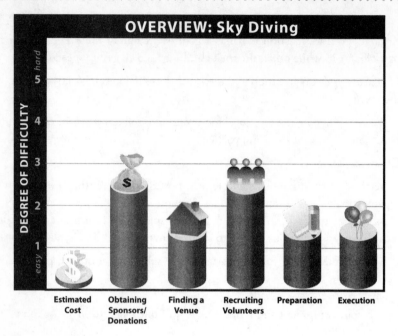

Sponsors/Donations

- E-mail family and friends a letter asking them to donate to help reach your goal to help your organization and make the skydive happen. Send them a link to your fundraising account on **www.skydive4free.com**.

Recommended Volunteer

1 to make the jump

Preparation

1. Register your group at **www.skydive4free.com**.

2. Choose your fundraising goal. This organization will set you up online to start raising a minimum of $500 toward your free skydive. When a minimum of $500 is raised, an individual from your organization will take a tandem skydive (one during which the skydiver is attached to a skydive instructor) in support of your cause. The more money raised, the higher the percentage of funds your organization will receive. Based on the amount of $500, approximately 50 percent of your fund raising will go to your organization. A campaign raising $1,000 would see about 70 percent of the money pledged. If you raise $5,000, your organization would see about 90 percent of the money pledged.

3. Advertise by sending e-mails and letters, posting fliers, putting a notice on your organization's website, and making an announcement in your newsletter. Send press releases to local media outlets like newspapers and magazines, and contact

local TV news and radio stations to request coverage and publicity. When you market your skydive, be sure to direct people to your website or your listing on **www.skydive4free.com**.

4. Collect donations toward your goal until you hit your target.

Execution

1. Once the fundraising goal is met, arrange to have someone from your organization jump from a plane with an instructor.

2. Send contributors photographs of the jump or invite them to watch the jumper land.

Tip(s)

- Buy the DVD of the skydiver's experience, and have a viewing party. Charge a few dollars each for organization members and the skydiver's friends to come watch. Sell drinks, popcorn, and other snacks. Get the next person to sign up and commit to a dive for your organization.

Soccer Tournament

Let participants go for the goal while helping you meet your fundraising goal. Charge a fee for teams to enter a soccer tournament. You can also have a kicking competition to see who can make the most goals. Make sure to offer other activities for families during the event.

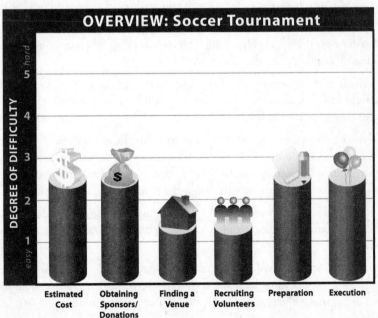

Special Materials/Equipment

- Soccer equipment (goals, soccer balls)

Sponsors/Donations

- Sporting goods stores are excellent sponsors for such events.
- Local sporting social clubs are also possible sponsors and may be able to help with equipment.

Possible Venue(s)

City parks with soccer fields are good venues. Schools are also excellent places to hold such events.

Recommended Volunteer

5 to 7+ to serve as committee heads for the venue, sponsors/donations, advertising, entry fees, and setup. You will also need a number of people on hand at the event to help with officiating.

Preparation

Prep Time: 6 months to 1 year

1. Start with a central committee of five to seven people who will serve as committee heads for the venue, sponsors/donations, advertising, registration and ticket sales, entertainment, setup, and cleanup.

2. Decide when to have the event. Before you settle on a date, find out what else is going on in your community, and avoid conflicts.

3. Determine your budget. How much are you looking to raise, and what are you willing to spend to raise that amount?

4. Search for your perfect venue. If you have to change the date of your event to get the right venue, make sure, again, that you will have no competition from similar events that may be scheduled.

5. You need to decide exactly what kind of tournament you will have. Decide if you will have youth soccer, adult soccer, boys and girls, full team soccer, six-on-six soccer. You will probably want to have advice from someone in your organization who is familiar with the game to design the structure of your tournament.

6. If you decide to serve food, plan your menu. Four months before the event, schedule a caterer, recruit people to cook, or ask restaurants or grocery stores to donate food.

7. Select what activities will occur at your event. Decide if you will have other fundraising mechanisms in place such as T-shirts, raffles, and/or silent auction. Decide if teams will pay a fee to play in the tournament, and if so, how much they will pay.

8. Decide what the tournament winners will receive and use that as an incentive to get teams to participate in your event.

9. Pick an announcer — either an organization member or a local sports celebrity. A celebrity can help you market the event.

10. Advertise by sending e-mails and letters, posting fliers, putting a notice on your organization's website, and making an announcement in your newsletter. Send press releases to local media outlets like newspapers and magazines, and contact local TV news and radio stations to request coverage and publicity. Programs are a good idea for events such as this because you can sell advertising and raise money through advertising dollars. If you plan on having programs, be sure you give yourself enough lead-time to get all of the program information together in time to get the program printed before the event. This is a task to be handled by your event marketing committee.

11. Use the event's theme in everything from marketing, to graphic design of tickets and programs, to venue decorations.

12. Have your various committees meet regularly and keep the lines of communication open.

13. Three months out from the event, print tickets and have everyone in your organization sell tickets. Offer an incentive to the individuals who sell the most tickets.

14. If you need any special equipment such as sound, lights, staging, or seating, this is a good time to reserve these items. Do this as you think about how the venue will be set up for the event.

15. Do a walk-through of the venue a month before the event to check if all the venue systems work and ask when you can get in to decorate.

16. Write a script to serve as your minute-by-minute flow of activities for the event. Plan a time to thank your sponsors and distribute information promoting your organization.

17. Hold a meeting with all event volunteers and go over the tasks and schedule. Be clear on what you expect every volunteer to do. Tell volunteers what to wear for the event. Get everyone's contact information (phone number and e-mail) in case you need to communicate any changes or reminders.

Execution

1. Come in early to decorate, set up equipment and food, and check the lighting and sound systems.

2. Have volunteers collect tickets as well as sell more tickets at the event.

3. Follow your script to carry out all planned activities.

4. Initiate cleanup at the designated end time.

Tip(s)

- A carnival can serve as a nice way to obtain additional profits for your organization.

Variation(s)

- Hold a baseball, softball, or Wiffle ball tournament.
- Have a flag football tournament.

Water Sports Challenge

Arrange for a local water sports center to provide a discount on morning or afternoon waterskiing or windsurfing. Obtain sponsors to donate to your charity based on the amount of time participants are able to stay standing. If some people are not avid water-skiers, in good spirits, have them seek sponsorship for the amount of times they fall.

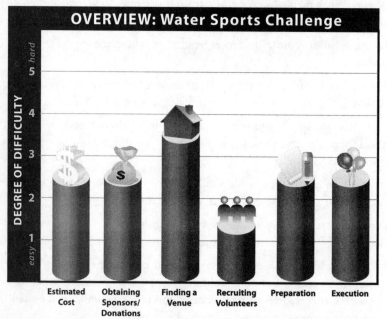

Sponsors/Donations

- Find a water sports center to lend their equipment and facility.
- Seek sponsorships from local sporting goods stores or sports drink distributors.

Possible Venue(s)

A good water sports center is key.

Recommended Volunteer
5+ to arrange for the venue, hospitality, and marketing

Preparation
Prep Time: Up to 1 year

1. Start with about five volunteers to arrange for the venue, participation, and advertising.

2. Decide when to have the event. Before you settle on a date, find out what else is going on in your community, and avoid conflicts.

3. Determine your budget. How much are you looking to raise, and what are you willing to spend to raise that amount?

4. Start seeking sponsors and donations immediately.

5. Search for your perfect venue. If you have to change the date of your event to get the right venue, make sure, again, that you will have no competition from similar events that may be scheduled.

6. If you decide to serve food, plan your menu. Four months before the event, schedule a caterer, recruit people to cook, or ask restaurants or grocery stores to donate food.

7. Select what activities will occur at your event. You may want a live or silent auction or a raffle.

8. Make a backup plan in case the weather is bad during your event.

9. Pick an emcee — either an organization member or a local celebrity. A celebrity can help you market the event.

10. Three months before the event, advertise by sending e-mails and letters, posting fliers, putting a notice on your organization's website, and making an announcement in your newsletter. Send press releases to local media outlets like newspapers and magazines, and contact local TV news and radio stations to request coverage and publicity.

11. Use the event's theme in everything from marketing, to graphic design of tickets and programs, to venue decorations.

12. Have your various committees meet regularly and keep the lines of communication open.

13. Three months out from the event, print tickets and have everyone in your organization sell tickets. Offer an incentive to the individuals who sell the most tickets. Plan for a central ticket location at the event, where supporters can purchase tickets and then exchange tickets for activities.

14. If you need any special equipment, such as seating, sound, light, or stage equipment, this is a good time to reserve these items. Do this as you think about how the venue will be set up for the event.

15. Do a walk-through of the venue a month before the event to check if all the venue systems work and ask when you can get in to decorate.

16. Write a script to serve as your minute-by-minute flow of activities for the event. Plan a time to thank your sponsors and distribute information promoting your organization.

17. Hold a meeting with all event volunteers and go over the tasks and schedule. Be clear on what you expect every volunteer to do. Tell volunteers what to wear for the event. Get everyone's contact information (phone number and e-mail) in case you need to communicate any changes or reminders.

Execution

1. Come in early to decorate, set up equipment and food, and check the lighting and sound systems.

2. Have volunteers collect tickets as well as sell more tickets at the event.

3. Follow your script to carry out all planned activities.

4. Initiate cleanup at the designated end time.

Tip(s)

• Most likely, you will raise the most funds by holding your event on a weekend. To get the most desirable date, you may have to pay the water sports center for the use of their facility and charge your supporters a fee that covers the cost of admission plus a donation to your organization.

• Most water sports centers have concession stands, so any food and drink that you plan to bring in will take business away from their concessions. Make arrangements regarding food and drink when you negotiate your facility usage.

Chapter 18

Themed Events

This chapter includes events that capture a theme, providing a fun get away for your supporters. The projects you will find in this chapter include:

- Beach Bash
- Casino Night
- Go Green Party
- International Day
- Night in Paris
- Renaissance Fair
- Superhero Fair
- '20s Dinner Party

- Black Tie Gala
- Fabulous New York Fundraiser
- Harry Potter Extravaganza
- Medieval Banquet
- Picture Perfect Party
- Spa Day
- Toga Party
- Without a Clue Party

Beach Bash

This fundraiser is ideal for communities by the coast. Arrange for popular bands to perform and organize volleyball tournaments with entry costs and cash prizes for the winners. Hold a babes and hunks contest, and have people pay a small fee to cast their vote. Have a drink company provide refreshments at the event, and get a local radio station to broadcast live from the beach to draw more people to attend.

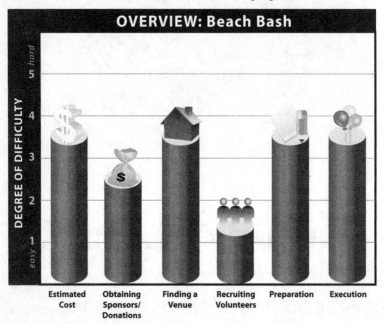

Special Materials/Equipment

- Stage (for live bands)
- Sound equipment (microphone, speakers)
- Volleyball equipment

Sponsors/Donations

- Local sports drink distributors are perfect sponsors for these events. Ideally, you want sponsorship dollars to allow these sponsors to spread their names all over your event. They get advertising and you get their support.

Possible Venue(s)

Seek the best beach in your community for throwing a party.

Recommended Volunteer

10+ including 5 to 7 to serve as committee heads for the venue, food, decorations, sponsors/donations, advertising, ticket sales, entertainment, setup, and cleanup.

Preparation

Prep Time: Up to 1 year

1. Start with a central committee of five to seven people who will serve as committee heads for the venue, food, decorations, sponsors/donations, advertising, ticket sales, entertainment, setup, and cleanup.

2. Decide when to have the event. Before you settle on a date, find out what else is going on in your community, and avoid conflicts.

3. Determine your budget. How much are you looking to raise, and what are you willing to spend to raise that amount?

4. Start seeking sponsors and donations immediately.

5. Search for your perfect venue. If you have to change the date of your event to get the right venue, make sure, again, that you will have no competition from similar events that may be scheduled. You may charge an admission to the beach if the beach venue is set up in such a way to allow you to charge admission.

6. Six months before the event, choose your menu and schedule the caterer, if you decide to serve food. Consider arranging a picnic or barbecue and charging per plate. Having a central ticket location is a good idea. Supporters can purchase tickets at a central booth and then exchange tickets for food.

7. Select what activities will occur at your event, such as a volleyball tournament and a babes and hunks contest. You may also have a sand castle building contest, live or silent auction, or raffle. You may want to book a band or DJ.

8. Have a back-up plan in case the weather is bad, like a nearby indoor hall to relocate to.

9. Pick an emcee — either an organization member or a local celebrity. A celebrity can help you market the event.

10. Three months prior to the event, advertise by sending e-mails and letters, posting fliers, putting a notice on your organization's website, and making an announcement in your newsletter. Send press releases to local media outlets like newspapers and magazines, and contact local TV news and radio stations to request coverage and publicity.

11. Use the event's theme in everything from marketing, to graphic design of tickets and programs, to venue decorations.

12. Have your various committees meet regularly and keep the lines of communication open.

13. Three months out from the event, print tickets and have everyone in your organization sell tickets. Offer an incentive to the individuals who sell the most tickets.

14. If you need any special equipment, such as seating, sound, light, or stage equipment, this is a good time to reserve these items. Do this as you think about how the venue will be set up for the event.

15. Do a walk-through of the venue a month before the event to check if all the venue systems work and ask when you can you get in to decorate.

16. Write a script to serve as your minute-by-minute flow of activities for the event. Plan a time to thank your sponsors and distribute information promoting your organization.

17. Hold a meeting with all event volunteers and go over the tasks and schedule. Be clear on what you expect every volunteer to do. Tell volunteers what to wear for the event. Get everyone's contact information (phone number and e-mail) in case you need to communicate any changes or reminders.

Execution

1. Come in early to decorate, set up equipment and food, and check the lighting and sound systems.

2. Have volunteers collect tickets as well as sell more tickets at the event.

3. Follow your script to carry out all planned activities.

4. Initiate cleanup at the designated end time.

Black Tie Gala

Guests can enjoy a formal evening of dinner, a live jazz band, and a silent auction for luxurious experiences like spa retreats while you ring in the money from ticket sales.

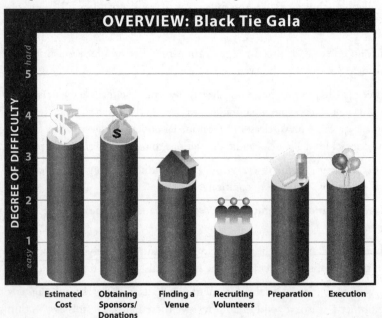

Special Materials/Equipment
- Stage
- Sound equipment (microphone, speakers)
- Tables and chairs

Sponsors/Donations
- Find a major supporter to sponsor the entire event or to cover the cost of the venue.
- Seek several sponsors for tables. A sponsor might purchase a table that seats 10 for dinner and give the tickets to employees, friends, or family.
- Have sponsors donate big-ticket items to auction for the silent auction, like trips, large electronics, or jewelry.

Possible Venue(s)
A hotel is a great place because it usually has a large ballroom, a caterer, and an in-house sound system and lighting.

Recommended Volunteer
10 to 15+ including 5 to 7 to serve as committee heads for the venue, food, decorations, sponsors/donations, advertising, ticket sales, entertainment, setup, and cleanup

Preparation
Prep Time: 6 months to 1 year

1. Start with a central committee of five to seven people who will serve as committee heads for the venue, food, decorations, sponsors/donations, advertising, ticket sales, entertainment, setup, and cleanup.

2. Decide when to have the event. Before you settle on a date, find out what else is going on in your community, and avoid conflicts.

3. Determine your budget. How much are you looking to raise, and what are you willing to spend to raise that amount?

4. Start seeking sponsors and donations immediately.

5. Search for your perfect venue. If you have to change the date of your event to get the right venue, make sure, again, that you will have no competition from similar events that may be scheduled.

6. If you decide to serve food, plan your menu. Four months before the event, schedule a caterer, recruit people to cook, or ask restaurants or grocery stores to donate food.

7. Plan what additional fundraisers and entertainment will occur at your event. You may want a live or silent auction, raffle, or band.

8. Pick an emcee — either an organization member or a local celebrity. A celebrity can help you market the event.

9. Three months in advance, advertise by sending e-mails and letters, posting fliers, putting a notice on your organization's website, and making an announcement in your newsletter. Send press releases to local media outlets like newspapers and magazines, and contact local TV news and radio stations to request coverage and publicity.

10. Use the event's theme in everything from marketing, to graphic design of tickets and programs, to venue decorations.

11. Have your various committees meet regularly and keep the lines of communication open.

12. Three months out from the event, print tickets and have everyone in your organization sell tickets. Offer an incentive to the individuals who sell the most tickets.

13. If you need any special equipment, such as seating, sound, light, or stage equipment, this is a good time to reserve these items. Do this as you think about how the venue will be set up for the event.

14. Do a walk-through of the venue a month before the event to check if all the venue systems work and ask when you can get in to decorate.

15. Write a script to serve as your minute-by-minute flow of activities for the event. Plan a time to thank your sponsors and distribute information promoting your organization.

16. Hold a meeting with all event volunteers and go over the tasks and schedule. Be clear on what you expect every volunteer to do. Tell volunteers what to wear for the event. Get everyone's contact information (phone number and e-mail) in case you need to communicate any changes or reminders.

Execution

1. Come in early to decorate, set up equipment and food, and check the lighting and sound systems.

2. Have volunteers collect tickets as well as sell more tickets at the event.

3. Follow your script to carry out all planned activities.

4. Initiate cleanup at the designated end time.

Tip(s)

- Send out a "save-the-date" card or e-mail a month or two before the event. This card will let people know the event, date, place, and maybe even what entertainment might be featured. The trick with the save-the-date card is to send it out early enough to give your potential audience the heads-up about your event, but not so early that they will forget about it.

Casino Night

Go "all in" on this fun evening of casino games. Casino nights are popular and simple to promote, so it is a safe bet that your organization will be successful. Consider making it into an annual occurrence.

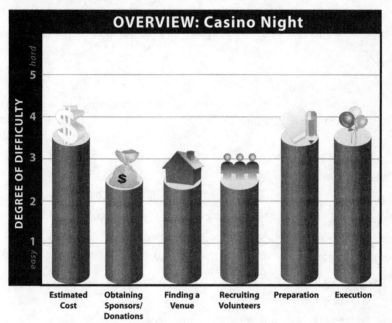

Special Materials/Equipment

- Casino games
- Chairs
- Poker chips
- Card tables
- Multiple decks of playing cards

Sponsors/Donations

- Ask party supply houses if you can rent games and chips for free or for a reduced price. Many cities also have companies that will offer equipment and personnel to assist you in your event.

- Solicit sponsors and items for auction, and arrange plans for a catered dinner.

- Try to find a company, business, or individual who might sponsor the entire event. The sponsorship cost could cover the cost of the venue and any rentals you may have to obtain to outfit the venue.

- Each player can sign up sponsors to pay a per-game sponsorship pledge to the player or simply pledge the player's evening.

- Consider finding people and businesses to sponsor a game (such as a roulette sponsor) or a card table. You can get, say, 20 sponsors to donate $100 per game.

- Try getting donations of cash or big-ticket items such as flat-screen TVs or even a car that will be used for a silent auction or raffle at the event.

Possible Venue(s)

A casino, hotel, recreation room, or any place that has the space and permits gambling is good.

Recommended Volunteer

10+ including committees to handle the venue, sponsors/donations, advertising, money, games, setup, and cleanup

Preparation

Prep Time: 3 to 6 months

1. Start with a central committee of five people to handle the venue, sponsors/ donations, advertising, money, games, setup, and cleanup.

2. Decide when to have the event. Before you settle on a date, find out what else is going on in your community, and avoid conflicts.

3. Determine your budget. How much are you looking to raise, and what are you willing to spend to raise that amount?

4. Start seeking sponsors and donations immediately.

5. Search for an appropriate venue that permits gambling. If you have to change the date of your event to get the right venue, make sure, again, that you will have no competition from similar events that may be scheduled.

6. Four months before the event, choose your menu and schedule the caterer, if you decide to serve food and drinks.

7. Plan what casino games you will feature, and whether you will offer a poker tournament, auction, and/or raffle.

8. Determine the rules of play for each of the games you offer. Your organization has to determine how you will make money from the event and how the players will benefit from winning. You might charge an entrance fee for each player and take a percentage of each game.

9. Advertise by sending e-mails and letters, posting fliers, putting a notice on your organization's website, and making an announcement in your newsletter. Send press releases to local media outlets like newspapers and magazines, and contact local TV news and radio stations to request coverage and publicity.

10. Use the event's theme in everything from marketing, to graphic design of tickets and programs, to venue decorations.

11. Have your various committees meet regularly and keep the lines of communication open.

12. Assign volunteers to run games, and make sure they are comfortable with the rules of the game in order to prevent misunderstandings during play.

13. Three months out from the event, print tickets and have everyone in your organization sell tickets. Offer an incentive to the individuals who sell the most tickets.

14. If you need any special equipment, such as seating, sound, light, or stage equipment, this is a good time to reserve these items. Do this as you thimk about how the venue will be set up for the event.

15. Do a walk-through of the venue a month before the event to check if all the venue systems work and ask when you can get in to decorate.

16. Write a script to serve as your minute-by-minute timeline of activities for the event, and set a closing time. Be sure to plan a time to announce winners, thank your sponsors, and distribute information about your organization.

17. Hold a meeting with all event volunteers and go over the tasks and schedule. Be clear on what you expect every volunteer to do. Tell volunteers what to wear for the event. Get everyone's contact information (phone number and e-mail) in case you need to communicate any changes or reminders.

Execution

1. Come in early to decorate, set up tables and games, and check the lighting and sound systems.

2. Have volunteers collect tickets at the door as well as sell more tickets at the event.

3. Follow your script to carry out all planned activities.

4. Initiate cleanup at the designated end time.

Tip(s)

- Events such as this are good for utilizing many different ways of raising funds. If you begin planning early, you can include a poker tournament, silent auction, and raffle.
- Set up side tables that people can buy into when they get eliminated from their original card game table. This is a good way to make a few extra dollars and it keeps people at your event from beginning to end.

Fabulous New York Fundraiser

Have guests take a trip to New York without the expenses of traveling. Sell tickets for admission to the event. Decorate your venue with skyscraper backdrops, bright lights, billboards, city street signs, and maybe even a few taxi cabs (or pictures of them).

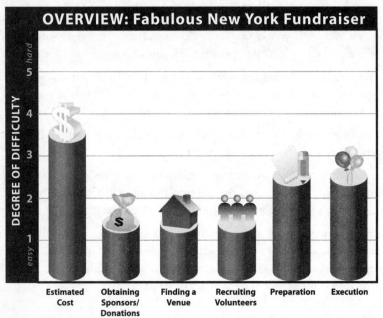

Special Materials/Equipment

- New York decorations
- Sound system (microphone, speakers)
- Banquet tables and chairs

Sponsors/Donations

- The best donation that you might possibly get is an event or venue sponsor. Otherwise, seek sponsors for each banquet table.

Possible Venue(s)

If you want to go all out, have the event at an upscale hotel in your community, or any venue with a fancy banquet room.

Recommended Volunteer

10+ volunteers can work as committees to organize the overall event, the decorations committee, food and beverage committee, the entertainment committee, and the marketing and ticket committee

Preparation

Prep Time: 6 months to 1 year

1. Start with a central committee of five to seven people who will serve as committee heads for the venue, food, decorations, sponsors/donations, advertising, ticket sales, entertainment, setup, and cleanup.

2. Decide when to have the event. Before you settle on a date, find out what else is going on in your community, and avoid conflicts.

3. Determine your budget. How much are you looking to raise, and what are you willing to spend to raise that amount?

4. Start seeking sponsors and donations immediately.

5. Search for your perfect venue. If you have to change the date of your event to get the right venue, make sure, again, that you will have no competition from similar events that may be scheduled.

6. If you decide to serve food, plan your menu. Four months before the event, schedule a caterer, recruit people to cook, or ask restaurants or grocery stores to donate food. You can serve New York cut steaks, drink Manhattans, and have New York Cherry Cheesecake for dessert.

7. Select what activities will occur at your event. You may want a live or silent auction, raffle, or band. Consider having a local theater company perform some Broadway show tunes.

8. Pick an emcee — either an organization member or a local celebrity. A celebrity can help you market the event.

9. Advertise by sending e-mails and letters, posting fliers, putting a notice on your organization's website, and making an announcement in your newsletter. Send press releases to local media outlets like newspapers and magazines, and contact local TV news and radio stations to request coverage and publicity.

10. Use the event's theme in everything from marketing, to graphic design of tickets and programs, to venue decorations.

11. Have your various committees meet regularly and keep the lines of communication open.

12. Three months out from the event, print tickets and have everyone in your organization sell tickets. Offer an incentive to the individuals who sell the most tickets.

13. If you need any special equipment, such as seating, sound, light, or stage equipment, this is a good time to reserve these items. Do this as you think about how the venue will be set up for the event.

14. Do a walk-through of the venue a month before the event to check if all the venue systems work and ask when you can get in to decorate.

15. Write a script to serve as your minute-by-minute flow of activities for the event. Plan a time to thank your sponsors and distribute information promoting your organization.

16. Hold a meeting with all event volunteers and go over the tasks and schedule. Be clear on what you expect every volunteer to do. Tell volunteers what to wear for the event. Get everyone's contact information (phone number and e-mail) in case you need to communicate any changes or reminders.

Execution

1. Come in early to decorate, set up equipment and food, and check the lighting and sound systems.

2. Have volunteers collect tickets as well as sell more tickets at the event.

3. Follow your script to carry out all planned activities.

4. Initiate cleanup at the designated end time.

Variation(s)

- Hold a Foggy London Fundraiser.

Go Green Party

This hot topic is a cool way to help the earth while raising money for your organization. Gather a group of friends and start a community beautification initiative. Have volunteers and supporters of your efforts make donations to your organization. Host a party featuring a premier of a popular nature program, and educate participants about smarter living habits. Have computers set up at the party, and encourage people to e-mail local, state, and federal officials, campaigning for a greener tomorrow.

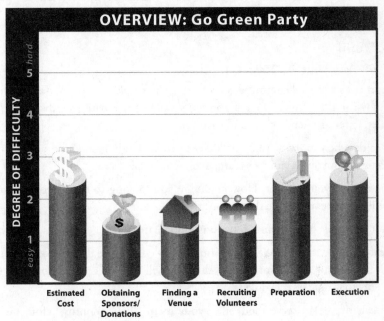

Special Materials/Equipment

Depending on the beautification project you choose, you may need:

- Trash bags
- Sandblaster (for grafitti)
- Plants
- Gloves
- Paint
- Shovels

For party:

- Lighting
- Projection equipment
- Sound equipment (microphone, speakers)
- Educational materials/video
- Computers

Sponsors/Donations

- Local environmental groups might be good sponsors for this event.
- Also, if there is a local business that markets itself as a supporter of environmental issues, you might try speaking to them about sponsoring your event.

Possible Venue(s)

If you are planning your event to take place during warm weather months, consider holding your event outside in a city park. If your event is at a time of the year when you are better off planning for an indoor party, choose a place where you can best highlight your message.

Recommended Volunteer

5 to 7+ to serve as committee heads for the venue, food, decorations, sponsors/ donations, advertising, ticket sales, entertainment, setup, and cleanup

Preparation

Prep Time: 6 months to 1 year

1. Start with a central committee of five to seven people who will serve as committee heads for the venue, food, decorations, sponsors/donations, advertising, ticket sales, entertainment, setup, and cleanup.

2. Decide when to have the event. Before you settle on a date, find out what else is going on in your community, and avoid conflicts.

3. Determine your budget. How much are you looking to raise, and what are you willing to spend to raise that amount?

4. Start seeking sponsors and donations immediately.

5. Search for your perfect venue. If you have to change the date of your event to get the right venue, make sure, again, that you will have no competition from similar events that may be scheduled.

6. If you decide to serve food, plan your menu. Four months before the event, schedule a caterer, recruit people to cook, or ask restaurants or grocery stores to donate food. Try to serve food with environmentally friendly plates, utensils, and napkins (biodegradable, reusable, or made from recycled material).

7. Select some activities for the party. You may want a live or silent auction, raffle, band, or guest speaker. Promote environmentally friendly products when possible.

8. Pick an emcee — either an organization member or a local celebrity. A celebrity can help you market the event.

9. Advertise by sending e-mails and letters, posting fliers, putting a notice on your organization's website, and making an announcement in your newsletter. Send press releases to local media outlets like newspapers and magazines, and contact local TV news and radio stations to request coverage and publicity.

10. Use the event's theme in everything from marketing, to graphic design of tickets and programs, to venue decorations.

11. Have your various committees meet regularly and keep the lines of communication open.

12. Three months out from the party, print tickets and have everyone in your organization sell tickets. Offer an incentive to the individuals who sell the most tickets.

13. If you need any special equipment such as sound, lights, staging, or seating, this is a good time to reserve these items. Do this as you think about how the venue will be set up for the event.

14. Do a walk-through of the venue a month before the event to check if all the venue systems work and ask when you can get in to decorate.

15. Write a script to serve as your minute-by-minute flow of activities for the event. Plan a time to thank your sponsors and distribute information promoting your organization.

16. Hold a meeting with all event volunteers and go over the tasks and schedule. Be clear on what you expect every volunteer to do. Tell volunteers what to wear for the event. Get everyone's contact information (phone number and e-mail) in case you need to communicate any changes or reminders.

Execution

1. Come in early to decorate, set up equipment and food, and check the lighting and sound systems.

2. Have volunteers collect tickets as well as sell more tickets at the event.

3. Follow your script to carry out all planned activities.

4. Initiate cleanup at the designated end time.

Variation(s)

- Have the party after completing a beautification project. Sell tickets at a discounted price to those who participate in the project. Beautification could include renting a sandblaster to erase graffiti from buildings; picking up litter from a street, beach, park, or your organization's parking lot; painting old buildings; and doing landscaping.

Harry Potter Extravaganza

Host a Harry Potter themed party, and watch your guests light up with excitement as they enter this fantasy world. Ask a local magician to perform and teach guests tricks and magic spells at a magic-themed bar. Cover your venue with wizard decorations and other pictures in the Harry Potter theme. Have guests dress up as their favorite Harry Potter character. Charge an admission fee.

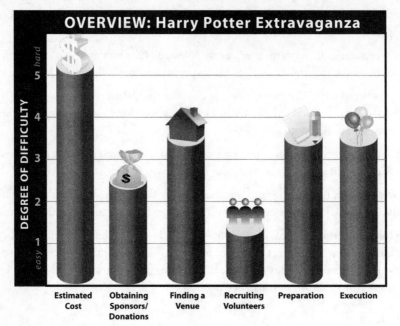

OVERVIEW: Harry Potter Extravaganza

DEGREE OF DIFFICULTY — *easy* to *hard*

- Estimated Cost
- Obtaining Sponsors/Donations
- Finding a Venue
- Recruiting Volunteers
- Preparation
- Execution

Special Materials/Equipment

- Hogwarts decorations
- Harry Potter-themed food service items

Sponsors/Donations

- Local theaters and performing arts organizations or theatrical prop companies are great places to seek donations of costumes and props for this event.
- Local bookstores may also be good places to seek sponsorships.

Possible Venue(s)

Large old churches, community buildings, or schools could be good venues.

Recommended Volunteer

10 to 15+ including 5 to 7 people to oversee the venue, food, decorations, sponsors/donations, advertising, ticket sales, entertainment, setup, and cleanup

Preparation

Prep Time: 6 months to 1 year

1. Start with a central committee of five to seven people who will serve as committee heads for the venue, food, decorations, sponsors/donations, advertising, ticket sales, entertainment, setup, and cleanup.

2. Decide when to have the event. Before you settle on a date, find out what else is going on in your community, and avoid conflicts.

3. Determine your budget. How much are you looking to raise, and what are you willing to spend to raise that amount?

4. Start seeking sponsors and donations immediately.

5. Search for your perfect venue. If you have to change the date of your event to get the right venue, make sure, again, that you will have no competition from similar events that may be scheduled.

6. If you decide to serve food, plan your menu. Four months before the event, schedule a caterer, recruit people to cook, or ask restaurants or grocery stores to donate food.

7. Select what activities will occur at your event. You may want a live or silent auction, raffle, or band. You may consider having music and dancing.

8. Pick an emcee who can pose as Professor Dumbledore — either an organization member or a local celebrity. A celebrity can help you market the event.

9. Advertise by sending e-mails and letters, posting fliers, putting a notice on your organization's website, and making an announcement in your newsletter. Send press releases to local media outlets like newspapers and magazines, and contact local TV news and radio stations to request coverage and publicity.

10. Use the event's theme in everything from marketing, to graphic design of tickets and programs, to venue decorations.

11. Have your various committees meet regularly and keep the lines of communication open.

12. Three months out from the event, print tickets and have everyone in your organization sell tickets. Offer an incentive to the individuals who sell the most tickets.

13. If you need any special equipment such as sound, lights, staging, or seating, this is a good time to reserve these items. Do this as you think about how the venue will be set up for the event.

14. Do a walk-through of the venue a month before the event to check if all the venue systems work and ask when you can get in to decorate.

15. Write a script to serve as your minute-by-minute flow of activities for the event. Plan a time to thank your sponsors and distribute information promoting your organization.

16. Hold a meeting with all event volunteers and go over the tasks and schedule. Be clear on what you expect every volunteer to do. Tell volunteers what to wear for the event. Get everyone's contact information (phone number and e-mail) in case you need to communicate any changes or reminders.

Execution

1. Come in early to decorate, set up equipment and food, and check the lighting and sound systems.

2. Have volunteers collect tickets as well as sell more tickets at the event.

3. Follow your script to carry out all planned activities.

4. Initiate cleanup at the designated end time.

Tip(s)

*   Be aware that Harry Potter is a copyrighted character and you should only use the names and likenesses of the popular characters in ways that are not in violation of copyright laws.

Variation(s)

*   For those who prefer vampires and werewolves, try a Twilight Party.

International Day

Celebrate diversity by hosting a day featuring food, music, and speakers from around the world.

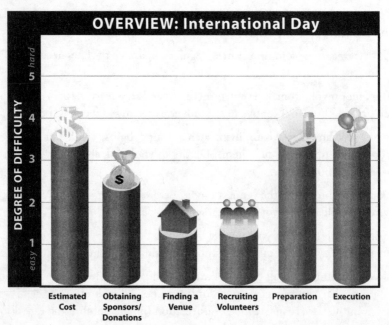

Special Materials/Equipment

- International food
- International music
- International decorations (i.e. flags, travel brochures)

Sponsors/Donations

- Many larger urban areas have international consulates or representatives that may wish to sponsor your event.
- Many cultural groups have social organizations committed to helping the community-at-large better understand their cultures by sponsoring the event.

Possible Venue(s)

Social halls, churches, schools, and hotels are possible venues.

Recommended Volunteer

15+ including 5 to 7 to serve as committee heads for the venue, food, decorations, sponsors/donations, advertising, ticket sales, entertainment, setup, and cleanup

Preparation

Prep Time: 6 months to 1 year

1. Start with a central committee of five to seven people who will serve as committee heads for the venue, food, decorations, sponsors/donations, advertising, ticket sales, entertainment, setup, and cleanup.

2. Decide when to have the event. Before you settle on a date, find out what else is going on in your community, and avoid conflicts.

3. Determine your budget. How much are you looking to raise, and what are you willing to spend to raise that amount?

4. Start seeking sponsors and donations immediately.

5. Search for your perfect venue. If you have to change the date of your event to get the right venue, make sure, again, that you will have no competition from similar events that may be scheduled.

6. If you decide to serve food, plan your menu. Four months before the event, schedule a caterer, recruit people to cook, or ask restaurants or grocery stores to donate food.

7. Select what activities will occur at your event. You may want a live or silent auction, raffle, or band.

8. Pick an emcee — either an organization member or a local celebrity. A celebrity can help you market the event.

9. Advertise by sending e-mails and letters, posting fliers, putting a notice on your organization's website, and making an announcement in your newsletter. Send press releases to local media outlets like newspapers and magazines, and contact local TV news and radio stations to request coverage and publicity.

10. Use the event's theme in everything from marketing, to graphic design of tickets and programs, to venue decorations.

11. Have your various committees meet regularly and keep the lines of communication open.

12. Three months out from the event, print tickets and have everyone in your organization sell tickets. Offer an incentive to the individuals who sell the most tickets.

13. If you need any special equipment such as sound, lights, staging, or seating, this is a good time to reserve these items. Do this as you think about how the venue will be set up for the event.

14. Do a walk-through of the venue a month before the event to check if all the venue systems work and ask when you can get in to decorate.

15. Write a script to serve as your minute-by-minute flow of activities for the event. Plan a time to thank your sponsors and distribute information promoting your organization.

16. Hold a meeting with all event volunteers and go over the tasks and schedule. Be clear on what you expect every volunteer to do. Tell volunteers what to wear for the event. Get everyone's contact information (phone number and e-mail) in case you need to communicate any changes or reminders.

Execution

1. Come in early to decorate, set up equipment and food, and check the lighting and sound systems.

2. Have volunteers collect tickets as well as sell more tickets at the event.

3. Follow your script to carry out all planned activities.

4. Initiate cleanup at the designated end time.

Variation(s)

- Theme the night around one country, such as by having an Italian Spaghetti Dinner and Opera, or an Evening in Ireland featuring a band that plays Irish jigs and waltzes.
- Plan an International Speakers Dinner featuring speakers from a variety of countries.

Medieval Banquet

Host a banquet where silverware is a foreign concept. Instead of fancy dishes, serve classic finger foods like chicken wings and other forms of meat, and maybe even a whole roast pig and some ale. Decorate with armor, weapons, and pictures of knights and dragons. Charge a fee for admission and dinner.

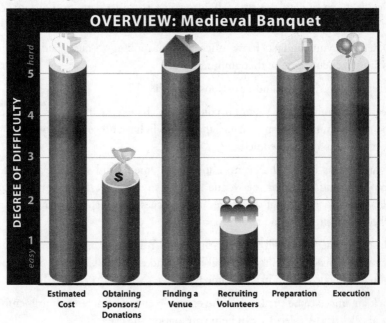

Special Materials/Equipment
- Medieval decorations
- Long tables
- Medieval-style dinner food
- Chairs

Sponsors/Donations
- Local theaters and performing arts organizations are suitable places to seek donations of costumes and props.

Possible Venue(s)
Large old churches, community buildings, or schools make for good locations.

Recommended Volunteer
10 to 15+ including 5 to 7 to serve as committee heads for the venue, food, decorations, sponsors/donations, advertising, ticket sales, entertainment, setup, and cleanup

Preparation

Prep Time: 6 months to 1 year

1. Start with a central committee of five to seven people who will serve as committee heads for the venue, food, decorations, sponsors/donations, advertising, ticket sales, entertainment, setup, and cleanup.

2. Decide when to have the event. Before you settle on a date, find out what else is going on in your community, and avoid conflicts.

3. Determine your budget. How much are you looking to raise, and what are you willing to spend to raise that amount?

4. Start seeking sponsors and donations immediately.

5. Search for your perfect venue. If you have to change the date of your event to get the right venue, make sure, again, that you will have no competition from similar events that may be scheduled.

6. Four months before the event, choose your menu and schedule the caterer. If you are doing the event at a venue that does not offer catering services, plan on identifying a caterer that specializes in barbecues and/or specialty meats. Having a whole roast pig is a good choice.

7. Select what activities will occur at your event. You may want a live or silent auction or raffle. Consider having medieval music and dancing. Consider finding a jester who can juggle and do bawdy comedy.

8. Pick an emcee to be the king of the court — either an organization member or a local celebrity. A celebrity can help you market the event.

9. Advertise by sending e-mails and letters, posting fliers, putting a notice on your organization's website, and making an announcement in your newsletter. Send press releases to local media outlets like newspapers and magazines, and contact local TV news and radio stations to request coverage and publicity.

10. Use the event's theme in everything from marketing, to graphic design of tickets and programs, to venue decorations.

11. Have your various committees meet regularly and keep the lines of communication open.

12. Three months out from the event, print tickets and have everyone in your organization sell tickets. Offer an incentive to the individuals who sell the most tickets.

13. If you need any special equipment such as sound, lights, staging, or seating, this is a good time to reserve these items. Do this as you think about how the venue will be set up for the event.

14. Do a walk-through of the venue a month before the event to check if all the venue systems work and ask when you can get in to decorate.

15. Write a script to serve as your minute-by-minute flow of activities for the event. Plan a time to thank your sponsors and distribute information promoting your organization.

16. Hold a meeting with all event volunteers and go over the tasks and schedule. Be clear on what you expect every volunteer to do. Tell volunteers what to wear for the event. Get everyone's contact information (phone number and e-mail) in case you need to communicate any changes or reminders.

Execution

1. Come in early to decorate, set up equipment and food, and check the lighting and sound systems.

2. Have volunteers collect tickets as well as sell more tickets at the event.

3. Follow your script to carry out all planned activities.

4. Initiate cleanup at the designated end time.

Variation(s)

- Hold a Roman Toga Banquet.
- Have a Western Chuck Wagon Banquet.

Night in Paris

Revive the romantic vibes of Paris by hosting a French dinner. For a set admission fee, guests can enjoy fine French cuisine, such as French bread, cheese, and wine. Decorate the venue with items reminiscent of Paris, like an Eiffel Tower replica and pictures of the city.

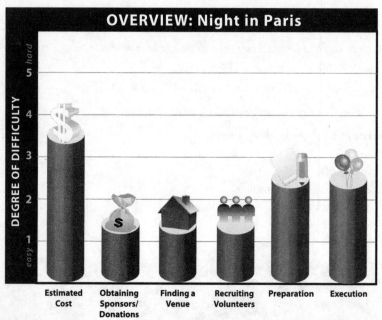

OVERVIEW: Night in Paris

DEGREE OF DIFFICULTY (easy 1 — hard 5)

Estimated Cost | Obtaining Sponsors/Donations | Finding a Venue | Recruiting Volunteers | Preparation | Execution

Special Materials/Equipment
- Parisian decorations
- Banquet tables
- Sound system (microphone, speakers)
- French food
- Chairs
- Specialty lighting

Sponsors/Donations
- The best donation is that of a venue.
- Find sponsors for each banquet table.
- Seek out event sponsors.

Possible Venue(s)
Consider having it at an upscale hotel in your community, or at any venue with a fancy banquet room.

Recommended Volunteer
10 to 15+ to take care of the venue, food, decorations, sponsors/donations, advertising, ticket sales, entertainment, setup, and cleanup

Preparation

Prep Time: 6 months to 1 year

1. Start with a central committee of five to seven people who will serve as committee heads for the venue, food, decorations, sponsors/donations, advertising, ticket sales, entertainment, setup, and cleanup.

2. Decide when to have the event. Before you settle on a date, find out what else is going on in your community, and avoid conflicts.

3. Determine your budget. How much are you looking to raise, and what are you willing to spend to raise that amount?

4. Start seeking sponsors and donations immediately.

5. Search for your perfect venue. If you have to change the date of your event to get the right venue, make sure, again, that you will have no competition from similar events that may be scheduled.

6. Four months before the event, choose your menu and schedule the caterer. Consider serving popular French items like escargot, champagne, and crème brulèe.

7. Select what activities will occur at your event. You may want a live or silent auction, raffle, or band. Consider having a local theater company perform in the manner of a French theater.

8. Pick an emcee — either an organization member or a local celebrity. A celebrity can help you market the event.

9. Advertise by sending e-mails and letters, posting fliers, putting a notice on your organization's website, and making an announcement in your newsletter. Send press releases to local media outlets like newspapers and magazines, and contact local TV news and radio stations to request coverage and publicity.

10. Use the event's theme in everything from marketing, to graphic design of tickets and programs, to venue decorations.

11. Have your various committees meet regularly and keep the lines of communication open.

12. Three months out from the event, print tickets and have everyone in your organization sell tickets. Offer an incentive to the individuals who sell the most tickets.

13. If you need any special equipment, such as seating, sound, light, or stage equipment, this is a good time to reserve these items. Do this as you think about how the venue will be set up for the event.

14. Do a walk-through of the venue a month before the event to check if all the venue systems work and ask when you can get in to decorate.

15. Write a script to serve as your minute-by-minute flow of activities for the event. Plan a time to thank your sponsors and distribute information promoting your organization.

16. Hold a meeting with all event volunteers and go over the tasks and schedule. Be clear on what you expect every volunteer to do. Tell volunteers what to wear for the event. Get everyone's contact information (phone number and e-mail) in case you need to communicate any changes or reminders.

Execution

1. Come in early to decorate, set up equipment and food, and check the lighting and sound systems.

2. Have volunteers collect tickets as well as sell more tickets at the event.

3. Follow your script to carry out all planned activities.

4. Initiate cleanup at the designated end time.

Picture Perfect Party

Guests at this fundraising event will have the opportunity to be captured in unique photo settings. Re-create movie scenes in your venue where guests can feel like true stars and have their photos taken. Be sure to include great food, and even an auction for valuable items once belonging to celebrities. Have drama clubs in the community help create props and scenery and make this event a night to remember. Charge a fee for general admission.

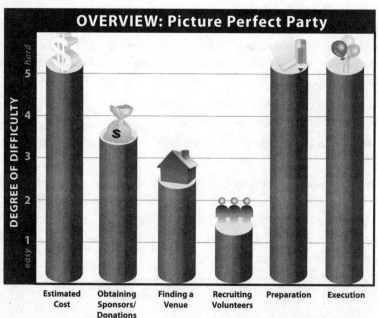

OVERVIEW: Picture Perfect Party

Special Materials/Equipment
- Sets
- Costumes
- Props
- Photography equipment

Sponsors/Donations
- A professional photographer and a local theater company can offer valuable assistance.

Possible Venue(s)
Schools, churches, social clubs or any large open space where you can have a variety of things happening at the same time will work well for this event. Ideally, choose a venue that you have access to 24 hours in advance. It is important that your scenery and items associated with your photo shoots are in place and ready to go before you open your doors.

Recommended Volunteer
15+ to handle the venue, photo shoots (photographer, costumes, props, and scenery), hospitality, and marketing. A few of these committees will have to be staffed rather heavily in the final planning phases and in the execution.

Preparation
Prep Time: 6 to 8 months

1. Start with a central committee of five to seven people who will serve as committee heads for the venue, food, decorations, sponsors/donations, advertising, ticket sales, entertainment, setup, and cleanup.

2. Decide when to have the event. Before you settle on a date, find out what else is going on in your community, and avoid conflicts.

3. Determine your budget. How much are you looking to raise, and what are you willing to spend to raise that amount?

4. Start seeking sponsors and donations immediately.

5. Search for your perfect venue. If you have to change the date of your event to get the right venue, make sure, again, that you will have no competition from similar events that may be scheduled.

6. If you decide to serve food, plan your menu. Four months before the event, schedule a caterer, recruit people to cook, or ask restaurants or grocery stores to donate food.

7. Decide what photo options to offer. Prepare a menu of photo choices your supporters can select from, including scenery, costumes, props, and makeup. You can design scenes from movies, TV, comics, or fantasy shots. If you arrange for multiple photo stages, you can have supporters book a specific stage at a specific time when they purchase advance tickets.

8. Prepare events that supporters can engage in while they wait for their photo shoots and after they are done with their shoots. You may have entertainment such as a band or a movie. If you plan for a silent auction, and/or raffle, offer items that are related to the event. Signed celebrity photos or costume items once worn by celebrities in famous movies are great for this event. Internet searches for celebrity press agents will set you in the right direction in this regard.

9. Pick an emcee — either an organization member or a local celebrity. A celebrity can help you market the event.

10. Advertise by sending e-mails and letters, posting fliers, putting a notice on your organization's website, and making an announcement in your newsletter. Send press releases to local media outlets like newspapers and magazines, and contact local TV news and radio stations to request coverage and publicity.

11. Use the event's theme in everything from marketing, to graphic design of tickets and programs, to venue decorations.

12. Have your various committees meet regularly and keep the lines of communication open.

13. Three months out from the event, print tickets and have everyone in your organization sell tickets. Offer an incentive to the individuals who sell the most tickets.

14. If you need any special equipment such as sound, lights, staging, or seating, this is a good time to reserve these items. Do this as you think about how the venue will be set up for the event.

15. Do a walk-through of the venue a month before the event to check if all the venue systems work and ask when you can get in to decorate.

16. Write a script to serve as your minute-by-minute flow of activities for the event. Plan a time to thank your sponsors and distribute information promoting your organization.

17. Gather your team prior to the evening's event to do a last minute run-down of the schedule. Emphasize with your photo crew how important it will be to stay on schedule, especially if you are expecting a large crowd. Be clear on what you expect every volunteer to do. Tell volunteers what to wear for the event. Get everyone's contact information (phone number and e-mail) in case you need to communicate any changes or reminders.

Execution

1. Come in early to decorate, set up equipment and food, and check the lighting and sound systems. Double-check the cameras and all technical systems. Be sure you have back-up systems in place. Have an individual or two on hand as technical troubleshooters.

2. Have volunteers collect tickets as well as sell more tickets at the event.

3. Follow your script to carry out all planned activities.

4. Initiate cleanup at the designated end time.

Tip(s)

- Consider doing this event in the fall and staging a Grinch or Christmas Story scene. Offering to help people take care of their holiday card needs is a good incentive to bring people to your event.

Renaissance Fair

Have guests dress in attire from the Renaissance era while enjoying all the elements of the time period. Host games and activities and charge a fee to participate. Set a price to dine without silverware, and watch as your guests let loose.

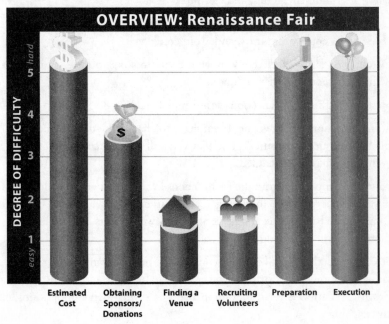

Special Materials/Equipment

- Renaissance costumes
- Props

Sponsors/Donations

- Contact local businesses to act as event sponsors. Set sponsorship levels and offer potential sponsors advertising rights and other perks to make sponsorship attractive.

Possible Venue(s)

A park with natural amphitheater is ideal because it will allow you to have a Renaissance performance in a natural setting while not having to worry about bringing seating in.

Recommended Volunteer

15 to 20+ including 5 to 7 to serve as committee heads for the venue, food, decorations, sponsors/donations, advertising, ticket sales, entertainment, setup, and cleanup

Preparation

Prep Time: Up to 1 year

1. Start with a central committee of five to seven people who will serve as committee heads for the venue, food, decorations, sponsors/donations, advertising, ticket sales, entertainment, setup, and cleanup.

2. Decide when to have the event. Before you settle on a date, find out what else is going on in your community, and avoid conflicts.

3. Determine your budget. How much are you looking to raise, and what are you willing to spend to raise that amount?

4. Start seeking sponsors and donations immediately.

5. Search for your perfect venue. If you have to change the date of your event to get the right venue, make sure, again, that you will have no competition from similar events that may be scheduled.

6. Four to six months before the event, choose your menu and schedule the caterer, if you decide to serve food. Pig roasts, turkey legs, and other foodstuffs that approximate Renaissance foods are always crowd-pleasers. Research and interview those who will be serving food at your event.

7. Select what activities will occur at your event. You may want a live or silent auction, raffle, or band. For performers, you can talk to local theater groups, music groups, clowns, and athletes. Consider puppet shows, strong men competitions, animals, and dancing.

8. Plan how you will handle transactions related to food and games. Having a central ticket location is a good idea. Supporters will purchase tickets at a central booth and then exchange tickets for food and games.

9. Pick an emcee to act as king — either an organization member or a local celebrity. A celebrity can help you market the event.

10. Advertise by sending e-mails and letters, posting fliers, putting a notice on your organization's website, and making an announcement in your newsletter. Send press releases to local media outlets like newspapers and magazines, and contact local TV news and radio stations to request coverage and publicity.

11. Use the event's theme in everything from marketing, to graphic design of tickets and programs, to venue decorations.

12. Have your various committees meet regularly and keep the lines of communication open.

13. Three months out from the event, print tickets and have everyone in your organization sell tickets. Offer an incentive to the individuals who sell the most tickets.

14. If you need any special equipment such as seating, sound, light, or stage equipment, this is a good time to reserve these items. Do this as you think about how the venue will be set up for the event.

15. Do a walk-through of the venue a month before the event to check if all the venue systems work and ask when you can get in to decorate.

16. Write a script to serve as your minute-by-minute flow of activities for the event. Plan a time to thank your sponsors and distribute information promoting your organization.

17. Hold a meeting with all event volunteers and go over the tasks and schedule. Be clear on what you expect every volunteer to do. Tell volunteers what to wear for the event. Get everyone's contact information (phone number and e-mail) in case you need to communicate any changes or reminders.

18. Make a backup plan. Setting a rain date for an event such as this is generally not possible. Decide what steps will be taken if rains come during your event.

Execution

1. Come in early to decorate, set up equipment and food, and check the lighting and sound systems.

2. Have volunteers collect tickets as well as sell more tickets at the event.

3. Follow your script to carry out all planned activities.

4. Initiate cleanup at the designated end time.

Spa Day

Have participants relax and get pampered during a fundraising event at a spa, salon, barbershop, or beauty vocational school. Beauticians can commit to donating a portion of their proceeds for a day or a specified number of hours to your cause. Supporters can receive a wide range of treatments, including manicures, foot treatments, massages, hair treatments, and facials.

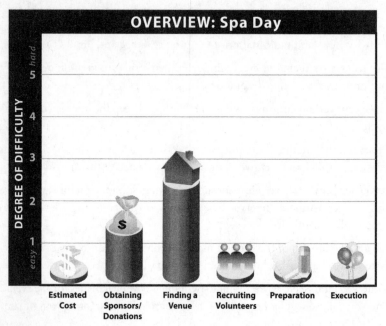

OVERVIEW: Spa Day

(DEGREE OF DIFFICULTY — from *easy* 1 to *hard* 5)

Estimated Cost — Obtaining Sponsors/Donations — Finding a Venue — Recruiting Volunteers — Preparation — Execution

Sponsors/Donations

- Approach beauty supply stores, women's apparel stores, nail salons, and other beauty-related businesses to donate cash or services in exchange for publicity during the event.
- Ideally, you would like a high-end spa to sponsor your event. You can sell tickets for admission to the spa, and the spa will draw people in who have never been there and make money from the sale of spa items such as soaps, lotions, and oils. If you plan your event for a time that is considered and "off time" for the spa and you can offer them a full house of your supporters that may become new spa patrons, they will be more than happy to do the event.
- Other great donations toward this event would be a variety of soaps, lotions, and bath oils to use as gifts or raffle items.

Possible Venue(s)

Hair salons, barbershops, and beauty vocational schools are appropriate. A mall or shopping center might also be willing to donate space where stylists can work, which would give the event great visibility.

Recommended Volunteer

1 to 3 to arrange with the spa, advertise the event, and be present during the fundraiser to talk with patrons about your organization's activities and thank them personally for their contribution

Preparation

Prep Time: 2 months+

1. Decide when to have the event. Before you settle on a date, find out what else is going on in your community, and avoid conflicts.

2. Determine your budget. How much are you looking to raise, and what are you willing to spend to raise that amount?

3. Search for your perfect venue. If you have to change the date of your event to get the right venue to donate its services, make sure, again, that you will have no competition from similar events that may be scheduled.

4. Select what activities will occur at your event. You may want a live or silent auction or raffle. Find donations of spa items for these activities and for gifts.

5. Advertise by sending e-mails and letters, posting fliers, putting a notice on your organization's website, and making an announcement in your newsletter. Send press releases to local media outlets like newspapers and magazines, and contact local TV news and radio stations to request coverage and publicity.

6. Three months out from the event, print tickets and have everyone in your organization sell tickets. Offer an incentive to the individuals who sell the most tickets.

7. Plan a time to thank your sponsors and distribute information promoting your organization.

Execution

1. Have volunteers collect tickets as well as sell more tickets at the event.

2. Let the spa pamper your participants.

3. Thank your sponsors and distribute information about your organization.

Tip(s)

- Plan your event around a special occasion, like Mother's Day, prom, or graduation, and advertise it as a great gift idea or great place to come to prepare for an occasion.

Variation(s)

- Suggest that the salon staff offer mini services, like a 15-minute hair trim, at a discount off the standard, full-service rate. That way, the stylists (who often are self-employed) will be able to perform more services while donating to your cause.

Superhero Fair

Whether held indoors or outdoors, this fundraiser will be a hit for all ages. Charge a fee for admission to the event, and offer activities geared toward superhero themes, like a contest for who can hit closest to a target with silly string (Spider-Man), a cape-decorating station (Superman), superhero face painting, and a costume contest for which kids dress up as their favorite superhero. Provide treats and prizes fit for a superhero for winners of the games.

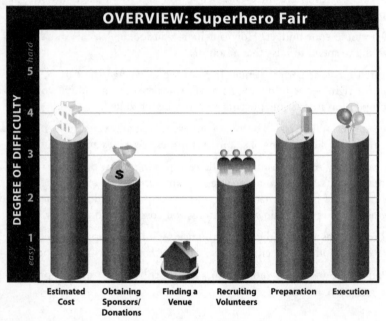

Special Materials/Equipment
- Superhero decorations
- Game equipment

Sponsors/Donations
- Ask party supply stores to donate superhero-themed toys and decorations.

Possible Venue(s)
Your organization's home parking lot or a field is a great venue, whether your organization is a church, a school, or a community center.

Recommended Volunteer
10+ to serve as committee heads for game planning, decorations, setup, ticket sales, advertising, running games, food, entertainment, and cleanup

Preparation

Prep Time: 10 months to 1 year

1. Start with a central committee of five to seven people who will serve as committee heads for the venue, food, decorations, sponsors/donations, advertising, ticket sales, entertainment, setup, and cleanup.

2. Decide when to have the event. Before you settle on a date, find out what else is going on in your community, and avoid conflicts.

3. Determine your budget. How much are you looking to raise, and what are you willing to spend to raise that amount?

4. Start seeking sponsors and donations immediately.

5. Search for your perfect venue. If you have to change the date of your event to get the right venue, make sure, again, that you will have no competition from similar events that may be scheduled.

6. If you decide to serve food, plan your menu. Four months before the event, schedule a caterer, recruit people to cook, or ask restaurants or grocery stores to donate food.

7. Decide what will occur at your event. Offer activities geared toward superhero themes, like a contest for who can hit closest to a target with silly string (Spider-Man), a cape-decorating station (Superman), superhero face painting, and a costume contest for which kids dress up as their favorite superhero. Provide treats and prizes fit for a superhero for winners of the games. You may also want a live or silent auction or a raffle.

8. Advertise by sending e-mails and letters, posting fliers, putting a notice on your organization's website, and making an announcement in your newsletter. Send press releases to local media outlets like newspapers and magazines, and contact local TV news and radio stations to request coverage and publicity.

9. Use the event's theme in everything from marketing, to graphic design of tickets and programs, to venue decorations.

10. Have your various committees meet regularly and keep the lines of communication open.

11. Three months out from the event, print tickets and have everyone in your organization sell tickets. Offer an incentive to the individuals who sell the most tickets.

12. If you need any special equipment, such as seating, sound, light, or stage equipment, this is a good time to reserve these items. Do this as you think about how the venue will be set up for the event.

13. Do a walk-through of the venue a month before the event to check if all the venue systems work and ask when you can get in to decorate.

14. Write a script to serve as your minute-by-minute flow of activities for the event. Plan a time to thank your sponsors and distribute information promoting your organization.

15. Hold a meeting with all event volunteers and go over the tasks and schedule. Be clear on what you expect every volunteer to do. Tell volunteers what to wear for the event. Get everyone's contact information (phone number and e-mail) in case you need to communicate any changes or reminders.

Execution

1. Come in early to decorate, set up equipment and food, and check the lighting and sound systems.

2. Have volunteers collect tickets as well as sell more tickets at the event.

3. Follow your script to carry out all planned activities.

4. Initiate cleanup at the designated end time.

Toga Party

Bring the Roman Empire back to life with a toga party. Sell tickets before the event, and ask that all guests show up dressed in togas. For dinner, offer a buffet served from a banquet table located at the center of your venue. Sell laurel wreaths to top off participants' outfits.

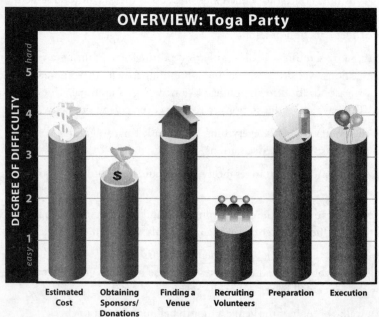

Special Materials/Equipment
- Medieval decorations
- Food service items

Sponsors/Donations
- Local theaters, performing arts organizations, and theatrical companies might be great places to seek donations of costumes and props for this event.

Possible Venue(s)
Large old churches, community buildings, or schools are good places to have it.

Recommended Volunteer
10+ including 5 to 7 to serve as committees that will organize the overall event, the decorations committee, food and beverage committee, the entertainment committee, the marketing and ticket committee

Preparation
Prep Time: 6 months to 1 year

1. Start with a central committee of five to seven people who will serve as committee heads for the venue, food, decorations, sponsors/donations, advertising, ticket sales, entertainment, setup, and cleanup.

2. Decide when to have the event. Before you settle on a date, find out what else is going on in your community, and avoid conflicts.

3. Determine your budget. How much are you looking to raise, and what are you willing to spend to raise that amount?

4. Start seeking sponsors and donations immediately.

5. Search for your perfect venue. If you have to change the date of your event to get the right venue, make sure, again, that you will have no competition from similar events that may be scheduled.

6. Four months before the event, choose a Roman menu and schedule the caterer, if you decide to serve food.

7. Select what activities will occur at your event. You may want a live or silent auction, raffle, or band. Consider having Roman music and dancing as well as finding entertainers who can perform bits of Roman-era comedies. Sell laurel wreaths made from gold paper or fake vines for headpieces to complete participants' outfits, or set up a wreath-making station and charge people to make their own wreaths.

8. Pick an emcee to act as Caesar — either an organization member or a local celebrity. A celebrity can help you market the event.

9. Advertise by sending e-mails and letters, posting fliers, putting a notice on your organization's website, and making an announcement in your newsletter. Send press releases to local media outlets like newspapers and magazines, and contact local TV news and radio stations to request coverage and publicity.

10. Use the event's theme in everything from marketing, to graphic design of tickets and programs, to venue decorations.

11. Have your various committees meet regularly and keep the lines of communication open.

12. Three months out from the event, print tickets and have everyone in your organization sell tickets. Offer an incentive to the individuals who sell the most tickets.

13. If you need any special equipment, such as seating, sound, light, or stage equipment, this is a good time to reserve these items. Do this as you think about how the venue will be set up for the event.

14. Do a walk-through of the venue a month before the event to check if all the venue systems work and ask when you can get in to decorate.

15. Write a script to serve as your minute-by-minute flow of activities for the event. Plan a time to thank your sponsors and distribute information promoting your organization.

16. Hold a meeting with all event volunteers and go over the tasks and schedule. Be clear on what you expect every volunteer to do. Tell volunteers what to wear for the event. Get everyone's contact information (phone number and e-mail) in case you need to communicate any changes or reminders.

Execution

1. Come in early to decorate, set up equipment and food, and check the lighting and sound systems.

2. Have volunteers collect tickets as well as sell more tickets at the event.

3. Follow your script to carry out all planned activities.

4. Initiate cleanup at the designated end time.

Tip(s)

- Hold a toga-decorating contest, and supply markers, buttons, sequins, ribbons, etc.

Variation(s)

- Have a White Night where everyone wears white.
- Host an Olympics Party modeled after ancient Olympic games and outfits.

'20s Dinner Party

Travel back in time to the roaring '20s for a fun night of flapper dresses, fedoras, fine food, silent movies, and poker or craps games. Participants can take pictures in a photo booth or have Polaroids taken to help them remember the event. Teach guests a popular dance from the era, like the Charleston. Charge a general admission fee as well as small cost for taking pictures.

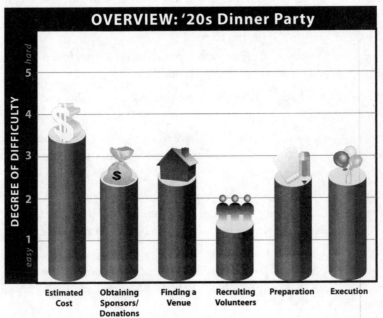

Special Materials/Equipment:

- '20s decorations
- Sound system (microphone, speakers)
- Silent movie and projector
- Tables and chairs
- '20s music
- Dance floor
- Poker or craps games
- Photo booth and Polaroid camera

Sponsors/Donations

- A local historical society might be a good place to begin looking for sponsorships and donations to use for the evening.

Possible Venue(s)

A '20s-era hotel, social building, or hotel in your community might be the perfect venue.

Recommended Volunteer

10 to 15+ including 5 to 7 to serve as committee heads for the venue, food, decorations, sponsors/donations, advertising, ticket sales, entertainment, setup, and cleanup

Preparation

Prep Time: 6 months to 1 year

1. Start with a central committee of five to seven people who will serve as committee heads for the venue, food, decorations, sponsors/donations, advertising, ticket sales, entertainment, setup, and cleanup.

2. Decide when to have the event. Before you settle on a date, find out what else is going on in your community, and avoid conflicts.

3. Determine your budget. How much are you looking to raise, and what are you willing to spend to raise that amount?

4. Search for your perfect venue. If you have to change the date of your event to get the right venue, make sure, again, that you will have no competition from similar events that may be scheduled.

5. Select what activities will occur at your event. You may want a live or silent auction, raffle, or band. The 1920s are famous for having great swinging jazz music. If you plan to have live music at your party, be sure to book your band at least six months in advance.

6. If you decide to serve food, plan your menu. Four months before the event, schedule a caterer, recruit people to cook, or ask restaurants or grocery stores to donate food.

7. Pick an emcee — either an organization member or a local celebrity. A celebrity can help you market the event.

8. Advertise by sending e-mails and letters, posting fliers, putting a notice on your organization's website, and making an announcement in your newsletter. Send press releases to local media outlets like newspapers and magazines, and contact local TV news and radio stations to request coverage and publicity.

9. Use the event's theme in everything from marketing, to graphic design of tickets and programs, to venue decorations.

10. Have your various committees meet regularly and keep the lines of communication open.

11. Three months out from the event, print tickets and have everyone in your organization sell tickets. Offer an incentive to the individuals who sell the most tickets.

12. If you need any special equipment such as sound, lights, staging, or seating, this is a good time to reserve these items. Do this as you think about how the venue will be set up for the event.

13. Do a walk-through of the venue a month before the event to check if all the venue systems work and ask when you can get in to decorate.

14. Write a script to serve as your minute-by-minute flow of activities for the event. Plan a time to thank your sponsors and distribute information promoting your organization.

15. Hold a meeting with all event volunteers and go over the tasks and schedule. Be clear on what you expect every volunteer to do. Tell volunteers what to wear for the event. Get everyone's contact information (phone number and e-mail) in case you need to communicate any changes or reminders.

Execution

1. Come in early to decorate, set up equipment and food, and check the lighting and sound systems.

2. Have volunteers collect tickets as well as sell more tickets at the event.

3. Follow your script to carry out all planned activities.

4. Initiate cleanup at the designated end time.

Variation(s)

- You can have a dinner party celebrating another popular era, like the '70s or '80s.

Without a Clue Party

In this interactive fundraiser, guests will be clueless as to why they are there. Leave clues in different areas of the venue that point to the purpose of the event. For example, place plant sticks in centerpieces with clues, or put more hints on napkins and underneath plates. Provide each guest with a mini spyglass as a party favor and decorate tables with question mark shaped candles. Charge guests an admission fee.

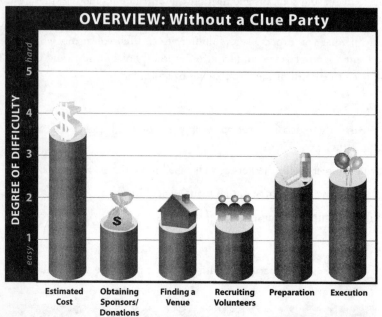

Special Materials/Equipment

- Decorations and clues
- Sound system (microphone, speakers)
- Banquet tables and chairs

Sponsors/Donations

- The best donation that you might possibly get is an event sponsor, or at least a venue sponsor or sponsors for each banquet table.

Possible Venue(s)

Consider having it at an upscale hotel in your community, or any venue that may have a fancy banquet room.

Recommended Volunteer

10 to 15+ including 5 to 7 to serve as committee heads for the venue, food, decorations, sponsors/donations, advertising, ticket sales, entertainment, setup, and cleanup.

Preparation

Prep Time: 6 months to 1 year

1. Start with a central committee of five to seven people who will serve as committee heads for the venue, food, decorations, sponsors/donations, advertising, ticket sales, entertainment, setup, and cleanup.

2. Decide when to have the event. Before you settle on a date, find out what else is going on in your community, and avoid conflicts.

3. Determine your budget. How much are you looking to raise, and what are you willing to spend to raise that amount?

4. Start seeking sponsors and donations immediately.

5. Search for your perfect venue. If you have to change the date of your event to get the right venue, make sure, again, that you will have no competition from similar events that may be scheduled.

6. If you decide to serve food, plan your menu. Four months before the event, schedule a caterer, recruit people to cook, or ask restaurants or grocery stores to donate food.

7. Select what activities will occur at your event. You may want a live or silent auction, raffle, or band.

8. Pick an emcee — either an organization member or a local celebrity. A celebrity can help you market the event.

9. Advertise by sending e-mails and letters, posting fliers, putting a notice on your organization's website, and making an announcement in your newsletter. Send press releases to local media outlets like newspapers and magazines, and contact local TV news and radio stations to request coverage and publicity.

10. Use the event's theme in everything from marketing, to graphic design of tickets and programs, to venue decorations.

11. Have your various committees meet regularly and keep the lines of communication open.

12. Three months out from the event, print tickets and have everyone in your organization sell tickets. Offer an incentive to the individuals who sell the most tickets.

13. If you need any special equipment, such as seating, sound, light, or stage equipment, this is a good time to reserve these items. Do this as you think about how the venue will be set up for the event.

14. Do a walk-through of the venue a month before the event to check if all the venue systems work and ask when you can get in to decorate.

15. Write a script to serve as your minute-by-minute flow of activities for the event. Plan a time to thank your sponsors and distribute information promoting your organization.

16. Hold a meeting with all event volunteers and go over the tasks and schedule. Be clear on what you expect every volunteer to do. Tell volunteers what to wear for the event. Get everyone's contact information (phone number and e-mail) in case you need to communicate any changes or reminders.

Execution

1. Come in early to decorate, set up equipment and food, and check the lighting and sound systems.

2. Have volunteers collect tickets as well as sell more tickets at the event.

3. Follow your script to carry out all planned activities.

4. Initiate cleanup at the designated end time.

Chapter 19

Miscellaneous

These events call for more planning, but offer a variety of interesting and memorable events. The projects you will find in this chapter include:

- ◉ Cash-for-Jewelry Party
- ◉ Community Cleanup
- ◉ Craft Fair
- ◉ Designer Home Display
- ◉ Donate Your Vehicle
- ◉ Flea Market
- ◉ Fortune-Telling Fun
- ◉ Historic Home Tours
- ◉ Park Day
- ◉ Rent a Puppy

Cash-for-Jewelry Party

Provide participants with the opportunity to sell old or broken jewelry they no longer wear for cash. Excited guests can will watch as their unwanted gold, silver, and platinum jewelry is tested, weighed, valued, and purchased by an appraiser from a company like American Gold & Diamond Buyers. Your organization receives 10 percent of the total purchase, everyone leaves richer, and no one has to buy anything.

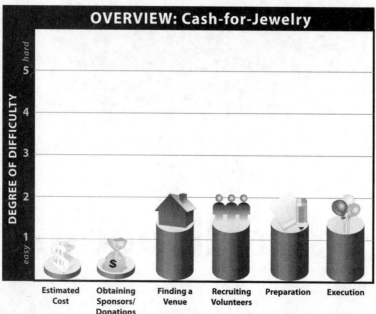

OVERVIEW: Cash-for-Jewelry

DEGREE OF DIFFICULTY — easy to hard (1 to 5)

Estimated Cost | Obtaining Sponsors/ Donations | Finding a Venue | Recruiting Volunteers | Preparation | Execution

Sponsors/Donations

- Find a jeweler with an appraiser who is willing to come to your event and give your organization a percentage of the total value of the metal it buys from your guests.

Possible Venue(s)

You can do this at someone's home or you can arrange for a larger gathering and a dinner at a hotel or restaurant.

Recommended Volunteer

1 to 2+ to contact a jeweler and arrange for the buy-back party

Preparation

Prep Time: 3 months

1. Contact a company like American Gold & Diamond Buyers, who works with nonprofits to help arrange jewelry buy-back parties, and schedule an event date that an appraiser can attend.

2. Search for your perfect venue.

3. Choose your menu and schedule the caterer, if you decide to serve food.

4. Select what additional activities will occur at your event. You may want a live or silent auction, raffle, or band.

5. Advertise by sending e-mails and letters, posting fliers, putting a notice on your organization's website, and making an announcement in your newsletter. Ask guests to bring unwanted gold and other jewelry with them to your event and receive cash for the items they bring. Send press releases to local media outlets like newspapers and magazines, and contact local TV news and radio stations to request coverage and publicity.

6. Use the event's theme in everything from marketing, to graphic design of tickets and programs, to venue decorations.

Execution

1. Let the appraiser buy guests' jewelry.

2. Serve food and run additional planned activities.

3. Receive a check from American Gold & Diamond Buyers for 10 percent of the total purchase from the event.

Tip(s)

- To raise even more money, charge an event admission fee.

Community Cleanup

Promote your organization as a community steward and collect money for your good works at the same time with a garbage collection effort. Have community members sponsor participants by pledging a set price (from 1 cent up) for every piece of trash that participants collect. Tidy up a neighborhood, park, beach, or business district.

Special Materials/Equipment

- Garbage bags
- Brooms
- Tally sheets (for each volunteer to record the amount of garbage collected)
- Gloves
- Sandblaster (for graffiti)

Sponsors/Donations

- Have each volunteer find sponsors to donate money for each hour of cleaning the volunteer commits to and completes.
- Ask people to donate a certain amount of money for each bag of trash (or can, bottle, or piece of refuse) collected.
- Ask a local hardware store or other type of store to donate supplies. Be sure to recognize them as sponsors during your activity.
- Collect additional sponsors during the event by setting out a table or booth near your clean up with information about your organization.
- Consider taking sponsorship pledges on your website.

Possible Venue(s)

Parks, urban neighborhoods, school grounds, scenic drives, or beaches are all possible locations. Your efforts will be welcomed in plenty of community places.

Recommended Volunteer

5 to 10+ to help with the clean up

Preparation

Prep Time: 2 months

1. Choose a location where your clean-up efforts will be best appreciated, and obtain permission from the venue.

2. Select a date for your event.

3. Prepare sponsorship forms that members of your group can use to gather monetary sponsorships for their activities. (Examples of pledge forms can be found in the appendix of this book.)

4. Advertise by sending e-mails and letters, posting fliers, putting a notice on your organization's website, and making an announcement in your newsletter. Send press releases to local media outlets like newspapers and magazines, and contact local TV news and radio stations to request coverage and publicity.

5. Four to six weeks in advance, have volunteers approach local stores to get supplies donated.

6. Have volunteers obtain pledges. Set up a PayPal on your website for additional monetary donations.

7. Plan a recognition party for all volunteers who part in the event. Consider planning a barbecue or picnic for after the clean up.

8. Arrange for a way to remove any trash you may collect.

Execution

1. Meet in a specified location at a specific time to go over planned activities and clean-up locations. Make sure all volunteers have the tools and equipment needed.

2. Send people out in teams with the proper equipment to do the clean up.

3. Arrange to meet at the end of the day in a specified location for the recognition party.

Tip(s)

- Remind volunteers to try not to disturb the people occupying the area you are cleaning.
- Bring brooms and dustpans to sweep up glass and unsanitary refuse.

Craft Fair

Showcase a variety of crafts and charge exhibitioners a fee to set up a booth at the event. Sell tickets for admission, and offer other fundraising activities at the fair, such as bake sales or raffles.

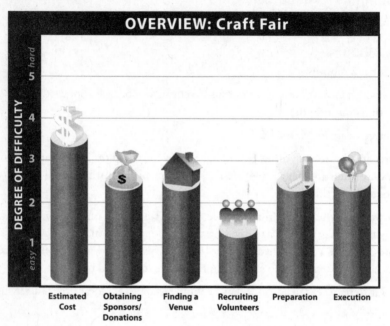

Special Materials/Equipment

- Tables or booths (to display the crafts)

Sponsors/Donations

- Identify a corporate or business sponsor to cover the venue cost and/or the cost of display materials. Craft dealers are often good places to go for such support.

Possible Venue(s)

Nice hotels that offer large banquet rooms accommodate such a need in terms of space and possible catering. For an outdoor event, try city parks or town squares. If you are going to be showing high-end crafts, be sure that you offer the craft artisans and dealers a secure venue.

Recommended Volunteer

10 to 20 starting with a committee of 10 individuals who will serve as committee heads for the venue, food, sponsors/donations, advertising, ticket sales, entertainment, craft artisans and dealers, security, setup, and cleanup.

Preparation
Prep Time: 8 to 12 months

1. Start with a central committee of 10 people who will serve as committee heads for the venue, food, sponsors/donations, advertising, ticket sales, entertainment, craft artisans and dealers, security, setup, and cleanup.

2. Decide when to have the event. Before you settle on a date, find out what else is going on in your community, and avoid conflicts.

3. Determine your budget. How much are you looking to raise, and what are you willing to spend to raise that amount?

4. Start seeking sponsors and donations immediately.

5. Search for your perfect venue. If you have to change the date of your event to get the right venue, make sure, again, that you will have no competition from similar events that may be scheduled.

6. Consider your options and decide how you will raise funds. Beside selling admission tickets, you can sell booths to dealers and collectors. You can also consider taking a percentage of each sale the dealer makes at the event. Crafts can be appraised before they are priced for sale at your fundraiser. An independent third party professional appraiser should do the appraisal.

7. If you decide to serve food, plan your menu. Four months before the event, schedule a caterer, recruit people to cook, or ask restaurants or grocery stores to donate food.

8. Select what activities will occur at your event. You may want a live or silent auction, raffle, or band.

9. Pick an emcee — either an organization member or a local celebrity. A celebrity can help you market the event.

10. As you settle on the dealers and collectors, plan to put a catalogue together. The catalogue will help to market your event and it will guide your supporters through your event. You should be prepared to print your catalogue three months prior to your event. The catalogue can pay for itself if you sell ad space in it.

11. Three months prior to the event, advertise by sending e-mails and letters, posting fliers, putting a notice on your organization's website, and making an announcement in your newsletter. Send press releases to local media outlets like newspapers and magazines, and contact local TV news and radio stations to request coverage and publicity.

12. Use the event's theme in everything from marketing, to graphic design of tickets and programs, to venue decorations.

13. Have your various committees meet regularly and keep the lines of communication open.

14. Three months out from the event, print tickets and have everyone in your organization sell tickets. Offer an incentive to the individuals who sell the most tickets. When you decide your ticketing structure, you might want to consider a

"private showing" period prior to the announced event time. These tickets will be priced a little higher and offer the purchaser early admittance to view the crafts and speak with the artists and sellers.

15. If you need any special equipment, such as seating, sound, light, or stage equipment, this is a good time to reserve these items. Do this as you think about how the venue will be set up for the event.

16. Do a walk-through of the venue a month before the event to check if all the venue systems work and to set up. Map out where each dealer will be stationed. It also helps if the craft artisans and dealers can attend this walk-through to address any last minute needs.

17. Write a script to serve as your minute-by-minute flow of activities for the event. Plan a time to thank your sponsors and distribute information promoting your organization.

18. Hold a meeting with all event volunteers and go over the tasks and schedule. Be clear on what you expect every volunteer to do. Tell volunteers what to wear for the event. Get everyone's contact information (phone number and e-mail) in case you need to communicate any changes or reminders.

Execution

1. Come in early to set up equipment and food, and check the lighting and sound systems.

2. Have volunteers collect tickets as well as sell more tickets at the event.

3. Follow your script to carry out all planned activities.

4. Initiate cleanup at the designated end time.

Tip(s)

- To appeal to the craft artisans and dealers, offer to pass along any mailing list you generate from this event.

- Also, meet with the craft artisans and dealers individually to work out any marketing hooks that will help you to advertise your event and their items.

- Consider offering a wide selection of crafts — a little something for everyone — to increase the appeal of the show and increase the likelihood that the craft artisans and dealers will find new customers.

Designer Home Display

Locate an empty home and contact several interior designers. Each will provide a new design for one room. Charge participants for home viewings, and increase profits by hosting an opening night preview to the home for special guests with a luncheon or auction. You can also provide guests a chance to meet with the designers for tips for their homes.

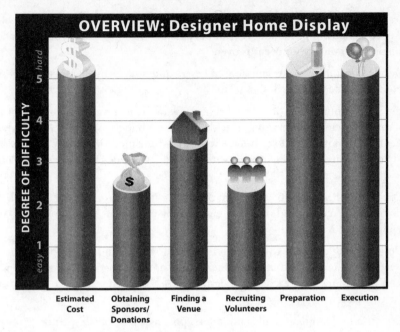

Special Materials/Equipment

- Paint, art, and other furnishings requested by the designers

Sponsors/Donations

- An upscale home realtor who will help you find a choice home that is the right style and size for your event is the ideal sponsor.

Possible Venue(s)

Find an empty house with design potential in a convenient location.

Recommended Volunteer

10+ volunteers assigned to assist designers. Start with a coordinating committee of 3 to 5 individuals to handle the venue, the designers, marketing, and hospitality.

Preparation

Prep Time: 6 months to 1 year

1. Start with a coordinating committee of three to five individuals to handle the venue, the designers, marketing, and hospitality.

2. Determine your budget. How much are you looking to raise, and what are you willing to spend to raise that amount?

3. Start seeking sponsors and donations immediately.

4. Search for your perfect venue. Make a written agreement with the owner of the property about what can and cannot be done. Make note of how you should leave the property once your event is over.

5. Decide how many rooms you have to design and how many designers you wish to work with. Identify the design team.

6. Lay some ground rules for the designers. Before you approach designers, put all of the requirements in writing. Decide what their budgets will be. Decide what, if anything, is not acceptable. Decide what their timelines will be. Ask the designers what materials they will require within their given budget. Have the designers document their work.

7. Consult the designers for a realistic timeframe of when to have the event. Before you settle on a date, find out what else is going on in your community, and avoid conflicts.

8. Decide whether or not to have food served at your open house. Your event may benefit from music. You may consider a raffle or silent auction. Schedule viewings with discussions with each of the designers. Ask the design team to plan to be at the entire event.

9. Advertise by sending e-mails and letters, posting fliers, putting a notice on your organization's website, and making an announcement in your newsletter. Send press releases to local media outlets like newspapers and magazines, and contact local TV news and radio stations to request coverage and publicity.

10. Use the event's theme in everything from marketing, to graphic design of tickets and programs, to venue decorations.

11. Have your various committees meet regularly and keep the lines of communication open.

12. Three months out from the event, print tickets and have everyone in your organization sell tickets. Offer an incentive to the individuals who sell the most tickets.

13. If you need any special equipment, such as seating, sound, light, or stage equipment, this is a good time to reserve these items. Do this as you think about how the venue will be set up for the event.

14. Do a walk-through of the venue a month before the event to check if all the venue systems work and ask when you can get in to decorate.

15. Write a script to serve as your minute-by-minute flow of activities for the event. Plan a time to thank your sponsors and distribute information promoting your organization.

16. Hold a meeting with all event volunteers and go over the tasks and schedule. Be clear on what you expect every volunteer to do. Tell volunteers what to wear for the event. Get everyone's contact information (phone number and e-mail) in case you need to communicate any changes or reminders.

Execution

1. Come in early to decorate, set up equipment and food, and check the lighting and sound systems.

2. Have volunteers collect tickets as well as sell more tickets at the event.

3. Follow your script to carry out all planned activities.

4. Initiate cleanup at the designated end time.

Tip(s)

- Do not forget to recognize and promote the design team, and thank the owner of the property.
- Remember: the larger the home, the higher your costs will be. Be sure that your team understands the agreement with the owner of the property and leaves the property as requested.

Donate Your Vehicle

Whether that old car that you want to get rid of is running or not, Donation Line will rev up a donation for your organization by auctioning it off. One of the largest vehicle donation centers in America, Donation Line auctions donates vehicles and gives your organization a percentage of the sales. The center also accepts trucks, boats, RVs, motorcycles, jet skis, and snowmobiles. Donors are compensated with IRS tax deduction documentation.

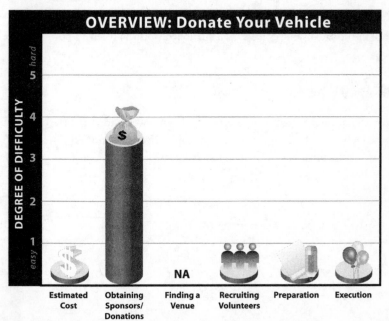

Special Materials/Equipment
- Used vehicles

Sponsors/Donations
- Contact supporters, volunteers, members of your organization, and used vehicle vendors for donations.

Recommended Volunteer
1 to 4 to put together an initial mailing requesting donations

Preparation
1. Log on to **www.DonationLine.com** for easy instructions and copy-ready fliers about the program.

2. Register online by providing your organization's information. Donation Line will review your information and contact you.

3. Advertise by sending e-mails and letters, posting fliers, putting a notice on your organization's website, and making an announcement in your newsletter. Send press releases to local media outlets like newspapers and magazines, and contact local TV news and radio stations to request coverage and publicity.

Execution
1. Refer supporters to **www.DonationLine.com** to donate their vehicles and name your organization as the beneficiary.

2. Once the donated vehicles have been auctioned, you will receive a portion of the sales.

Flea Market

Offer a range of booths featuring everything from jewelry to art to fresh fruit. People will be attracted to the market for its bargain prices and unique offerings. Set up concession stands throughout the venue to increase profits.

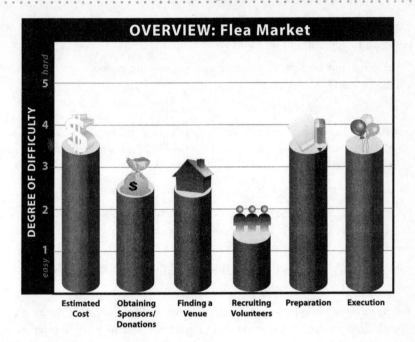

Special Materials/Equipment
- Booths, tables, or other means to display goods

Sponsors/Donations
- Find a corporate or business sponsor to cover the venue cost and/or the cost of display equipment.
- Consider inviting local folk, jazz, or blues musicians to play for a passing of the hat.

Possible Venue(s)
City parks and town squares can be ideal outdoor venues for a flea market. You can also have it in your organization's parking lot.

Recommended Volunteer
10 to 15+ to take care of the venue, food, sponsors/donations, advertising, ticket sales, entertainment, setup, and cleanup

Preparation
Prep Time: 8 months to 1 year

1. Start with a central committee of five to seven people who will serve as committee heads for the venue, food, sponsors/donations, advertising, ticket sales, entertainment, display/setup, and cleanup.

2. Decide when to have the event. Before you settle on a date, find out what else is going on in your community, and avoid conflicts.

3. Determine your budget. How much are you looking to raise, and what are you willing to spend to raise that amount?

4. Start seeking sponsors and donations immediately.

5. Search for your perfect venue. If you have to change the date of your event to get the right venue, make sure, again, that you will have no competition from similar events that may be scheduled.

6. Decide what types of vendors you might feature, and book vendors.

7. Four months before the event, choose your menu and food arrangements, if you decide to serve food. You can arrange with food vendors to buy space in the same way that you sell other vendors space.

8. Select what additional activities will occur at your event. You may want a live or silent auction, raffle, or band.

9. Advertise by sending e-mails and letters, posting fliers, putting a notice on your organization's website, and making an announcement in your newsletter. Send press releases to local media outlets like newspapers and magazines, and contact local TV news and radio stations to request coverage and publicity.

10. Use the event's theme in everything from marketing, to graphic design of tickets and programs, to venue decorations.

11. Have your various committees meet regularly and keep the lines of communication open.

12. Map out a space for each seller to display his or her merchandise.

13. Three months out from the event, print tickets and have everyone in your organization sell tickets. Offer an incentive to the individuals who sell the most tickets.

14. If you need any special equipment, such as seating, sound, light, or stage equipment, this is a good time to reserve these items. Do this as you think about how the venue will be set up for the event.

15. Do a walk-through of the venue a month before the event to check if all the venue systems work and ask when you can get in to decorate.

16. Write a script to serve as your minute-by-minute flow of activities for the event. Plan a time to thank your sponsors and distribute information promoting your organization.

17. Hold a meeting with all event volunteers and go over the tasks and schedule. Be clear on what you expect every volunteer to do. Tell volunteers what to wear for the event. Get everyone's contact information (phone number and e-mail) in case you need to communicate any changes or reminders.

Execution

1. Have vendors arrive early to set up.

2. Follow your script to carry out all planned activities.

3. Initiate cleanup at the designated end time.

Tip(s)

*   Meet with the vendors individually well in advance of your event to work out any marketing hooks that will help you to market your event and help them to market their items. Do everything you can to make this a win/win event for your organization as well as the vendors.

*   Offer a little something for everyone to increase the appeal of the show and increase the likelihood that the vendors will find new customers.

Fortune-Telling Fun

Your organization will foretell a memorable fundraiser in its future by hiring a fortune-teller, astrologer, or tarot card, palm, or tea-leaf reader. Charge guests for each fortune told. Set up an area for each reader, and create appropriate lighting and other special effects at each table. Candles and black lights can also be used to increase the effects.

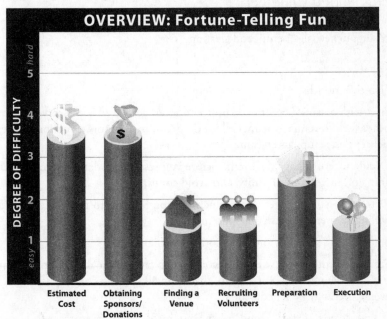

Special Materials/Equipment
- Mysterious decorations
- Tarot cards, a crystal ball, or tea leaves (depending on the activity)

Sponsors/Donations
- Try getting a fortune-teller, astrologer, or tarot card, palm, or tea-leaf reader to donate his/her services.
- Contact a local bar and ask that they donate the venue to your organization for an evening. Generally, you will charge admission to the bar and the bar will make money on the liquor sales. You can make other arrangements with the bar, such as increasing the price of drinks and you getting a percentage of drink sales, but you have to make it attractive to them, as well. If you plan your event for a night that is considered and "off night" for the bar, such as a Monday or Tuesday, and you can guarantee them a full house of your supporters, they likely will be more than happy to do the event.

Possible Venue(s)
This event is best held in a bar or club, especially one with a quiet back room for fortune telling.

Recommended Volunteer
5 to 7+ to handle the venue, fortune-tellers, decorations, sponsors/donations, advertising, ticket sales, setup, and cleanup

Preparation
Prep Time: 2 months+

1. Start with a central committee of five to seven people who will serve as committee heads for the venue, fortune-tellers, decorations, sponsors/donations, advertising, ticket sales, setup, and cleanup.

2. Decide when to have the event. Before you settle on a date, find out what else is going on in your community, and avoid conflicts.

3. Determine your budget. How much are you looking to raise, and what are you willing to spend to raise that amount?

4. Start seeking sponsors and donations immediately.

5. Search for your perfect venue. If you have to change the date of your event to get the right venue, make sure, again, that you will have no competition from similar events that may be scheduled.

6. If you decide to serve food, plan your menu. Four months before the event, schedule a caterer, recruit people to cook, or ask restaurants or grocery stores to donate food.

7. Plan whether to have fortune-tellers go from table to table offering to tell the fortunes, or set up in specific locations for your supporters to sit with them. If you are in a venue with a quiet back room, see if you can arrange for several séance sessions or past-life readings.

8. Select what other activities will occur at your event. You may want a live or silent auction, raffle, or band.

9. Pick an emcee — either an organization member or a local celebrity. A celebrity can help you market the event.

10. Advertise by sending e-mails and letters, posting fliers, putting a notice on your organization's website, and making an announcement in your newsletter. Send press releases to local media outlets like newspapers and magazines, and contact local TV news and radio stations to request coverage and publicity.

11. Use the event's theme in everything from marketing, to graphic design of tickets and programs, to venue decorations.

12. Have your various committees meet regularly and keep the lines of communication open.

13. Three months out from the event, print tickets and have everyone in your organization sell tickets redeemable for a fortune telling. Offer an incentive to the individuals who sell the most tickets.

14. If you need any special equipment such as sound, lights, staging, or seating, this is a good time to reserve these items. Do this as you think about how the venue will be set up for the event.

15. Do a walk-through of the venue a month before the event to check if all the venue systems work and ask when you can get in to decorate.

16. Write a script to serve as your minute-by-minute flow of activities for the event. Plan a time to thank your sponsors and distribute information promoting your organization.

17. Hold a meeting with all event volunteers and go over the tasks and schedule. Be clear on what you expect every volunteer to do. Tell volunteers what to wear for the event. Get everyone's contact information (phone number and e-mail) in case you need to communicate any changes or reminders.

Execution

1. Come in early to decorate, set up equipment and food, and check the lighting and sound systems.

2. Have volunteers collect tickets as well as sell more tickets at the event.

3. Follow your script to carry out all planned activities.

4. Initiate cleanup at the designated end time.

Variation(s)

- Host a Magic Night featuring magicians.
- Have a Hypnotist Night, and get your message across in a humorous way ("Donate to the cause!").

Historic Home Tours

Provide participants the chance to tour historic homes or other establishments in unique neighborhoods. Charge a fee for admission to the tour. Offer a program book to supporters.

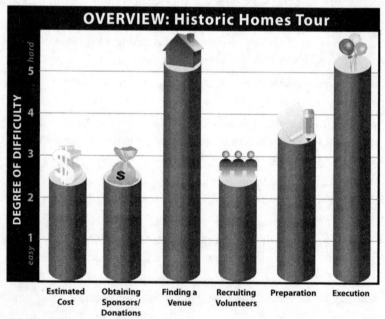

Special Materials/Equipment

- Bus or other large vehicle (to transport groups of people from place to place)
- Catalogue that includes information about the historic homes

Sponsors/Donations

- Sponsors may include realtors, historical societies, and neighborhood associations.

Possible Venue(s)

Find numerous historical venues (homes or buildings) located reasonably close together.

Recommended Volunteer
5+ to arrange the tour stops, marketing, and hospitality

Preparation
Prep Time: 4 months

1. Identify a potential date and tour stops.

2. Research the historic homes that you have scheduled for your event. Put together a guide catalogue that includes information about the homes and the neighborhoods the homes are in. The home's residents can help you with this task. You can also look for help from a local historical society and local records such as newspapers. Be sure that you clear all information with the home's owners.

3. When you make arrangements with the home residents and/or owners, be specific about what it is you are going to do. If you plan on bringing more than one group through the house, arrange set times for viewings.

4. Put together a schedule of viewings.

5. If you are going to hire a limousine or bus to transport your group from one place to another, hire that service as soon as you know your schedule.

6. If you plan on leaving from a set location, think about additional activities that may occur at your point of departure. Perhaps you may include food, drink, educational information, and a raffle or silent auction.

7. Consider who will be the tour guide — a member of your organization or a local historian handle. If the latter is the way you choose to go, start looking for your ideal tour guide early. He or she can help you market your event.

8. Start selling tickets three months out from the event. This should be a task done by everyone in your organization. Offer an incentive to the individual(s) who sell the most tickets.

9. Do a walk-through of the various homes a day or so before the event and make notes of the location needs that you have not considered.

10. Write a script to serve as your minute-by-minute flow of activities for the event. Plan a time to thank your sponsors and distribute information promoting your organization.

11. Hold a meeting with all event volunteers and go over the tasks and schedule. Be clear on what you expect every volunteer to do. Tell volunteers what to wear for the event. Get everyone's contact information (phone number and e-mail) in case you need to communicate any changes or reminders.

Execution
1. Be in contact with all involved parties the day of the event before it begins. Let the home owners know you are on your way.

2. Have a member of your organization stay at the point of departure and be reachable all through the event, especially if you are doing multiple tours.

3. Follow your script to carry out all planned activities.

4. Let the volunteer at the point of departure know when you are on your way back. This will allow for greater hospitality, as well as letting those waiting to go on the tour know that you are running on time. This is important especially if you are managing with one bus.

Tip(s)

• Promoting this event through the local historical society may bring many new supporters to your organization.

Park Day

Organize a barbecue in your community park for locals, and host fun games like flag football, Frisbee, tug-of-war, sack races, water balloon tosses, and more. In addition to being a fundraiser, this event is easily a "friend" raiser for your organization.

Special Materials/Equipment

• Sound equipment (microphone, speakers)
• Game/activity equipment (i.e. football, Frisbee, rope etc.)

Sponsors/Donations

- Ask attendees to bring a dish to share for a potluck meal, or ask local vendors for food donations for the event.
- Try for some kind of media sponsorship. Radio stations are good places to start, and they will bring in music for dancing. They may consider doing live remote broadcasts from your event.

Possible Venue(s)

Ideally, find a local park with a large, open grassy areas for games and a pavilion for a place to eat and some shelter from the sun and rain. A large parking lot works as well.

Recommended Volunteer

10 to 15 including 5 to 7 people to plan the venue, food, decorations, sponsors/donations, advertising, ticket sales, entertainment, setup, and cleanup

Preparation

Prep Time: 4 to 6 months

1. Start with a central committee of five to seven people who will serve as committee heads for the venue, food, decorations, sponsors/donations, advertising, ticket sales, entertainment, setup, and cleanup.

2. Decide when to have the event. Before you settle on a date, find out what else is going on in your community, and avoid conflicts.

3. Determine your budget. How much are you looking to raise, and what are you willing to spend to raise that amount?

4. Start seeking sponsors and donations immediately.

5. Search for your perfect venue. If you have to change the date of your event to get the right venue, make sure, again, that you will have no competition from similar events that may be scheduled.

6. If you decide to serve food, plan your menu. Four months before the event, schedule a caterer, recruit people to cook, or ask restaurants or grocery stores to donate food.

7. Plan activities and gather equipment for games. Create a back-up plan in case it rains.

8. Three months prior to the event, advertise by sending e-mails and letters, posting fliers, putting a notice on your organization's website, and making an announcement in your newsletter. Send press releases to local media outlets like newspapers and magazines, and contact local TV news and radio stations to request coverage and publicity.

9. Use the event's theme in everything from marketing, to graphic design of tickets and programs, to venue decorations.

10. Have your various committees meet regularly and keep the lines of communication open.

11. Three months out from the event, print tickets and have everyone in your organization sell tickets. Offer an incentive to the individuals who sell the most tickets.

12. If you need any special equipment, such as seating, sound, light, or stage equipment, this is a good time to reserve these items. Do this as you think about how the venue will be set up for the event.

13. Do a walk-through of the venue a month before the event to check if all the venue systems work and ask when you can get in to decorate.

14. Write a script to serve as your minute-by-minute flow of activities for the event. Plan a time to thank your sponsors and distribute information promoting your organization.

15. Hold a meeting with all event volunteers and go over the tasks and schedule. Be clear on what you expect every volunteer to do. Tell volunteers what to wear for the event. Get everyone's contact information (phone number and e-mail) in case you need to communicate any changes or reminders.

Execution

1. Come in early to decorate, set up equipment and food, and check the lighting and sound systems.

2. Have volunteers collect tickets as well as sell more tickets at the event.

3. Follow your script to carry out all planned activities.

4. Initiate cleanup at the designated end time.

Variation(s)

- Host a block party on your street and invite neighbors to participate.
- Create games of chance that people will donate, say, $1 a chance to take part in.
- Invite community members to showcase their antique cars in a designated area for a fee. Offer prizes for oldest car, best in show, etc.

Rent a Puppy

Ask your local puppy shelter to rent out puppies for a few hours. Explain your cause and that you will be offering people in the community a chance to play with the puppies. Set up a table or booth at a school or park and offer puppy playtime for $5 per 30 minutes. Make sure all animals are leashed.

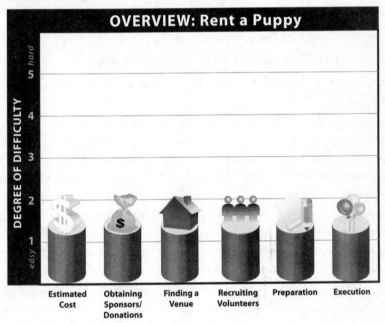

Special Materials/Equipment
- Dog leashes
- Booth equipment
- Toys

Sponsors/Donations
- Local pet stores, humane societies, and/or pet supply outlets are all potential sponsors for this event. Offer the puppy supplier a good bit of positive advertising for participating.

Possible Venue(s)
A city park with a good amount of foot traffic would be an ideal venue for this event.

Recommended Volunteer
3 to 5+ to take care of the venue, puppies, and marketing

Preparation

Prep Time: 1 month

1. Find a puppy supplier, like a pet store or animal shelter.

2. Identify a date and venue for your event.

3. Create a sign that will be posted to let people know about the event and your organization.

4. Construct an area for the puppies to play.

5. Identify a rain date to fall back on in case of bad weather.

6. Decide whether you will have additional fundraisers at the event, like a raffle or bake sale.

7. Two weeks before your event, advertise by sending e-mails and letters, posting fliers, putting a notice on your organization's website, and making an announcement in your newsletter. Send press releases to local media outlets like newspapers and magazines, and contact local TV news and radio stations to request coverage and publicity.

8. Arrange for a way to transport the puppies from the pet store or shelter to your venue. Be sure to have set times of pick-up and drop with the pet store or shelter. If the puppy supplier would like its sign displayed at your event to advertise its facility, pick it up when you pick up the puppies.

9. Decide how you will collect money for your event on site. Have starter bills ready for making change, and set up a donation jar.

10. Hold a meeting with all event volunteers and go over the tasks and schedule. Be clear on what you expect every volunteer to do. Tell volunteers what to wear for the event. Get everyone's contact information (phone number and e-mail) in case you need to communicate any changes or reminders.

Execution

1. Make sure the puppies arrive before the event's start time, and have everything set up.

2. Follow your script to carry out all planned activities.

3. Initiate cleanup at the designated end time.

Tip(s)

- When you put your booth together, be sure that you have a complete enclosure and that all of your puppies are leashed. You do not want to lose or chase any of your furry charges.

- Bring poop bags, and be sure to clean up after the puppies.

Chapter 20

Advice from the Experts

Organizing an Auction

Kathleen Boshar Reynolds
Director of Development
Boys & Girls Club of Lawrence

For nearly three years, Reynolds has been a part of an organization that serves 3,500 youths per year. Ever since 1891, the main goal of The Boys & Girls Club of Lawrence has been to help troubled youth in the community by providing educational and recreational activities.

Reynolds said her organization recruits volunteers using various methods, including newsletters, contacting schools and colleges, and word-of-mouth. Additionally, her group uses e-mail blasts to promote events and attract participants.

Auctions have been the most effective form of fundraising for the organization. With 400 people in attendance, it is no wonder the club's auction was the best fundraising event.

"The reason is that it raises a lot of money," Reynolds said of the auction. "People have fun at the event, and we reach new potential donors through the event."

Many people were involved in making the event a success. Reynolds said it took 30 committee members plus an additional 25 people to help that night.

"Active community leaders serve on the committee and work with staff to raise close to $500,000 in one evening. Committee and staff reach out to its directors, community leaders and personal contacts," Reynolds said.

However, corporate giving has been the most ineffective fundraising strategy.

"We haven't spent a lot of energy on this initiative, but we are working on a plan right now to engage local, regional, state, and national business with the club," Reynolds said.

She said it is important to have a committee that is dedicated to the cause for a successful fundraiser. However, having an excessive amount of events may not be a good idea, Reynolds said.

"Avoid burning people out with too many fundraising activities in one year."

For small nonprofits wanting to raise money in this tough economy, Reynolds advised to beware of excess spending.

"Watch your expenses. You don't need a lot of 'pretty' to raise money."

Building Relationships with Donors

Amanda Barnard
Community Director
March of Dimes in Putnam and Marion County

In 1938, President Franklin D. Roosevelt asked the nation to donate money to support polio research, in an attempt to stop the polio epidemic affecting the nation. Since then, the March of Dimes has been fighting to improve babies' health by combating birth defects, premature birth, and infant mortality.

Now a Community Director for this organization, Amanda Barnard began her career with March of Dimes as a college intern and has been with the nonprofit for more than 2 years.

"We carry out our mission through research, community services, education and advocacy to save babies' lives," Barnard said. "March of Dimes researchers, volunteers, educators, outreach workers, and advocates work together to give all babies a fighting chance against the threats to their health."

Each year, the organization holds their signature event, known as "March for Babies." Several cities have hosted this event, including 900 communities in all 50 states of the U.S., as well as Puerto Rico.

Aside from the monumental march, the March of Dimes holds other special events during the year. To recruit volunteers, Barnard said her organization simply asks for support.

"Family, friends, co-workers, community leaders, school clubs, civic organizations, and church groups are all great places to start," Barnard said. "Networking is key here."

Word-of-mouth has been the best strategy to attract new participants for this organization. Barnard said they also use different forms of media, such as e-mail blasts, Facebook, Twitter, and LinkedIn to bring attention to their cause. Additionally, the organization will make calls to business leaders in the community to ask for support, but this is a last resort.

When it comes to developing an effective strategy for fundraising, Barnard said she believes listening is essential.

"The most effective fundraising occurs after you have first developed a relationship with your volunteer or donor. You can't build a relationship without ever taking the time to listen to the other party's needs."

On the other hand, cold calling is a strategy that has provided the organization with minimal success.

"If you have a person or business that you want to make contact with, find out more about them before you call," Barnard suggests. "Do whatever it takes to get the initial meeting by any means other than a cold call."

Finding quality volunteers who are dedicated and personally enthusiastic about the cause are key to an organization's success, Barnard said. Your group should feel comfortable letting the volunteers make key decisions that impact events.

Barnard said the most important things for small organizations to remember during these hard economic times is to not give up or be afraid to ask for donations.

"Give your donors the chance to decide for themselves what they value. If you believe in your cause, chances are that other people will as well."

Finding the Right Event for Your Organization

Irene Rabinowitz
Executive Director
Helping Our Women
Provincetown, MA

Since 1993, Helping Our Women has been a nonprofit organization assisting women with chronic, life threatening, or disabling conditions. Executive Director Irene

Rabinowitz has been with the group for more than 14 years.

The organization developed a Fundraising Committee to come up with events. Rabinowitz said local business owners sometimes make offers to help with fundraisers, such as restaurant dinners.

HOW uses an e-newsletter to attract participants to its events. Rabinowitz said they also advertise through the local and regional newspapers, and even promote events on local cable.

In terms of their strongest event, fundraising dinners have proven the most successful.

"For our donors, we find that the dinners with music and dancing give our supporters a fine dining experience and a night to network with other business people," Rabinowitz said. "We also raffle off a one-of-a-kind piece of fine handmade jewelry."

Rabinowitz said refusing to help publicize an event created the most problems for her organization's efforts.

"Our failures have sometimes come because board members come up with an idea, ask the staff to implement it, and then do not help to promote the event. This happened last summer and it was frustrating for the staff and the volunteers who helped."

To have a successful fundraiser, Rabinowitz said it is important to know your donor base and have a consistent message for your organization. Most importantly, she said to never assume that techniques used by another organization will also benefit yours.

"Do not lose sight of the investment of staff, board, and volunteer resources," Rabinowitz said. "Nonprofits sometimes go to local business leaders too many times in one year and wear out their welcome."

For small organizations looking to raise money for their cause, Rabinowitz advises to carefully identify target donors and eliminate events that have lost power over time.

"It is difficult to let go of events because optimism is what runs small nonprofits, but the return on investment must be considered."

Quality Events at Affordable Prices

Karen Haven
Development Coordinator
Hospice of Marion County, Inc.

With 450 employees and more than 550 volunteers, The Hospice of Marion County, Inc. has been providing comforting care to Marion County residents in the final stages of life since 1983. Development Coordinator Karen Haven has been with the nonprofit since June 2001.

When brainstorming for upcoming events, Haven said her organization observes what other nonprofits have come up with, and they are also open to suggestions from members of the community. Researching trends also help the group come up with fundraisers.

Furthermore, the organization makes full use of local media to promote their events. Hospice of Marion County, Inc. uses the Star Banner newspaper, *Ocala Magazine*, and *Ocala Style* to raise awareness for their cause.

"Depending on the kind of event it is dictates our advertising," she said. "You have to go where your client is."

Haven said her organization strives to give all attendees a quality event for an affordable price. Additionally, she said they always make sure to have adequate sponsorship monies ahead of time to avoid falling short in funds.

Aside from being financially prepared, Haven said it is important to have a sense of humor, especially during an event.

"Things never go as planned. Just as long as your attendees don't know there has been a catastrophe in the backroom, you conceal the damage because the show must go on."

People have had a strong influence on Haven when it comes to planning events. She said many times, others will try and influence how you fundraise and what events you plan.

"You have to learn to have a very thick skin in this business. In the beginning, I really let people's comments affect me — not so much anymore. All you can do is your best."

Another goal of the Hospice is to establish a friendly relationship with members of the community.

"For Hospice of Marion County, we call our events fundraisers and friend-raisers at the same time," Haven said. "Of course our goal is to make money, but we also want to show people how organized our events are run and how friendly our employees and volunteers are."

The best event held by the nonprofit, Haven said, was their Steel Horse Stampede Motorcycle Run in 2001, which made about $22,000 in profits.

"We had 503 motorcycles participate and fed over 700 people at this event. Our farthest rider came from New Mexico, oldest rider was 76, and the youngest was 10. It took 100 volunteers to run this the day of the event."

Overall, Haven said having expenses planned in advance proves highly beneficial for any fundraising event.

"Stay focused and do your planning. Events should cost you 10 to 20 cents on the dollar to be profitable. Go to events in surrounding areas and see if a particular event is really for your organization."

Generating Creative Events

Catherine Shimony
Co-Founder and Co-director
Global Goods Partners
New York, NY

Global Goods Partners is a far-reaching, nonprofit organization with more than 40 community-based partner organizations located in more than 20 countries throughout Africa, Asia, the Americas, and the Middle East. Their mission, in developing countries, is to combat poverty, promote social justice, and encourage women's empowerment and independence. Here in the U.S., their efforts are focused upon education and advocacy.

The organization was founded in 2005. Co-founder Catherine Shimony said the nonprofit hosts events created by staff, volunteers, students, and their families. Past creative events have included a Fair Trade Fashion Show, house parties, and bead parties aimed at creating products to sell to benefit GGP's cause and promote knowledge of their mission.

Shimony said the organization has had no problems recruiting volunteers all throughout the year. Aside from having a space on their website for volunteer listings, the nonprofit uses other techniques to gain support.

"We have advertised for volunteers on Idealist and at local universities. We also receive volunteers via word of mouth and from our nonprofit partnerships," she said.

Shimony said the most effective fundraiser is one that will reach the largest amount of people. She said her group has had much success with their internet-based program.

"A successful event is a strategy with a specific target audience, being prepared to reach that audience and making sure the audience understands your mission," she said.

Every year, the organization holds what is called a Holiday Fair Trade Marketplace. Shimony said this event is always highly successful.

"We publicize it far and wide, and this year we added a panel presentation that covered topics related to our work. It took approximately one month to organize, 8 volunteers at the event and sales range from $8,000 to $12,000 for the day."

For small nonprofits looking for strategies to raise money, Shimony said being original and obtaining adequate publicity is key.

"Come up with a unique event, know your target audience, check the local events in your community so you don't conflict with other events, and do a lot of advertising leading up to the event."

One Large Event Instead of Many Small Events

Liliane Stransky
President & Founder
Step By Step Foundation, Inc.

Liliane Stransky founded the Step By Step Foundation in 1994. The mission of this organization is to provide aid to underprivileged children by offering support in areas such as health, nutrition, water, and education. The nonprofit strives to promote programs that impact child development around the world.

Stransky said members of the organization, including the Board of Directors and volunteers, generate fundraising ideas. Step By Step also makes sure to stay up to date on the latest fundraising techniques, including the use of social media platforms.

The group has a mailing list for events, and Stransky said they always let friends know about upcoming fundraisers.

"We use free media, including public relations, social media, and e-mail primarily. We find those media have the most responsiveness and provide a way to continuously engage people."

Stransky said it is much more effective to focus on large-scale event planning for fundraisers rather than planning several smaller events throughout the year.

"We're a relatively small organization, so we need to focus our resources. We also supplement those activities with ongoing mainstream activities on social media such as Facebook, and public relations."

Common mistakes that many nonprofits make when planning fundraisers are lacking creativity, not having a steady control on finances, bad organization and execution tactics, and simply not planning far enough ahead of the event, Stransky said.

The best event held by her organization was the "All In For Charity 2010" poker tournament and casino night, Stransky said. Held in Palm Beach, Florida, this event cost about $20,000 and involved almost 40 volunteers. Stransky said event planning began in March 2009, and the event did not take place until the end of January 2010.

"We needed this much time to secure sponsors, select the right partners and vendors, generate awareness of the event, and to coordinate all of the logistics for the event."

Aside from managing expenses and planning ahead of time, Stransky advises small nonprofits not to burn out by creating numerous events.

"Less is more. Focus on doing a high-profile event that will appeal to sponsors and be the talk of the town. If you can't do a stand-alone event, tap into other events that are happening in relevant locations."

Take the Stress Out of Organizing Volunteers

Karen Bantuveris
Founder and CEO
VolunteerSpot

Karen Bantuveris is the founder and CEO of VolunteerSpot, an organization supporting more than 200,000 volunteers in 40 states who contribute to local nonprofits, schools, and religious organizations. Through their website, **www.VolunteerSpot.com**, gathering volunteers is made simple for any organization.

"It's a time-saving, sanity-saving tool for all kinds of fundraisers, including carnivals, walk-a-thons, fun runs, art and music festivals, silent auctions, and more," Bantuveris said.

Before launching her organization in 2009, Bantuveris was a working mom who joined the PTA as a board member when her daughter began school.

"Shocked at all the little things that made volunteering a hassle, and fueled by frustration with reply-all e-mails, clipboards, online groups, and late night reminder messages, I decided to do something about it."

Upon introduction, VolunteerSpot's mission was to make grassroots community service simple and power the initiative. Bantuveris said her organization's streamlining efforts have decreased coordination time by 85 percent and enhanced volunteer turnouts by 20 percent.

Additionally, Bantuveris said her site is easy to use.

"No waiting for approvals and passwords, no software to install, just easy, free scheduling and sign up tools for everyday heroes making a difference."

Appreciating volunteers is extremely important to the success of any nonprofit organization, Bantuveris said. She said these volunteers, who give their time and efforts to your cause but might not have funds to support your group, might very well become your most devoted donors in the future.

"Make the most of their volunteer experience by engaging them with good communication practices from the start, giving them meaningful work to do, inviting them to bring their friends, and thanking them and seeking their feedback for improvement when the fundraiser is over," Bantuveris said.

Matching Entertainment with Worthy Causes

Christina L. Pollack
Co-Chairwoman, Auction Party 2008
Junior League of Monterey County
Monterey, CA

The Junior League of Monterey County has been around for 49 years. The nonprofit organization strives to promote volunteerism and encourage women's development. Their goal is to prepare volunteers to improve the community through action and effective leadership skills.

Pollack has been with the JLMC for three years. She said the group comes up with fundraising events through their Finance Council, made up of chairwomen from various fundraising committees in the organization. During regular meetings, the council evaluates different fundraising campaigns and holds a vote on which events to begin, continue, or cease.

When it comes to recruiting volunteers, Pollack said the JLMC has a requirement for its own members to complete finance hours. This means members volunteer at various fundraisers held by the organization throughout the year.

The group aims to promote its events by sending out e-mails to members. Additional methods of advertising for the JLMC include distribution of newsletters, mailed invitations, and communication via the website. The nonprofit even has a Public Relations Chairwoman, who specifically deals with creating press releases and sending them out to local media platforms.

Pollack co-chaired a successful fundraiser for the group back in 2008. The event, "An Evening of Comedy," featured celebrity stand-up comedians from the NBC show, *Last Comic Standing*. Wine and hors d'oeuvres were served upon entering the venue, followed by comedic performances and a silent auction, where luxurious prizes such as spa packages and hotel stays were given away.

"This fun-filled event had audiences laughing out loud, while supporting a great organization that benefits the community," Pollack said. "The successful event attracted 300 attendees, and raised approximately $8,000 for underprivileged women and children in Monterey County."

Pollack said the event allowed supporters to enjoy world-class entertainment while helping a worthy cause in the process.

"A comedic trio offered a full evening of entertainment that accompanied a silent auction, cocktail reception, and no shortage of smiles."

Comedy Nights Offer Solid, Weather-proof Fundraisers

Tom Starling, Ed.D.
President and CEO
Mental Health Association of Middle Tennessee

With programs reaching the entire state, The Mental Health Association of Middle Tennessee aims to promote mental health and well being by offering education, service, and advocacy to all citizens of Tennessee. The organization, led by President and CEO Tom Starling, has been in operation for 64 years.

Starling said it is wise to organize a diverse group of professionals who will develop a group's fundraisers.

"The key is to develop a recruitment and retention subcommittee that can manage and thank attendees, in hopes of recruiting them onto next year's planning committee."

Aside from turning to board members, appointing a key member of the community as your organization's honorary chair will aid in the process of recruiting volunteers, Starling said. He suggests the chairman or chairwoman should name two to three volunteers.

Furthermore, Starling said methods of promoting events could include placing ads in newspapers, community calendar listings, use of local radio, and most importantly, word of mouth. He also said nonprofits should avoid sending out extravagant invitations.

"A solid first-year event should result in creating some buzz, and that's when nonprofits should approach next year's corporate chairs and potential planning committee members."

To host a successful event, Starling said nonprofits should keep things simple.

"Mistakes to avoid include extravagant invitations, not thanking volunteers and sponsors throughout the year, not sending 'save the date' notices well in advance of the invitations, and nickel-and-diming attendees with auctions, T-shirts, and mementos."

Throughout his experience with nonprofit organizations, Starling said he has participated in numerous events, including walks, concerts, and wine tastings. However, he said he believes the best event is a comedy night, because the fundraiser can be catered toward families or strictly adults.

"A good comedian is less than $2,000, doesn't require any choreography, isn't dependent on the weather, and oftentimes you can split travel expenses with a comedy club that wants to use the comedian after you."

Overall, Starling said organizations should avoid putting on pricey special events, especially in these hard economic times.

"Special events take a lot of staff time and their success may be weather dependent. It's not enough to net $10,000 if you've used $10,000 of staff time to develop a worthwhile event."

Use Professionals to Make Your Event a Success

Esther Gillette
Vice President
Peninsula Temple Sholom Women
Burlingame, CA

The Women of Peninsula Temple Sholom has been raising funds to aid their community, both inside and outside the synagogue, for more than 55 years. The organization has provided assistance by offering scholarships for children to attend camps and schools. Additionally, the group collected funds to construct a new kitchen in their synagogue to assist Home at Heart, a hospitality network serving meals to the homeless in the San Francisco Bay Area.

Vice President Esther Gillette has been with the organization for approximately 4 years. Although the group's board members decide on a date for fundraising events to avoid clashing with other community activities, Gillette said the primary decision for an event's "feel" generally rests with her.

"It does vary from year to year and we have had everything from Casino Nights to Casbah (Moroccan night) to most recently a Western event, complete with line dancing and a jail that people had to pay bail to be released."

To obtain volunteers, Gillette said the event organizer asks friends to assist on different committees. Then, if the event calls for additional support and is highly detailed, the group turns to volunteers among their pool of members.

Aside from asking friends to participate in fundraisers, Gillette said her group posts on Twitter and Facebook, and distributes fliers and e-mails to attract attention.

"We reach out to sister communities as well to see if they want to attend," she said. "Usually, if there is an interesting speaker that is coming, then we have a greater external attendance."

When planning a fundraiser, Gillette said it is essential to rely on professionals.

"If you want to have a successful event, it is worth working with people that provide a service on a regular basis," she said. "Don't have cousin Joe come play music for you or have your Grandma Sara bake dessert just to save on costs."

Gillette said poor communication leading up to your event can ruin your plans. She said that it is important to create excitement throughout the community before your fundraiser. Nevertheless, overkill tactics such as bombarding people with e-mails is not necessary.

To ensure the success of your event, Gillette said to be sure it is fun and interesting.

"People want a good time, especially if they are paying a small fortune to attend your event," she said. "Try and do everything in theme, and carry the motif through from pre-planning to post thank you's. People will remember it better and be more likely to

give next time."

On the other hand, Gillette said to avoid making the assumption that all friends will be able to lend a helping hand. She also said breaking down tasks into smaller assignments will prevent anyone from feeling bombarded in your group. Lastly, Gillette suggested to always have several back-up plans at your disposal.

Gillette said her organization's most successful event was their Moroccan Night, or Casbah.

"We netted over $350,000. The event was fun and top-notch. We had over 250 people, live Berber music, the right cuisine, a marketplace, live auction, henna tattoo artist, beautiful décor, professional auctioneer, and honored speaker."

Most importantly, Gillette said to appreciate any and all donations, regardless of the amount.

"Just because someone is donating $20 instead of $200 doesn't mean they don't care about your organization. Make sure to say thank you to your donors, teams, and participants!"

Appendices

Appendix A:
Pledge Form for Potential Sponsors

It's time for [Organization Name]'s [Year] [Event]!

[Day of the week], [Date] [Time]
[Place]

Dear Potential Sponsor,

I, [Name] am participating in the **[Organization Name]** **[activity]**. All proceeds will help fund **[list of activities]**. You can sponsor me for a specific amount and can name a maximum amount that you are willing to contribute. After the **[activity]**, I will inform you of what I did and collect your contribution. Please make checks payable to **[Organization Name]**. All contributions are tax-deductible.

Thank you!

Sponsor	Pledge (Example: $1.00 per lap)	Maximum Pledge	Amount Collected	Business Matching Pledge Amount

Participants:

To reach our goal, we hope that each participant finds 15 sponsors.

Please bring this form to our meeting on the day of the event, **[Day of the week]**, **[Date]**.

Double Your Contribution

The following is a list of employers who will match employees' contributions. Please ask everyone who sponsors you if his or her employer is on this list.

[Company Name]	[Company Name]	[Company Name]
[Company Name]	[Company Name]	[Company Name]
[Company Name]	[Company Name]	[Company Name]

Appendix B:
Rules for Participants Collecting Pledges

Annual [Organization Name] [Year] [Event]!

[Day of the week], [Date]

Our annual event is [description of event]

Our goal is to help [organization name] raise at least $ [amount] to fund [list of activities]. We hope that each participant in the event contributes to the best of his/her ability. If each participant raises $ [amount], we will achieve our goal. We're hoping to make this event the best ever, so the more contributions you raise, the more successful we'll be at achieving our goal. Thank you for your participation.

Rules

1. Participants may start collecting pledges as soon as they receive the pledge sheets. **Reminder: Pledge sheets need to be turned in on event day, [Day of the week], [Date].**

2. Pledges may be made by anyone. However, participants may not ask for pledges from any of the staff members of **[Organization Name]. Please ask everyone who pledges if his/her company has a matching gift fund policy.** Companies who match pledge gifts are listed on the back of the pledge sheet.

3. **Each sponsor making a pledge should write his/her name, pledge, and maximum pledge.** Students may collect the pledge in advance but must keep pledges until all are collected.

4. On the event day, each participant will be issued a summary of his/her participation, which will be the participant record of the event.

5. Upon completion of the event, participants will hand in their summaries. A volunteer will record each person's participation on the pledge sheet and return it. Participants may then collect outstanding pledges. **Please return pledge sheets with the money to [Organization Name] by [Day of the week], [Date] to [location].**

6. Participants are encouraged to dress appropriately for the event. Bring a hat and sunscreen if the weather is anticipated to be sunny, or bring rain gear if the weather is expected to be overcast.

We look forward to all our participants having a great time! For questions or concerns, or to volunteer, contact **[Coordinator]** at **[phone number]** or **[e-mail address]**.

Bibliography

www.fundraiser-ideas.net/art-fundraising/

www.fundraiserinsight.org/ideas/ballroom-dancing-lessons.html

www.profitquests.com/IdeasChristmasTreeSales.html

www.profitquests.com/IdeasOldChristmasTreePickups.html

www.donationline.com/index.htm

www.profitquests.com/IdeasStyleShows.html

www.profitquests.com/IdeasCelebrityLunch.html

www.fundraiser-ideas.net/

www.usafundraising.com

http://relay.acsevents.org/site/DocServer/Fundraising_A-Z.pdf?docID=113406

www.fundraiserhelp.com/charity-poker-tournament.htm

www.fundraiserhelp.com/car-raffle-tips.htm

www.fundraiserhelp.com/church-fundraiser-feastival.htm

www.fundraiserhelp.com/holiday-fundraising-3.htm

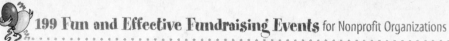

www.fundraiserhelp.com/chair-ity-fundraiser.htm

www.fundraiserhelp.com/casino-night-fundraiser.htm

www.fundraiserhelp.com/mystery-dinner-theater.htm

www.fundraiserhelp.com/wine-tasting-fundraiser.htm

www.fund-raising-ideas-center.com/art-show-fundraiser.html

www.fund-raising-ideas-center.com/fundraising-games-quiz-show.html

www.fund-raising-ideas-center.com/scavenger-hunt-non-profit-fundraising.html

www.fund-raising-ideas-center.com/artistic-charity-fundraiser.html

www.smartraise.com/fundraising/activities/gala-fundraiser

www.amnestyusa.org/get-activist-toolkit/run-your-group/
planning-a-fundraising-event/page.do?id=1101338

www.fundraiserhelp.com/silent-auction-tips.htm

www.mahalo.com/how-to-plan-a-masquerade-ball

www.charitybuzz.com/auctions

www.melanoma.org/get-involved/breakfast-and-book-signing-author-kelly-corrigan

www.unitedwayjanesville.org/files/Campaign%20Rally%20Ideas.pdf

www.unitedwayjanesville.org/files/Campaign%20Rally%20Ideas.pdf

www.fundraiser-ideas.net/taste-of-the-town/

www.fundraiser-ideas.net/creative-fundraising-ideas-exotic-meat-barbecue/

www.fundraiserhelp.com/mardi-gras-fundraiser.htm

www.fundraiserhelp.com/gardening-supplies-fundraiser.htm

www.fundraiserhelp.com/relay-for-life-fundraiser.htm

www.hubcapcafe.com/resources/car-clubs.htm

www.fundraiserhelp.com/relay-for-life-fundraiser.htm

www.fundraiserhelp.com/relay-for-life-fundraiser.htm

www.skydive4free.com

http://spa-parties.com/publicsparties.html

http://bradzockoll.tripod.com/youthworker/id16.html

www.ehow.com/way_5463096_banquet-theme-ideas.html

www.ehow.com/way_5187686_church-banquet-theme-ideas.html

www.evite.com/app/cms/ideas/flapper-party?_3

www.evite.com/app/cms/ideas/60s-party?_3

www.evite.com/app/cms/ideas/eco-friendly?_3

www.evite.com/app/cms/ideas/martini-party?_3

www.evite.com/app/cms/ideas/winter-wonderland?_3

http://party-games-etc.com/medieval/

www.party411.com/holidays-halloween97.html

www.party411.com/theme-chocolate-tasting.html

www.party411.com/theme-harrypotter-bm.html

www.party411.com/theme178.html

www.party411.com/theme149.html

www.party411.com/theme134.html

www.party411.com/theme22.html

www.party411.com/theme127.html

www.party411.com/theme13.html

www.party411.com/theme35.html

www.sclutheran.org/SC-WELCA/mother_daughter_banquet_ideas.htm

www.fundraising-ideas.org/DIY/UKCollection.htm

www.fund-raising-ideas-center.com/church-fund-raiser-flea-market.html

http://bachelorsoftalkeetna.org/bachelor-auction-and-ball.html

www.fundraisinghq.com/fire-department-fundraisers.html

www.dojiggy.com/s/Fundraising-Event-Ideas/

http://ezinearticles.com/?How-to-Hold-a-Successful-Fundraising-Holiday-Bazaar
&id=1614058

www.buzzle.com/articles/unique-fundraising-ideas-for-fundraising-activities.html

www.element11.org/index.php?option=com_frontpage&Itemid=1&limit=
5&limitstart=20

www.visitparksvillequalicumbeach.com/cms.asp?wpID=163&Yr=2009&Mnth=
11&Dy=&evID=112855

www.americancash4gold.com/

www.fund-raising-ideas-center.com/backwards-pageant-fundraiser.html

www.fundraising-ideas.org/DIY/scrabble.htm

http://familycrafts.about.com/od/pumpkingames/Pumpkin_Games.htmwww.
jlmontereycounty.org

www.ichope.com

http://sholom.org/getinvolved/women/

www.VolunteerSpot.com

www.stepbystepfoundation.com

www.globalgoodspartners.org

www.hospiceofmarion.com

www.helpingourwomen.org

www.lawrencebgc.com

Eileen Figure Sandlin is an award-winning writer and the author of 17 books, including 15 business start-up books. She has published more than 700 magazine and newspaper articles, as well as thousands of newsletter articles. Her writing specialties are health care, small business issues, and education. Sandlin holds a master's degree in journalism and is a professor of business communication at a major Midwest university.

Richard Helweg has more than 25 years experience working in the nonprofit sector as an artistic director, managing director, and executive director. He is an award-winning playwright and has recently written *...And Justice for All, A History of the Supreme Court*, a book for young readers, and *How to Get Your Share of the $30-Plus Billion Being Offered by U.S. Foundations*. Richard lives in Lincoln, Neb. with his wife, Karen, and sons, Aedan and Rory.

Index